Strengthening
Community

Strengthening Community

Social Insurance in a Diverse America

Kathleen Buto
Martha Priddy Patterson
William E. Spriggs
Maya Rockeymoore
Editors

NATIONAL ACADEMY OF SOCIAL INSURANCE
Washington, D.C.

9286730

Copyright © 2004
National Academy of Social Insurance
1776 Massachusetts Avenue, N.W., Washington, D.C. 20036

Strengthening Community: Social Insurance in a Diverse America
may be ordered from:

BROOKINGS INSTITUTION PRESS
1775 Massachusetts Avenue, N.W.
Washington, D.C. 20036
Tel.:   1-800/275-1447
        202/797-6258
Fax: 202/797-6004
Internet: www.brookings.edu

Library of Congress Cataloging-in-Publication data

   Strengthening community : social insurance in a diverse America /
Kathleen Buto . . . [et al.], editors.
     p.   cm.
   Based on papers delivered at the National Academy of Social Insurance's
15th annual conference, held January 30–31, 2003, at the National Press Club
in Washington, D.C.
   Includes bibliographical references and index.
    ISBN 0-8157-1281-2 (pbk. : alk. paper)
    1. Social security—United States—Congresses. 2. Minorities—United
States—Social conditions—Congresses. 3. Medicare—Congresses. I. Buto,
Kathleen. II. National Academy of Social Insurance (U.S.).
Conference (15th : 1999 Washington, D.C.)
   HD7125.S765 2003
   368.4'3'00973—dc22   2003022861

9 8 7 6 5 4 3 2 1

The paper used in this publication meets minimum requirements of the American National Standard for Information Sciences—Permanence of Paper for Printed Library Materials: ANSI Z39.48-1992.

Typeset in Times Roman

Composition by Stephen McDougal
  Mechanicsville, Maryland

Printed by Victor Graphics
  Baltimore, Maryland

Preface

This book is based on papers delivered at the National Academy of Social Insurance's fifteenth annual conference, held January 30–31, 2003, at the National Press Club in Washington, D.C. The conference examined how Medicare, Social Security, and state-administered programs accommodate America's growing diversity.

The academy received financial support for this conference from the Daimler-Chrysler Fund; the Foundation for Child Development; Johnson & Johnson; the Robert Wood Johnson Foundation; the W. K. Kellogg Foundation; the March of Dimes Foundation; Martha Priddy Patterson of Deloitte & Touche, LLP; the Mary Ross Bequest; and the TIAA-CREF Institute. Scholarship support for attendees from California came from the California Health Care Foundation.

As with all activities organized under its auspices, the academy takes responsibility for ensuring the independence of this book. Participants in the conference were chosen for their recognized expertise and with due consideration of the balance of disciplines appropriate to the program. The resulting chapters are the views of the presenters and are not necessarily the views of the officers, board, or members of the academy.

The editors would like to thank all the conference participants for sparking a lively discussion and debate. We also commend the academy staff for helping design stimulating sessions and for facilitating the smooth running of the conference, in particular, Jill Braunstein, Nelly Ganesan, Terry Nixon, Kate Robie, and Reggie Williams.

We appreciate the efforts of all those who made this book possible: the authors for their attention to the task of turning their presentations into chapters; Pamela Larson, Elizabeth Dulaney, and Shayna Robinson of the academy staff, who assisted the editors and organized the process; Janet Walker and the staff at the Brookings Institution Press; Kerry Kern, who edited the manuscript; Enid Zafran, who provided an index; and Carlotta Ribar, who proofed the pages.

—*KB, MPP, WS, MR*

Contents

Strengthening
Community

1

Introduction

Maya Rockeymoore

On January 16, 2003, exactly two weeks prior to the commencement of the fifteenth annual conference of the National Academy of Social Insurance (NASI), President George W. Bush filed briefs with the U.S. Supreme Court opposing affirmative action policies at the University of Michigan. His action helped set the stage for another round of legal and public debate about the continued relevance of affirmative action in the post–Civil Rights era. As the primary legal remedy constructed to compensate for past discrimination against African Americans and women, affirmative action had long been the flashpoint for Americans struggling with the policy implications of residing in a country with an uneven past with regard to race and gender relations. Mirroring the national debate, the NASI conference—"Strengthening Community: Social Insurance in a Diverse America"— allowed participants to explore issues of fairness, equity, and diversity in relation to the design, implementation, and outcomes associated with social insurance programs in contemporary America.

Several speakers discussed the influence of sociocultural factors on socioeconomic outcomes for diverse populations. Some—like Lee Hargraves and Brian Smedley—pointed out that differences in the treatment of racial and ethnic minorities based on factors such as race, country of origin, and language have contributed to contemporary "gaps" that span an array of socioeconomic indicators, including education, wealth, life expectancy, and health status. These indicators are central to the administration of social insurance programs because they not only help determine whether benefits are received at all but also the type and amount of benefits distributed. They also raise a provocative question that goes to the heart of discussion about social insurance and diversity: To what extent must social insurance programs address historical, social, and economic inequities to be viewed as fair?

Social Insurance and Disparities in Historical Context

U.S. Census Bureau figures, as presented by NASI panelist Nancy Gordon, indicate that the role of diversity in America is becoming even more important as the population share of Latinos and Asians continues to rise. Dramatically changing demographics underscore the significance of understanding how various populations interface with social insurance programs ostensibly designed to meet the needs of all American workers and their families at various stages in life. Do the programs actually meet the diverse needs of those who qualify for their benefits? Are the programs structured in a manner that maximizes outcomes for diverse populations? Is the system fair to all workers who contribute to social insurance programs?

Fairness was a topic that engaged NASI participants throughout the two-day conference. In his opening speech, Rep. Xavier Becerra (D-Calif.) highlighted the circumstance of undocumented Latino workers who contribute significant amounts to Social Security and Medicare yet receive no payable benefits in return due to their illegal status (chapter 2). Becerra pointed out that their contributions help to boost the Old Age Survivors and Disability Insurance (OASDI) and Hospital Insurance Trust Fund and help pay social insurance benefits to U.S. citizens. The equity of this approach has been questioned at the national level by President Vicente Fox of Mexico, who has responded by pressuring the Bush administration to find a solution that would fairly compensate undocumented workers for their social insurance contributions.

Samuel L. Myers Jr. presents a fascinating discussion about the philosophical underpinnings of perceived fairness in a diverse society (chapter 3). Taking readers through a series of hypothetical scenarios, he illustrates that fairness is a fluid concept that shifts when issues of race and gender are brought into the equation. Given this perspective, Myers underscores the importance of clearly defining the type of equality or fairness policy analysts seek to achieve when proposing to tinker with the structure of social insurance programs.

While the primary focus of conference participants was on the programmatic implications of racial and ethnic diversity, issues such as diversity in gender and family formations also informed the discussion of the assembled group. Pamela Herd's analysis of Social Security's adequacy for women in light of changed circumstances in marital, employment, income, and caretaker status provided important insight into program design strategies that could help reduce gender and class inequities. Others highlighted state-administered programs, such as temporary disability insurance (TDI) and Temporary Assistance for Needy Families (TANF), and discussed their adequacy in meeting the needs of working women. Clearly, issues related to gender, parental, and marital status continue to be important factors when one assesses the adequacy of social insurance programs in a diverse society. When one considers that these factors are often interconnected with race, ethnicity, and class, the challenge of constructing equitable programmatic remedies becomes even more complex.

In sum, the ultimate charge to the conference participants can be paraphrased from a question posed by Jerry Mashaw, who asked: "How do we think about diversity and social insurance in ways that are productive, both in recognizing and celebrating the diversity that we have in our population—and the strengths that it gives us—while at the same time understanding how diversity interacts with social insurance, can strengthen it, and can promote revisions that will strengthen it still further?" Indeed, how?

In order to have diversity inform and strengthen social insurance programs, it seems that American society must first agree on the value of equity across a diverse population as a social good. However, the highly contentious affirmative action debate makes it clear that the nexus between policy prescriptions and diversity goals uneasily remains at the fore of public attention a full thirty-nine years after passage of the Civil Rights Act of 1964. Although the country seems effectively divided on the issue, the NASI conference made a significant contribution to the national discussion by highlighting how issues of diversity remain central to the implementation of effective and equitable social insurance programs in the twenty-first century.

Equity and fairness in social insurance are generally considered fundamental concepts that guide the distribution of benefits. Yet when social insurance is viewed through the lens of diversity, the notion of what is fair and equitable becomes murky. As a result, it becomes important to clearly define the values that shape social insurance programs and the social goals they seek to achieve.

Myers brought the issues of equity and fairness into focus by challenging NASI conference participants to not only talk about desired diversity goals, like eliminating health disparities, but to also address why society should pursue these goals in the first place. As a professor who specializes in training policy professionals and program administrators in issues of social equity, Myers acknowledged the dearth of education about the role of equity and fairness in public administration curricula. As a result, he claimed there exists a level of ambiguity that has obscured the various ways that equity and fairness can be defined and measured in policy analysis.

Providing a brief overview of horizontal and vertical equity, Myers asserts that horizontal equity—identical outcomes for identical individuals—is most often considered the appropriate measure of equity in social insurance programs. But, he charges, these notions of equity are complicated by the nature of the outcomes. For example, in horizontal equity two people who make the same amount of money and contribute the same amount to a social insurance program should both receive an equal amount of money upon retirement. Vertical equity, on the other hand, seeks equality of outcomes for unequal persons. Myers cites progressive tax schemes, which allow lower income individuals to contribute a smaller share to the system but receive a higher benefit upon retirement, as one example of vertical equity. He claims that, while there is less agreement about the desirability of vertical equity, governments seeking to rectify social imbalances may pursue this form of equity. He also points out that these two forms of equity are measuring very different things.

But the notion of equal outcomes is not the first thing people think about when race is introduced as an element in the equation, according to Myers. When race comes up, the conversation necessarily turns to equal opportunity because it becomes evident that measuring outcomes begs the question: Equal outcomes based on what? Myers asserts that the basis of equal outcomes can be broadly defined as equal to individuals, equal to groups, or segments within that group. He argues that this concept of opportunity-based equity is further complicated by the notion of compensatory equity, or affirmative action, which is clearly based on factors such as when a group arrives in a country and how federal law treats that group. Myers asks: Is there a fair way to compensate people who have been disadvantaged because of federal law?

In addition to equity based on outcomes and opportunity, equity can also be defined in terms of procedural fairness. In this conception, neither outcomes nor opportunity matters as much as the equitable nature of the rules that govern the process.

Myers highlights Baumolian and Varian fairness as yet another way to think about equity. Under this concept, it is assumed that there can never be perfect equality. The idea of fairness shifts the equality of outcomes question to a focus on individual preferences and desires. Thus, according to Myers, equity is measured by the degree of envy that shapes people's perceptions about what is fair in our society. Using the current affirmative action debate as an example, he illustrates that while athletic or academic preferences are left unchallenged in higher education decisionmaking, racial preferences cause many to raise objections. Myers argues that this is because race invokes ideas of envy and changes individual perceptions about what is fair. Thus the concept of fairness becomes fluid depending on the terms of the debate and the degree of envy.

Myers suggests that the concept of efficient equity may provide a way to evaluate the merit of competing equity claims. Efficient equity assumes that when multiple ways to achieve a fairness objective exist, selecting the path that costs the least provides the most equitable outcome. Myers concludes that policy analysts must be willing to embrace alternative definitions of equity when addressing equity and social insurance in the context of diversity.

Examining the origins of contemporary social insurance programs can help to illuminate the social goals and values that went into their creation and implementation. What was the social philosophy espoused by those who championed the creation of programs like Social Security and Medicare? How were they seeking to change social outcomes for citizens? Were issues of diversity explicitly considered? Did they employ specific notions of equity and fairness in the development of the programs? What policy tools and processes did they use to achieve their goals? Robert C. Lieberman (chapter 4) and Jill Quadagno (chapter 5) discussed elements of these questions in reviewing the creation of the Social Security and Medicare programs.

Lieberman asserts that issues of diversity were discussed in the debates surrounding the formation of the Social Security program. At that time, however, racial and ethnic diversity in outcomes was not considered as much a desired social goal as was racial uniformity. Citing the congressional testimony of an NAACP official in 1935, Lieberman points out that policies that sought to exclude agricultural and domestic workers had the effect of excluding about 50 percent of the African American work force in the 1930s. In the South, where most blacks lived at the time, the figure would have been even higher, at about 60 percent.

As time progressed, Social Security laws were expanded to include the occupations in which African Americans were concentrated. Lieberman argues that political and financial pressures influenced the trend toward a racially and ethnically inclusive program. In essence, Social Security became so popular that even President Dwight D. Eisenhower, a Republican, considered it political suicide to repeal or change the program. Lieberman argues that the second reason for expanding the program rested on fiscal logic. The more uncovered workers brought into the system, the more payroll taxes the program could collect to help it meet its obligations. Additional fiscal pressures were brought on by a shift from the program's original emphasis on equity (horizontal) to adequacy, or vertical equity. According to Lieberman, repeated congressional acts to increase benefit amounts in an effort to protect them from inflationary erosion resulted in a benefit level that is currently about 50 percent above the original value of Social Security benefits.

Lieberman provides data illustrating how the number of nonwhites covered by Social Security increased over time. He also illustrates how the benefit levels of nonwhite retirees, while lower than those of whites, have gradually improved over time. Lieberman concludes by affirming his belief that Social

Security has served our diverse society fairly well and has promoted a social citizenship that has contributed to a strong middle class in the United States.

The Jill Quadagno chapter charts the evolution of the Medicare program and how its implementation facilitated the end of racial barriers in the U.S. health care system. Quadagno recounts racist practices in the medical profession that led to segregated facilities and equipment in hospitals, the refusal to bestow full staff privileges on African American doctors, and the exclusion of African American students from medical training programs. She points out that fourteen southern states designed their hospital systems around the separate but equal principle.

Quadagno notes that it took just six months in 1966 for almost every hospital in the country to begin admitting patients regardless of race. She questions why desegregation occurred so rapidly, especially in the face of the long-entrenched role of racial discrimination in the United States and in its health care system. While the 1963 *Simpkins* v. *Moses B. Cone Memorial Hospital* Supreme Court decision and the Civil Rights Act of 1964 helped set the stage for change, Quadagno argues that little progress was made in the desegregation of hospitals until the passage of Medicare.

With the program's passage, hospitals had to prove that they were not practicing racial discrimination in order to receive federal funds. Quadagno's research revealed that hospitals first had to certify that their facilities did not discriminate on the basis of race. The hospitals then received visits from federal workers who were charged with the task of determining whether the hospitals were in actual compliance with the law. As a result, more than 99.5 percent of all hospitals were certified when Medicare went into effect on July 1, 1966.

While a few hospitals attempted to skirt the law, continuous monitoring and the financial lure of Medicare funds ensured their compliance after a time. In her summary, Quadagno argues that the implementation of Medicare provides one example of how the government can achieve important social goals through carefully crafted social insurance programs.

The open discussion following the Lieberman and Quadagno presentations at the conference yielded a rich debate about whether program designers intentionally considered racial implications when they enacted and expanded Social Security and Medicare. Panel moderator Christopher Edley began this discussion by questioning the level of intentionality Social Security program designers possessed when they adopted the racially disparate occupational exclusions.

Lieberman responded that in his view the move to exclude agricultural and domestic workers was racially motivated. To support his assertion, he cites the fact that the categories were included when Roosevelt first sent the proposal to Congress but were later excluded during congressional committee sessions dominated by Southern Democrats who had a vested interest in maintaining the racial status quo. The administrative difficulties that would likely ensue with agricultural and domestic workers were also cited as a rationale for exclusion.

According to Quadagno, race played a minor role in the Medicare debate largely because southern opposition had lost steam after passage of significant civil rights legislation. Instead, she notes that when race was discussed it was to affirm that Medicare would comply with the Civil Rights Act.

In response to a question about how Medicare and Social Security have managed to escape charges of racism in their implementation, both Lieberman and Quadagno argued that the national administration of the programs and their formulaic nature allow them to resist the influence of local and regional prejudices. Quadagno argued that, in the case of Medicare, physicians might actually have opportunities to exhibit racial bias in the doctor's office. She noted that this form of discrimination is hard to track due to patient confidentiality issues. Data presented in a recent Institute of Medicine (IOM) report on health disparities, however, may provide some evidence of physician discrimination, as had been suggested in the discussion.

In discussing the accomplishments and future of the Medicare and Social Security programs, Lieberman underscored the importance of maintaining the support of a diverse coalition that can stave off political threats to the current system. He asks what it would mean for coalition politics if opposing forces were successful in splitting Social Security into privatized and public programs that would likely serve two very different populations. Quadagno ended her remarks by highlighting that Medicare has provided near universal health care coverage for people over the age of sixty-five since its passage.

The Implications of Growing Diversity

Part II of this volume provides an overview of the status of racial and ethnic minorities from a demographic, health, and income perspective. The chapters paint a statistical portrait of diverse populations that sets the context for subsequent panels that focus on how these variables interface with various aspects of social insurance policy.

Nancy Gordon synthesizes demographic trends from Census 2000 (chapter 6). She notes that with 281 million people, the U.S. population has grown significantly—particularly during the economic boom of the 1990s when America experienced its largest ever decade-to-decade increase. States in the South and West reflected the highest growth rates, and this trend seemed consistent with the demographic profile for where Latinos and Asians—the fastest growing and most "linguistically isolated" minority populations—choose to reside.

Gordon approaches the demographic overview of the country by first looking at the profile of the largest, most heterogeneous group in America—the non-Hispanic white population. She notes that this group's share of the U.S. population is declining in every state in the country. Nationally, white non-Hispanics dropped from 76 to 69 percent of the U.S. population. Despite their overall decline, this population still makes up the largest percentage of the population over the age of forty-five. Gordon notes that this trend will influence the profile of the elderly—a population concentrated in the Midwest, Florida, and some parts of the West—for some time to come.

Family formation is another area upon which Gordon focuses. Her data indicate that the number of single parents and the number of people living alone have been growing at rates faster than that of married couples. The ramifications of this trend will have a special impact on women, who make up the bulk of single-parent households and individuals living alone.

J. Lee Hargraves shifts the focus toward the life expectancy and health status of the U.S. population (chapter 7). He finds that diverse populations have different life expectancies—with whites and Asians more likely to live longer than African Americans and Hispanics. He attributes this to socioeconomic, life-style, and employment differentials among racial and ethnic subgroups. Hargraves notes that while mortality rates seem to indicate that the population is getting healthier, this conclusion is refuted by evidence showing that death rates have remained relatively unchanged over the past decade.

Health disparities among racial and ethnic subgroups reveal disease trends that have a startling impact on minority populations. Hargraves notes that the diabetes epidemic has had an especially devastating impact on African Americans and Native Americans and that complications from diabetes cause blindness, amputation, heart disease, and stroke—many of the conditions that cause individuals to become reliant on social insurance programs.

Hargraves discusses how research and health insurance status may help explain why health disparities exist. While socioeconomic variables cannot completely explain disparities, he argues that recent IOM studies help provide researchers with the tools they need to delve further into issues—like quality of care differentials—that may provide more explanation. In addition, Hargraves notes that African Americans and Latinos are much more likely than whites to be without health insurance, and when they do have coverage they are more likely to be enrolled in managed care plans. His research indicates that a lack of health insurance correlates to some degree to minority health disparities.

Hargraves speculates that this may be due to inadequate access to personal physicians, treatment, and regular, preventive care. He concludes that a lack of access to health care insurance plays a significant role in minority health disparities.

Building on the theme of racial and ethnic disparities, Cecilia Conrad examines the marginal labor force status of African Americans and Hispanics (chapter 8). She argues that the pattern of labor force vulnerability experienced by these groups is a poor fit for social insurance plans based on the labor force experiences of the non-Hispanic white population.

At a rate three times higher than those of non-Hispanic whites, poverty rates among blacks and Hispanics provide evidence of their vulnerability, according to figures cited by Conrad. Looking at median family income, she illustrates how the income of black and Hispanic families grew in both absolute and relative terms over the past two decades. Conrad cautions, however, that the rate of growth for Hispanics was slower relative to that of whites, and income disparities between the two groups showed a slight increase. Additionally, while median income for African Americans and Hispanics grew the fastest for those families in the top deciles of both groups, median income for families in the bottom deciles grew more slowly.

Conrad points out that income disparities within the bottom deciles appear to be closing among black, white, and Hispanic families. She explains that this is likely linked to proportional shifts in the number of female-headed households within each racial and ethnic group. The number of African-American, female-headed households dropped, while the share of white, female-headed households increased. The story is different for married couple families. Again, African American and white families in this group have similar median incomes, but the incomes for Hispanic married couple families are lower. Conrad attributes this disparity to the traditional one full-time earner model that Hispanic families are more likely to follow. She further posits that this phenomenon is partially hidden because, at the same time, these families are more likely to have multiple earners who are not the wife or mother. Thus, through extended-family and other arrangements, the median income of Hispanic families tends to be made up of multiple, low-income earners, and this unique arrangement has implications for the ability of social insurance programs to meet the needs of these families.

Conrad highlights wage differentials, labor force participation, and employer benefits as additional areas of vulnerability for women, blacks, and Hispanics. Despite the closing of disparities in median income, Conrad shows that wage differentials for black and Hispanic women compared to white women are actually widening. She also affirms that African American men have weak labor force attachment, as evidenced by their high unemployment rates, low employment-to-population ratios, and high rates of incarceration. Her data suggest that even though Hispanics have jobs, they are least likely to have pension benefits, and Hispanic women are less likely to have employer-sponsored health care. Thus, for some, having a job translates into little protection in terms of benefits.

In sum, Conrad finds that the manner in which blacks and Hispanics earn income and the source from which income is derived vary depending on a number of factors, such as differences in family formation, labor force attachment, and occupation. As a result, these groups are faring differently, and these differences have direct implications for the way in which social insurance programs are configured and benefits distributed.

Summary comments by Jerry Mashaw challenge readers to rethink social insurance and diversity by focusing on the nature of several fundamental tensions between social insurance and racial and ethnic diversity. First, he reflects on the fundamental similarity among all people and the perspective of diversity that highlights elements of difference among us. Second, he asserts that policy analysts tend to think about diversity in terms of discrete variables like age and labor force attachment rather than looking at these variables and their outcomes through the lens of race and ethnicity. The latter view highlights that not all groups fare similarly in social insurance schemes and, in fact, some fare worse. Mashaw points out that those who would like to undermine social insurance can readily capitalize on these disparate outcomes by using divisive political tactics.

As a means to counter divisive strategies, Mashaw challenges readers to think about ways to engage diversity and social insurance in a productive fashion so that racial and ethnic differences can be used to strengthen social insurance programs. According to Mashaw, this can be accomplished by focusing on social insurance not as discrete programs but as a family of programs that—while utilizing different policy tools—all work toward the same goal of minimizing the risks that all people face.

Donna Chiffriller and Audrietta Izlar of Verizon Communications also provided summary comments by highlighting their employer's commitment to diversity in the area of health care. Chifriller and Izlar note that their employer took notice when the Institute of Medicine released its "unequal treatment" study showing that minorities were more likely to receive a poorer quality of care than whites, even when health insurance status, income, and education remained the same. With more than 28 percent of Verizon's work force composed of racial and ethnic minorities, the company decided to launch a program seeking to eliminate minority health disparities among health care providers affiliated with the company. Izlar reports that Verizon's two-part action plan in this area includes holding health plans accountable and educating their employees and retirees about the problem. She concludes that the implications of growing diversity means that employers like Verizon must leverage their power over affiliated health plans to ensure that their employees receive quality health care that in turn contributes to their ability to operate at maximum performance levels.

Social Security in a Diverse America

In Part III panelists focused on illuminating how components of the Old Age Survivors and Disability Insurance (OASDI) program, also known as Social Security, affect diverse populations. From disability and domestic workers to privatization's impact on African Americans, the chapters present a range of issues pertinent to the role, function, and future of Social Security in the United States.

Lee Cohen, Eugene Steuerle, and Adam Carasso provide an analysis of the distributional effects of the retirement and survivor portions of the Social Security program (OASI) versus the disability component (DI) by gender, earnings, education, and race and ethnicity (chapter 9). The concept of distribution measures the amount of money transferred from one group to another through Social Security's progressive benefit structure. Using the Modeling Income in the Near Term simulation model, Cohen and his coauthors examine real earnings histories by employing two measures for distribution: internal rates of return and lifetime net benefits. He notes that these measures examine (horizontal) equity and not adequacy.

Cohen and his coauthors find that when analyzed alone, DI is more progressive than OASI. But, when combined, OASDI is only slightly more progressive than OASI alone primarily because DI is a relatively small program in comparison. Cohen claims that men, workers in the bottom earnings quintile, high school dropouts, and minorities benefit the most when DI is combined with OASI. Women, however, tend to have higher internal rates of return regardless of whether OASI is considered alone or with DI attached. He asserts that internal rates of return for women are worse under DI, however, because they have a lower take-up rate than men.

With regard to lifetime earnings, Cohen's data showed that OASI combined with DI increased the progressivity of the program for each cohort examined. Indeed, when one looks at the male cohort with the lowest lifetime earnings, Cohen's research indicates that the OASDI return rates for men have increased significantly over time. He explains that this increase is primarily due to increased DI take-up rates for low-earning men. In contrast, DI does not boost the progressivity between OASI and OASDI over time for women.

Cohen's research illuminates an interesting pattern when education is considered. When one assesses OASI, the returns for men with less education do not become progressive until DI is added to the equation. Cohen theorizes that this anomaly is a result of the higher mortality rates experienced by men with less education. Thus higher mortality rates have a regressive effect that cancels out the progressivity of the benefit formula. This finding did not hold true for women with less education because the extra benefits provided by spousal benefits raise the returns of high school dropouts above those of women with more education.

In the case of racial and ethnic minorities, Cohen shows that DI raises the rate of return for minorities while favoring men over women. He explains that this occurs because minorities are more likely to be among lower earners and because DI take-up rates are higher for minorities than for whites.

Partially in response to criticism about Social Security's inadequacy for women who raise children, Pamela Herd examines policy proposals that seek to compensate women for their care-giving role through Social Security retirement benefits (chapter 10). In her analysis, Herd points out that the two primary ways to earn benefits are as a worker or as the spouse of a worker. The marital benefit, however, is inherently problematic, according to Herd. Originally adopted to provide for women with husbands, she claims that marital benefits do not help African American and less educated women because they are less likely to be married and more likely to receive benefits as workers. Another problem in the construction of the marital benefit is that it provides a higher benefit for nonworking women married to a higher earner versus working women married to a man who earns less.

The care credit proposals examined by Herd seek to eliminate spousal benefits by assuming that all women work. The proposals also seek to link benefits to parental status as opposed to marital status. Herd says that this approach lessens the penalty for working women by rewarding them for their care-giving role. The proposals are different, however, in the extent to which they require women to work while raising children.

Herd first discusses the "breadwinner" model that allows women to drop five to nine zero-earning years from benefit calculations that consider the highest thirty-five years of earnings. She says that this approach penalizes women who work while raising children. The second proposal she highlights is the "universal breadwinner" model, which provides incentives for women to work while they are raising children. This proposal drops the lowest five to nine years of the thirty-five-year benefit calculation. The downfall of this approach, according to Herd, is that it rewards higher earners. The final "family care" proposal she examines rewards women regardless of whether or not they are working by allowing women to boost low earnings by $15,000 in those five to nine years when their earnings were below half of their median wage. She claims that this proposal levels the earnings differentials between low- and high-earning women.

Herd assesses each of these proposals in terms of adequacy, individual equity, and cost-effectiveness. She finds that each proposal is cost neutral because eliminating the spousal benefit covers the costs. To assess adequacy and equity, however, Herd looks at a 1992 health and retirement study merged with Social Security earnings and benefit records to understand the distributional impact of replacing spousal benefits with care credits. She finds that those most disadvantaged by current rules (African American and unmarried women) would have the best outcomes under the family care credit model. Women with the highest current benefits would do best under the universal breadwinner proposal. Finally, Herd asserts that the smallest percentage of women benefit from the breadwinner model.

According to Herd, individual equity and benefit adequacy are enhanced under the care credit proposals. She further asserts that this is primarily true because the proposals reward those who do more paid work. The downside of care credit proposals includes the loss of spousal benefits for women who rely on them, such as divorced women. When one assesses replacement rates, Herd's analysis reveals that married couples in the lowest lifetime earnings quartile experience an improvement in their replacement rates under the family care proposal but not under the universal breadwinner or breadwinner proposals.

Herd concludes that the family care model presents the best alternative, as it is the most progressive and results in the smallest benefit decreases. She cautions that, while no proposal is perfect, current policy options must take into account differences in the marital status and working patterns of today's women.

The work patterns of women and other vulnerable workers are the subject of Kilolo Kijakazi's presentation on unreported earnings (chapter 11). Her chapter highlights the problem of workers, especially domestic and farm employees, who fail to qualify for Social Security benefits because they do not contribute to payroll taxes and their employers do not report their earnings.

Women and racial and ethnic workers are the groups primarily affected by unreported earnings, according to Department of Labor statistics cited by Kijakazi. In 2001 women constituted 96 percent of the workers holding domestic jobs like child care and cleaning. Latinos were disproportionately represented among domestic workers (33 percent) and farm workers (42 percent).

She points out that while African Americans were not overrepresented among domestic workers, their historical presence in this occupation likely means that they compose a disproportionate share of those nearing retirement. This is problematic because their lifetime of hard work in unreported, low-wage jobs means that, in addition to not receiving Social Security retirement benefits, they are not likely to have income from pensions or investments.

Citing a lack of available literature on the subject, Kijakazi highlights the need for more studies to examine the prevalence and impact of unreported earnings. She claims that, in addition to the scope and impact of unreported earnings, these studies should explore the extent to which domestic and farm workers understand the reporting rules regarding the difference between self-employment and employment.

Maya Rockeymoore spoke on how African Americans would be affected by proposals to privatize Social Security, particularly plan three of the President's Commission to Strengthen Social Security. Pointing to the inadequacy of studies that use imputed data to assess the distributional impact of privatization proposals, Rockeymoore shared that she and her coauthors, Kilolo Kijakazi and Cheryl Hill Lee, sought to overcome these methodological limitations by using the Panel Survey of Income Dynamics to extract real earnings histories of individuals. The study, not included as a chapter in this book due to ongoing work, utilizes the SASSIM policy simulation model to estimate the distributional impact of plan three for African Americans.

In an effort to contextualize the broad policy environment, Rockeymoore reviewed arguments made for and against diverting funds from Social Security to create self-managed individual accounts invested in the stock market. According to Rockeymoore, those in favor of privatization argue that African Americans get a low rate of return from Social Security due to their higher mortality rates. As a result, they claim that African Americans would fare better with private accounts through which they can accumulate inheritable wealth. Those on the opposite side question these assumptions by arguing that African Americans actually receive a greater rate of return through Social Security's progressive benefit formula and the value added by its survivor and disability programs.

Due to the complex nature of the arguments, Rockeymoore stressed the need for careful research that can show the true impact of proposed plans on individuals. She says that this type of research is especially important because African Americans have unique earning patterns that would have direct implications for their benefit levels should the United States move toward a benefit structure that relies on stock market performance and steady account contributions over time. She concluded that policy analysts must be

careful about earnings assumptions as African Americans' lower and un-
steady earnings histories, due to higher unemployment rates, make them
vulnerable.

Kim Hildred provides summary commentary that reiterates the need for
practical research that can be useful to those who make policy decisions.
Hildred presents a series of criteria that can be used by Capitol Hill staff to
evaluate Social Security research. According to Hildred, policy research
should consider whether the research topic is timely, whether the research
approach is objective and its assumptions realistic, and whether the research
methodology is scientifically sound.

Hildred argues that policy research should help policymakers analyze
current policy as well as the impact of politically viable solutions. In addition,
it should balance concerns about cost, impact, and competing policy principles, such as the value of diversity versus equity. Hildred asserts that Cohen's
chapter provides important information that could help identify which groups
benefit the most from various aspects of Social Security. Of particular interest
to her was the interconnectedness of OASI and DI and how potential changes
to the system could affect this relationship.

Hildred lauds the Herd presentation as meeting all the criteria necessary for
relevant policy research. She expressed reservations, however, about whether
Herd's proposal to eliminate spousal benefits fit the political viability criterion.
Hildred agreed that the subject of Kijakazi's chapter was of interest to policymakers
and that more work needed to be done to highlight the implications of
unreported earnings. Finally, Hildred agrees with Rockeymoore's argument
about the need to examine realistic earning and work patterns but encourages
her to expand her research to examine other privatization proposals.

Kathryn Olson also provides commentary on this research, agreeing with
the criteria outlined by Hildred but providing additional comments about the
usefulness of outside policy research. According to Olson, policy research not
only helps policymakers evaluate policy alternatives, but it is also used as
ammunition to support a particular perspective in policy debates. She added
that policy research also serves an important role in illuminating the plight of
vulnerable populations.

Agreeing with Rockeymoore's thesis, Olson asserts that it is imperative that
researchers and policymakers look beyond blind averages to determine how
diverse workers will be affected by the variable nature of individual accounts.
In response to Herd, Olson questions whether the family care proposal serves
as a child-care credit or an income booster for low earners. She claims that
child-care credit proposals may also present administrative difficulties in
trying to assess and prove who has children.

Olson states that Kijakazi's work raises an important but understudied aspect of the social insurance system. She asserts that society needs to be concerned about those who do not receive Social Security due to unreported earnings because they are highly vulnerable. Furthermore, Supplemental Security Insurance (SSI) is not a good substitute for Social Security because it discourages savings through means testing and fails to provide early retirement benefits, survivor benefits, or Medicare benefits. Olson praises the Cohen chapter for filling important gaps in disability insurance research and reiterating the importance of disability insurance to American families.

The Impact of State-Administered Programs on Diverse Populations

Millions of Americans are dependent upon the benefits provided by state-administered programs like Temporary Assistance for Needy Families, unemployment insurance (UI), and Medicaid. The articles in Part IV focus on the importance of understanding how these programs address issues of diversity, equity, and adequacy, which are also pertinent to national programs.

In her analysis of state unemployment insurance, Cheryl Hill Lee discusses racial disparities in access to the programs (chapter 12). Citing figures that show African Americans, Latinos, and women as 6.7, 6.7, and 1.6 percent less likely, respectively, to receive UI benefits than white unemployed men, Hill Lee's chapter attempts to uncover the reasons for these differences in recipiency rates.

Using data from the 2001 Current Population Survey, Hill Lee examined UI benefits by race, age, gender, geography, education, and marital status. She finds that white men and women are more likely to receive UI benefits than African American and Hispanic men and women. African American men, however, are the least likely of all groups to receive UI. Hill Lee says that this is an area of special concern in light of the labor market discrimination and high unemployment rates that African American men also experience. Regionally, she shows that the Midwest and Northeast, followed by the West, have the highest rates of UI recipients. Hill Lee's data illustrate that the South, where the greatest percentage of African Americans in her sample lived, had the lowest UI recipiency rates.

Hill Lee provides evidence that the design of state policies has an effect on access to state unemployment insurance programs. For example, alternative base period policies—which calculate the most recently completed quarter of wages to assess UI eligibility and benefit levels for workers who do not qualify under the regular base period—disregard a half year's worth of an individual's earnings when determining UI eligibility. Whether states provide UI benefits for part-time employees is another example of a policy that affects access to benefits. According to Hill Lee twenty states allow part-time worker benefits. She highlights that part-time workers are disproportionately women and minorities who are unable to get full-time jobs due to child-care obligations and the nature of low-wage jobs. Low-wage earners and less educated, never married individuals are also the least likely to receive UI benefits.

Hill Lee conveys the results from her model estimating how much of the variability in UI recipiency rates could be attributed to state policies. She concludes that gender, race, and ethnic differences in access to UI benefits indicate problems in the administration of the program. She recommends extending UI benefits and addressing issues of bureaucratic discrimination as a way to close disparities in access.

Vicky Lovell provides an in-depth look at temporary disability insurance programs (chapter 13). According to Lovell, TDI short-term medical disability programs include workers' compensation and a program dedicated to covering illnesses and accidents outside of the workplace. Thirty-six percent of American workers had TDI coverage in 1996. Lovell reports that individuals covered by employment-based TDI programs tend to be unionized or highly educated professional and technical workers. Part-time, low-income, and less educated workers are the least likely to receive TDI coverage.

With only five states—California, New Jersey, Rhode Island, New York, and Hawaii—mandating employer TDI coverage, Lovell reports that the types of plans offered vary by eligibility criteria, plan structure and coverage, and worker exclusions. California is notable among the states that offer TDI as a result of its recent expansion to provide up to six weeks of paid family disability leave allowing workers to stay home to care for new babies or sick family members. There are also variations in the payroll tax rates for TDI programs. Lovell notes that the wages of high-income workers are not subject to full taxation.

Lovell adds that there are few demographic data available to determine who does and does not receive TDI coverage. She cites New Jersey Department of Labor statistics showing that women are the majority of TDI claimants. Indeed, the data show that paid maternity leave is the third highest reason for TDI claims. Lovell asserts that data are also inadequate regarding the denial of claims. While 40 percent of those denied benefits in New Jersey are denied on the basis of their unemployed status, Lovell argues that more demographic information is needed to determine whether there is a discriminatory impact based on race or ethnicity. She concludes that TDI programs are a key component of social insurance but should be expanded to provide for better adequacy and access.

Addressing state cash assistance programs, John Monahan provides an overview of diversity in the Temporary Assistance for Needy Families program (chapter 14). Monahan reiterates that while Aid to Families with Dependent Children, TANF's predecessor, was considered a federal program, in actuality the program was a federal-state matching-funds program with benefits that varied greatly by state.

Monahan points out that with the passage of TANF less than half of the block grant funds now provided to the states are allocated to actual cash assistance. Instead, state and local offices have discretion in directing TANF funds toward child care and other work supports. Monahan argues that, as a result of devolution, cash assistance programs have become diverse not only among states but also within states. Federal guidelines remain but only for establishing broad policies like work participation rates, benefit time limits, and restrictions for illegal immigrants.

Assessments of the TANF program have illustrated that, while many participants have left the rolls and joined the work force, most have moved into low-wage jobs. Given the depressed economic climate, Monahan outlines four groups that are particularly vulnerable: (1) welfare leavers who remain unemployed, (2) children living in households where mothers have gone to work, (3) those leavers who remain eligible but have lost their Medicaid and food stamp benefits, and (4) those TANF cases that are child-only or without adult caretakers. With regard to diverse populations, Monahan emphasizes that the share of Hispanics on the caseloads has increased, the share of whites has decreased, and the share of African Americans has remained relatively steady. When assessing the type of state policies that may correlate with the location of diverse populations, he also points out that African Americans tend to be concentrated in states with stricter policies. In addition, studies on those who leave welfare for work have shown that African Americans remain on the rolls longer than whites and are more likely to return to the rolls once they leave.

While federal law imposed a ban on providing TANF benefits to immigrants, Monahan relays that nineteen states have used state funds to provide some coverage for this population. He points out, however, that none of these replacement programs completely compensate for the loss of TANF benefits. Immigrant children, often American citizens born to noncitizens, suffer the most from this arrangement.

Monahan concludes by calling for more studies focused on how diverse groups are treated by "facially neutral" policies and on how to serve those families that fall through the cracks.

Access to health care coverage is the focus of Cindy Mann's presentation on diversity in state-based Medicaid programs (chapter 15). Mann begins by highlighting that racial and ethnic minorities composed a little more than 50 percent of the nonelderly uninsured population in 2001. She adds that low-income citizens made up an even larger percentage of that number. She attributes low rates of coverage among low-income and minorities to gaps in the employer-based health insurance system.

Mann argues that minorities' lower wages influence the type of employer-based health coverage they are offered, their ability to pay for that insurance, and even whether they are offered insurance at all. Despite popular perception, low-income workers may not be eligible for Medicaid due to strict eligibility criteria limiting participation. For example, Mann cites increased uninsured rates for former TANF recipients who lost Medicaid benefits even though they still earned wages below the poverty line. Mann says that this occurred because Medicaid income requirements are so strict that they often exclude those in need. She claims that prior to current budget crises, the Medicaid coverage of parents had improved to include almost twenty states that were covering parents up to the official poverty line.

With the passage of the Child Health Insurance Program (CHIP) in 1997, the coverage outlook for low-income children brightened considerably, according to Mann. She cites data showing that 84 percent of the nation's low-income children were now eligible for Medicaid—a vast improvement when compared to the percentage eligible prior to passage of CHIP. Mann cautions, however, that there are still poor children who are not eligible for Medicaid because they may live in a state where the laws do not extend coverage to persons making up to 200 percent of the poverty level or they may reside in immigrant families who are not eligible for coverage. Indeed, noncitizen, nonelderly individuals make up approximately 20 percent of the uninsured.

Mann warns that many states are seeking to cover budget shortfalls through savings found in Medicaid benefit and eligibility cuts. States are also seeking to find savings by limiting provider participation through cuts in their payment rates. Mann concludes by pointing out that increased restrictions in state Medicaid policies are likely to result in increased coverage disparities among low-income and minority groups.

Medicare and Health Disparities

As the only near universal health care coverage program in the United States, Medicare has helped meet the health needs of American seniors since 1966. Providing coverage to all individuals, regardless of race, income, or geography, Medicare is considered a true social insurance program. Yet there are still questions about whether Medicare provides the same quality of care for all participants. The articles in Part V aim to determine the presence, scope, and impact of health disparities within the Medicare program.

The implementation of Medicare has had a lasting effect on the health of elderly Americans and on the structure of health care in the United States. Paul Eggers begins his treatise on disparities in Medicare by first illustrating how the program has contributed since its passage to increased life expectancies among both African Americans and whites (chapter 16). While great strides have been made, Eggers notes that Medicare was built on an unequal, racialized system of care that has been in place for centuries. As a result, health disparities have been a persistent factor even within a social insurance program that has brought great benefits to many.

Eggers argues that several changes in Medicare led to a more in-depth analysis of health disparities. Implementation of the prospective payment system, which mandated the diagnosis related groups coding system, led to more analysis of the impact of the new payment system on vulnerable groups. Physician payment reform legislation reinforced the inclination to conduct more studies on the hospitalization rates of special populations. Both of these legislative initiatives, according to Eggers, improved hospital reporting systems and the quality of the data, which in turn allowed for better analysis of trends in hospital utilization and care. Additionally, efforts to improve racial coding have enhanced the research capacity of the Medicare database.

Eggers points to studies over time that demonstrated that, among other disparities, African Americans have higher hospitalization rates, less access to coronary angiography, higher per capita Medicare expenditures, and higher rates of end stage renal disease. Other indications of disparities were that African American seniors were much more likely to see a physician as a result of hospitalization instead of regular visits to a doctor's office, much more likely to be without supplemental insurance, and much more likely to report that they were in poor or fair health condition. Disparities in health screenings, such as mammography and pap smears, seem to have been reduced over time.

Eggers concludes by reiterating the need to utilize centers for Medicare and Medicaid services resources to track and monitor important health disparity indicators. He argues that this information will guide effective interventions to eliminate racial and ethic disparities in health care.

According to Nicole Lurie, health disparities in the Medicare program should be viewed primarily as a quality of care issue (chapter 17). She argues that this approach will help to highlight the importance of equity in care while neutralizing public dissension over health issues related to race and ethnicity.

One study highlighted by Lurie examined Health Plan Employer Data and Information Set measures to better understand the health care differences experienced by racial and ethnic groups in Medicare+Choice plans. Her study found that while mammography rates were improving for African Americans and Hispanics, they were very poor for Native Americans. On the other hand, the rate for Asian Americans seemed to be on par with or better than whites. Lurie cautioned, however, that this finding could be misleading when one assesses the rates among various Asian American subgroups. Lurie's data on diabetes follow-up care showed significant racial disparities in the receipt of hemoglobin A1C, and eye exams were worse for African Americans compared to whites. These disparities also held true when one looks at blood pressure control indicators and the receipt of ambulatory services.

A second study highlighted by Lurie used the Consumer Assessment of Health Plans Study data to examine self-reported information about patient satisfaction with Medicare+Choice and other health plans. The study found that African Americans were more likely to report greater levels of satisfaction with health care, their health plan, and with patient-provider communication. Asian Americans, on the other hand, had the worst reported ratings for each of the care measures.

Pointing to variances in the health disparity performance of health plans, Lurie argues that health plans can indeed move more aggressively to reduce and eliminate racial and ethnic health disparities. While managed care plans are not the answer, according to Lurie, federal leadership through Medicare and other programs can go a long way toward addressing the problem.

A panel of distinguished respondents addressed the issues highlighted in the Eggers and Lurie chapters. While each discussant agreed that Medicare has played a pivotal role in helping to reduce racial and ethnic disparities by providing health coverage for eligible beneficiaries, they highlighted different areas that need improvement. Linda Fishman drew on her expertise as a Senate health staffer to argue that federal resources are likely inappropriately or inefficiently deployed to effectively address health disparities. Citing many underutilized preventive care services, Fishman calls for innovative federal efforts to communicate the scope of benefits available to Medicare patients. A system of structured incentives, not punitive measures, provides the best way to improve the quality of care for all beneficiaries, says Fishman.

Brian D. Smedley supported Lurie's argument, underscoring the need to assess the extent of health disparities among all racial and ethnic minorities and their relevant subgroups. While the IOM report did not go far enough in this regard, according to Smedley, he argues that future research should be sensitive to this need. He further questions whether certain types of health plans have a differential impact on access and quality measures for racial and ethnic minorities. He cites a study showing that mandatory enrollment in Medicaid managed care resulted in reduced health care access for minorities when compared to whites enrolled in the same program and other minorities enrolled in Medicaid fee-for-service.

According to Smedley, structural factors like differences in source of care, health system policies, and rates of supplemental insurance are a possible source of health disparities. Differences in health provider treatment provide another possible source. For example, the IOM study showed that African Americans and Hispanics had health disparities even when they accessed the same private physician as a white patient. Smedley highlights that providers' prejudiced attitudes and biased behaviors can contribute to disparities. Finally, differences in patient preferences, attitudes, language, and cultural norms present other possible barriers to care contributing to health disparities.

Given the different possible sources of disparities, Smedley argues that multiple strategies are needed to address the problem. Raising public and provider awareness, implementing better physician training, providing translation services, strengthening data collection and monitoring, and reducing financial disincentives that may obstruct minority access to care are a few of Smedley's proposed remedies.

James Randolph Farris rounded out the commentary by sharing the steps his employer, the Centers for Medicare and Medicaid Services (CMS), is taking to address disparities. In an attempt to be more service oriented, CMS changed its name from the Health Care Financing Administration, established monthly meetings with health care provider and constituency groups, hired more knowledgeable physicians, and created more aggressive health promotion efforts. Additional quality improvement efforts include the introduction of nursing home and home health care quality initiatives and Quality Improvement Organizations (QIO) that monitor the effectiveness of CMS health interventions. This latter initiative works with hospitals and physicians to highlight the underutilization of important preventive care services in an attempt to eliminate racial and ethnic health disparities. Through the QIO initiative, CMS has also established race and ethnicity-specific working groups to develop culturally and linguistically appropriate interventions and materials.

Farris concluded by stressing that, while CMS has undertaken important steps to eliminate health disparities, the greatest threat to the nation's health and the greatest opportunity for improvement lie in addressing the health burdens experienced by historically disadvantaged populations.

Turning Diversity Research into Action

Policy-related research often yields rich data that can help legislators make better program decisions and inform the general public about the direct implications of programs and policies. Information generated by research can spur mass mobilization and social change. Despite the potential power of action inspired by quality research, there has been a general disconnect between quality research, policy debates, and public discourse. The articles in Part VI discuss how to use research findings to empower decisionmakers, bureaucrats, and citizens to act in a manner that improves the circumstances of diverse populations.

Leslie Norwalk provides an overview of the health insurance aspects of the social insurance system (chapter 18). Amid rising costs and uninsured rates, Norwalk argued for a revamped system that would provide quality health care coverage for all people. As a CMS employee, Norwalk outlined the various agency initiatives designed to eliminate racial and ethnic health disparities.

CMS efforts to lower barriers to health care access have included an aggressive outreach initiative targeting education, research, and data collection. According to Norwalk, examples of CMS outreach activities have included open door diversity forums between the CMS director and constituency groups, innovative partnerships with organizations and institutions serving racial and ethnic groups, and the development of Spanish language CMS materials among other efforts.

A number of CMS research projects have also been initiated to better understand racial and ethnic health disparities. Norwalk cited a research partnership with the Morehouse School of Medicine using Medicaid claims data to examine minority health issues. Another study focused on pregnancy-related care and outcomes for minority women on Medicaid, and another Medicaid project analyzed the utilization of cancer-related preventive health care services for women on Medicaid. Other notable studies include an analysis of the proportion of eligible Native Americans and Alaskan Natives enrolled in CMS programs and an examination of gender and racial disparities among Medicare recipients with chronic diseases. Norwalk concluded by reiterating the need for stronger outreach efforts, increased cultural competency, and improvements in the areas of health care access and quality.

James B. Lockhart III of the Social Security Administration (SSA) approached this issue from the perspective of a large bureaucracy that uses research to anticipate the impact of program changes and to improve services for a diverse clientele (chapter 19). With more than 50 million aged, impoverished, and disabled people served each month, SSA serves a wide range of people through the OASDI and SSI programs. Program beneficiaries are not only racially and ethnically diverse, but they also have varying economic circumstances and some are also linguistically diverse.

SSA employees also reflect the diversity of the agency's clientele. Lockhart noted that 10 percent of SSA field office employees and 23 percent of its telephone service center employees are bilingual. Additionally, the percentage of African Americans and Hispanics employed by the SSA is larger than their representation in the federal government or civilian labor force. According to Lockhart, the disabled also represent about 8.2 percent of the SSA work force.

Lockhart argued that the diversity of SSA program beneficiaries informs the nature of the research conducted by the agency. Variables such as race, ethnicity, gender, immigrant status, and income are regularly examined in conjunction with research assessing the impact of policy changes on various demographic groups. Lockhart points out that these demographic differences have an impact on such issues as lifetime earnings and savings rates as well as morbidity and mortality rates. All these factors are important for determining the equity of SSA-administered programs and understanding how program changes like proposals to reform the Social Security system are likely to affect different populations.

Lockhart also affirms that key issues related to diversity must also be addressed when one assesses proposals to create personal retirement accounts. In sum, Lockhart points out that life expectancy, widow benefits, low-income subsidies, and disability benefits are just a few of the diversity-related chal-lenges that must be analyzed in the context of Social Security reform.

Bringing the foundation perspective, Ruby Takanishi addresses how research on disparities and cultural differences can inform social insurance policy and bridge the gap between research and action (chapter 20). Her focus on immigrant families provides important insight into this often overlooked segment of the population. Statistics highlighted by Takanishi show that one of every five children—14 million children—lived in immigrant families in 2000. While some of those children are immigrants, approximately 75 percent of them were born in, and are citizens of, the United States. She notes that as the fastest growing segment of the population, children from immigrant families are expected to make up an even greater percentage of the labor force by the year 2035.

Given the demographic projections, Takanishi argues that it is important for the social insurance system to include policies that speak to the unique needs of children from immigrant families, who will make up a significant portion of the beneficiary population. She points out that economic, education, and health status are all factors that will influence how this population interacts with social insurance programs. Children living in immigrant families currently fare poorly in each of these areas. As a result, she argues that it is imperative that surveys and research studies include information about non–English-speaking Hispanic, Asian, and African immigrant families.

Takanishi discusses a number of policy options that would directly benefit immigrant families. She argues that policymakers should lift the ban on the receipt of welfare benefits for immigrant families as an important first step for helping them achieve economic self-sufficiency. Additionally, because a significant number of the nation's uninsured population includes immigrant children and citizen children living in immigrant families, state and federal health policies should take steps to provide health insurance coverage for this population. Takanishi also supports increasing food stamp availability to immigrant children and argues that more attention needs to be given to immigrant children's access to early education programs, the plight of undocumented immigrants, the adequacy and enforcement of minimum wage laws, and immigrant assimilation programs that support English language proficiency.

In conclusion, Takanishi claims that most social insurance policies need to be updated to accommodate the needs of an America more diverse than when the policies were enacted. She argues that, since policies greatly influence the life circumstances of individuals, merging advocacy with policy analysis is the most important way to improve the lives of children from immigrant families. Ray Suarez affirms Takanishi's conclusion in his commentary on America's changing demographic landscape. With more than 30 million foreign-born people living and working in the United States—approximately half from Mexico and other Latin American countries—Suarez questions how new immigration patterns will affect the immigrants and their chances for success in America. Suarez estimates that their increased presence is likely to have a later generational effect on social insurance programs. Undocumented workers contribute to social insurance programs without receiving benefits. But as subsequent generations become part of the system, they will be beneficiaries and costs will increase. Despite lacking access to social insurance benefits and facing burdens, many newly arrived immigrants, Suarez concludes, feel that America remains a land of opportunity—a place to establish roots not for their personal benefit but for that of future generations.

Conclusion

As the United States becomes increasingly diverse, it is imperative that researchers and policymakers give greater attention to the unique circumstances and needs of vulnerable populations. On the one hand, social insurance programs have provided some important benefits for diverse populations. However, as many conference participants noted, current policies have produced disparate outcomes that can have negative effects on the lives of traditionally underserved and overlooked groups. From education and health to labor market and immigration policies, minority populations have received the short end of the stick in their attempt to attain the "American dream." Thus, given their tenuous hold on many social indicators, racial and ethnic minorities, women, and non–English-speaking immigrants are just a few of the groups that research and policies must address if social insurance programs are to provide equitable and adequate services in the future.

Social Insurance and Disparities in Historical Context

The National Academy of Social Insurance conference drew from many perspectives that included personal, philosophical, and historical interpretations of the role of social insurance in a diverse American society. The insight stemming from these unique perspectives forms the basis for part one of this book.

In chapter 2, Rep. Xavier Becerra (D-Calif.) places a human face on the question of diversity and social insurance by acquainting us with the plight of immigrant workers—such as his parents—who work hard to make ends meet but receive negligible social insurance benefits in return.

In chapter 3, Samuel L. Myers Jr., from the Hubert H. Humphrey Institute of Public Affairs at the University of Minnesota, segues to a philosophical discussion about the importance of pursuing diversity goals in the U.S. social insurance system. Using a mix of empirical references and hypothetical scenarios, Myers challenges the policymakers to think carefully about the value of diversity as a social good and, in turn, how to effectively structure social insurance policies to meet fairness and equity goals.

In chapters 4 and 5 Robert C. Lieberman of Columbia University and Jill Quadagno of Florida State University provide thought-provoking historical accounts about the role of racial diversity in the implementation of the Social Security and Medicare programs. The ensuing dialogue hints at the ambiguity that remains in understanding how questions of race influence and have been affected by the implementation of social insurance programs.

2

Policymaking in
a Diverse America

Xavier Becerra

Public dialogue about social insurance frequently excludes millions of people living in the United States. Social insurance is extremely important to these individuals, but it is out of their reach. They are America's undocumented workers—people who do not have documents to be in this country but work every day, raise families, run businesses, own homes, get sick, get well, and try to get their children to college. They pay into Social Security and Medicare but never collect it because they do not qualify for certain benefits.

The Social Security system is running out of money and needs to be strengthened. It is important to note that this system has some extra money because many undocumented workers contribute to it based on a Social Security number or name that is not valid. They pump dollars into the Social Security trust funds but probably will never collect on it unless the system is changed. Public discourse is not now prepared to address this issue, but it should in the future.

Ninety percent of America was white in 1900. Today that number has dropped to less than 70 percent of the population. Now, 44 million Americans speak a language other than English at home; 28 million Americans are foreign born, up from 9.6 million just thirty years ago. Social Security, a crucial part of America's social insurance safety net, lifts 11 million seniors out of poverty. When Medicare was created in 1965 it immediately doubled the number of seniors who had health insurance to 50 percent. By 1970 the number of seniors with access to health care rose to 97 percent.

Now, more than ever, Americans must support and defend social insurance programs. The socioeconomic challenges faced by diverse Americans present a number of questions about the fairness of social insurance programs. The education gap is one example. Only 57 percent of Latinos twenty-five or older have received a high school diploma compared to 78 percent of African

Americans and 88 percent of whites. Furthermore, only 16 percent of African Americans and 10 percent of Latinos have received a four-year college degree. That compares to nearly 26 percent of whites.

Another example is the wage gap. Women still earn only about seventy-three cents for every dollar earned by a man. The median income for African Americans is about $29,000, about $33,000 for Latinos, and about $46,500 for whites. Controlling for education levels does not eliminate this gap. A white male with a master's degree makes on average $68,000, while a similarly qualified African American male makes $51,000 and a Latino male makes about $60,000.

Yet another challenge facing diverse America is the health care gap. Thirteen percent of white women, 23 percent of black women, and 42 percent of Latino women are uninsured.

There is also the foreign-born gap. The foreign-born represent 11 percent of our population. They make up 12.5 percent of the civilian work force, but some 43 percent of immigrants work in jobs paying less than $7.50 an hour. In contrast, only about 28 percent of the rest of the American work force makes less than this amount. The result of that gap leads to undeniable disparities, but there is variety even within the disparities. Upon entering a fast food chain, for example, one can take a look at the young men or women behind the counter and know that they probably are earning around the minimum wage. But once these individuals have earned $890 during the year, they start to pay into Social Security and their employer also pays into Social Security for those workers' future retirement needs.

On the other hand, one can go a few blocks away and find a homeowner that has an individual come in and clean. That domestic worker might work just as hard as the fast food employees and for as many hours, but chances are that at the end of the year neither the domestic worker nor the employer will have contributed at all to Social Security, thus neglecting the worker's retirement needs. This occurs not because it is the right policy but because politics influences the outcome in this manner. The case of Zoë Baird, who was nominated to be appointed attorney general under President Bill Clinton, high-lights the lack of political will to address the plight of domestic workers. When it was discovered that Baird paid her domestic worker "under the table," the laws were not changed to help the nannies and domestic workers of America but to help those who hire nannies and domestic workers so that none of those individuals, should they come for confirmation before the Senate, would have to face the question: "Did you pay Social Security taxes for your nanny?"

The law passed after the Baird debacle stated that workers do not qualify for Social Security unless they earn $1,400 from one particular employer in a year's time. Because most domestic workers work for multiple employers at any given time, they may never earn $1,400 from one employer in the course of a year and, therefore, never have an opportunity to save for retirement through the Social Security program.

Unfortunately, there is a disconnect between our growing diversity, existing disparities, and current policy proposals. It is bad enough that disparities and "Nanny-gates" are driving our policy. It seems that current proposals will move us even farther away from achieving social justice through social insurance. Recently President George W. Bush declared that Medicare is a binding commitment of a caring society. He could have included Social Security in his statement. Both programs are binding commitments because by their nature they are guaranteed.

President Bush is now proposing that we move toward private systems for Medicare and Social Security. In the case of Medicare, the president embraces a voucher system that requires seniors to join a private health plan to receive prescription drug benefits. Utilizing the private sector for this would increase the risk of higher premiums. With Social Security, his proposal is to divert tax dollars from the Social Security Trust Fund to the stock market—a plan that would subject this system to risk as well. Consider the evisceration of guarantees that occurs when individuals move from a system that tells them they have coverage to one that says they could get more, but only if they play the game and roll the dice.

Without Social Security disability insurance, 55 percent of individuals with disabilities would live in poverty. The Social Security disability benefit amounts to a $353,000 disability insurance policy for someone who is about twenty-five to thirty years of age. Under a privatized system for Social Security, endorsed by the president, this guarantee for people with disabilities might not be available. Furthermore, Social Security currently provides an annual benefit of more than $10,000 to aged widows; this would be eliminated under a private system as well.

It is important to note that existing Social Security benefits are not dependent on the whims of the stock market. That is a relief, considering the poor market performance over the last several years. A privatized system would, in effect, trade in a proven return for an unproven yield.

President Bush also said, "Let's talk about the next generation. Let's not leave our debts to our next generation." But a move away from the guaranteed systems of Social Security, Medicare, and other social insurance programs would mortgage away America's future. The president justifies this change by citing an imbalance in the system and unfairness in our tax policies. However, over the years U.S. corporate income taxes have actually gone down. In 1965

U.S. corporate income taxes represented about 4.1 percent of the gross domestic product. Today they make up only about 1.5 percent. Individual income taxes are also unfair. Currently the wealthiest 1 percent of Americans earns more than 18 percent of America's total pre-tax income. President Bush pushed another tax cut proposal that would cost about $320 billion over the next ten years. That loss of tax income is compounded by the $1.7 trillion tax cut proposal that was passed in 2001. In both cases most of the benefits go to people with the highest income levels in this country.

In the 2001 tax cut more than 30 percent of the tax relief went to the wealthiest 1 percent of Americans. Seventy-eight million taxpayers in the lowest 60 percent of the income scale got an average of $347 a year in savings from that tax cut. President Bush's $320 billion tax cut proposal in 2003 offered 60 percent of the benefits to the top 10 percent, and the top 1 percent of those with incomes averaging in excess of $1 million would receive more than $30,000 apiece. Furthermore, the president's tax cut also proposed to eliminate the tax on corporate dividends at a ten-year cost of about $350–370 billion. This amount is about equal to the cost of a Medicare prescription drug benefit.

At a time when we are trying to figure out how to pay for all these things and increase the availability of our social insurance programs, we should consider what is going on with Social Security and the payroll tax. Only 6 percent of Americans have income that is not fully taxed for purposes of Social Security. The Social Security payroll tax is levied only on earnings up to $72,000. The wealthiest 6 percent with incomes above this level, and not the poorest, of Americans benefit from this loophole. This lost tax money amounts to a very large sum, and we are beginning to see that our long-term ability to correct and improve programs that fall within the safety net of social insurance is eroding.

Privatizing Social Security will also incur a transitional cost, amounting to about $1 trillion over ten years. Prescription drug coverage for seniors will cost about an additional $1.8 trillion over ten years. Still, the president proposes to reduce tax revenue even further. When you add the $1.7 trillion tax cut of 2001 to the proposed 2003 tax cut approaching $1 trillion, the sum is enormous. Looking closely at this, it is clear that we are tinkering with a system that works very well but is not completely understood by the American public. Those who do understand the system have a responsibility for communicating this to the public.

Private enterprise has great power and has contributed enormously to where we are today. President Bush recently spoke about our children driving vehicles that would be powered by hydrogen fuel cells. We have moved from the first telephone lines to broadband and wireless communication, from discovering penicillin to examining the human genome. American enterprise has spurred innovation, and we are a great nation because people can use their entrepreneurial spirit to move forward. Still, there are things that private, for-profit companies cannot or will not do well.

In the end, a company that exists for profit has to look at its bottom line. Private companies face tough choices, and the bottom line is that their financial interests will come before the personal interests of individuals. For example, DSL has only penetrated urban populations, and there is a shortage of Medicare HMO operations in rural America. Private enterprise cannot guarantee fair, equal, and universal access to health care and a decent retirement income to all Americans. Now, more than ever, we can strengthen our diverse communities through social insurance programs that have worked and can work in a diverse America, but we have to defend them in order to see them work into the future.

Although he was born in the United States, I consider my father an immigrant. He was born in 1928 during the time of growing recession and then depression, and if it was hard for an American to find work, it was even harder for my Mexican grandfather. So he took his family back to Mexico right after my father's birth. My father got a sixth-grade education. He worked with his hands all his life, principally as a laborer, building the roads that we now drive on. He never made more than about $23,000, and together he and my mother earned in fifteen years what today my wife and I will earn in one year. Yet somehow, on their income, they were able to raise four children in a 580 square foot, one-bedroom home. Together they saw all four of their children enter college, and now, because of my work in Washington, they have met the president of the United States. This occurred not because they were educated or wealthy but because they were able to pass an opportunity to do better on to the next generation, both to their own children and to others. But now, the same opportunity would not be there for the next generation of young people trying to go to college, especially young people of color.

We have to deal with the challenge that we face today with diversity. Diversity also means disparity, not because it comes naturally with diversity but because our nation still has remnants of discrimination. Today there are many men and women like my father and mother, who have limited skills but work very hard. They are the people that will be supporting us when we retire. However, if 43 percent of our immigrant population continues to make $7.50 an hour or less, they will not contribute an adequate amount to Social Security to make the system sustainable, whether it is privatized or not. If we are serious about social insurance and the contract we have with America to provide a safety net, then we have to deal with the realities of our population today. We cannot will it or wish it away.

Today, while many people of color have tried to enter college, they have been denied. While many have tried to move up the corporate ladder, they have been denied. And many, like my parents, have worked more than forty years, and those that do not have financial-planning skills must rely on the next generation as they retire. When my father was in his prime as a worker, there were 5 workers for every retiree. Today we have 3.5 workers for every retiree, and that number is expected to fall to about 2.3 workers in the year 2025; by 2075 the estimate is less than 2 workers for every retiree in America.

Most people of color today are younger than most of the folks who are not black, Latino, or Asian. Thirty-five percent of Latinos are under the age of eighteen, compared to 32 percent of African Americans and only 24 percent of whites. The median age of Latinos in this country is ten years younger than that of the rest of the population. Since 1990 the nation's population has grown by about 13 percent, but for whites over that same time the increase has been less than half that rate. Forty-two percent of the population growth over the last decade is attributable to immigration.

We must address the fact that we have a growing number of people of color who will become our eighteen-year-olds preparing to go to college and our twenty-four-year-olds preparing to enter the work force full time. These populations are preparing to start contributing to Social Security and Medicare. If we do not account for their unique situation, we will not address the growing gap between what is necessary and what we are currently providing to ensure that social insurance is meaningful for everyone in the future.

As we consider diversity in America and the future of social insurance in the twenty-first century, there is more to worry about than just the fiscal policy of this country and the problems inherent in privatization proposals for Social Security or Medicare. We must also worry about providing our people with the tools they will need to succeed. We must provide what is needed to sustain them, whether it is school, vocational education, or opportunities. This is difficult to do when some people must live on $5.15 an hour. In Los Angeles, where many people flip hamburgers and clean homes, it is impossible to live on the minimum wage. Washington, D.C., is not much different, and may in fact be even more difficult. Yet the law tells people that they can work and they should survive on $5.15 an hour.

Social insurance is a very important subject, and the programs that constitute its safety net are very important. The president recently said that if you are seeking a job, there should be a job there for you. But we should go further. If you are not just seeking, but also actually working, you should have a livable wage. It is unreasonable to expect that the social insurance safety net will continue to exist if hard workers must contribute from an hourly wage of $5.15.

It is not Marxist to call for a livable wage, nor is it offensive. It is time to insist that the private sector and the government call an end to such a low wages. We must realize that many full-time workers earn the minimum wage and, as a result, have annual earnings that are $4,300 below the poverty level. The minimum wage has lost 35 percent of its purchasing power over the last twenty years. It is time to adopt a livable minimum wage, as eighty cities and counties have done already throughout America. Sixty-one percent of the workers who will benefit from this livable wage will be women, and another 30 percent of them represent minority groups, primarily black or Latino. This is not a novel idea. Today America is strong, and it is a better nation because of our diversity. We can strengthen the diverse American community by providing a livable wage and adequate social insurance.

Sooner or later it will dawn on America that a living wage, universal health care, and a guaranteed Social Security benefit are consistent with America's core values. Now, more than ever, we must recognize that our partners in making America's social programs work in the future will be those faces of diversity, and those who are making diversity work.

It is people like my mother and my father who have made this country great, although we did not recognize this during their generation. It is time for us to recognize that we owe it to them to provide them with an essential safety net, including Social Security, Medicare, and a living wage. As this problem is considered, we must pay attention to the "Nanny-gate" issue. There are millions of people who pay into Social Security but will never receive any benefits, and there are people who will work for generations cleaning our homes or driving our buses but will never quite be able to save enough to survive once they retire.

If we truly want to make diversity work and strengthen our communities, then as a nation we have to deal with the bottom line just like a private company does. The bottom line should be that social insurance must be guaranteed, and it must be backed by a guarantee that we will hold up people's dignity to work and earn a living. If we head in that direction, we will set the course for the next generation.

The scholars and experts in this field should talk to us in Congress so that that powerful Ways and Means Committee can pass legislation that will give all Americans a chance to say that we will do right by the fathers and mothers of America.

Questions

QUESTION: Would you comment on the fiscal situation that you see confronting the country that establishes the environment within which the debate about Medicare and Social Security reform is going to take place?

REP. BECERRA: We just got revised numbers on the size of the budget deficit for the coming year. We are now being told by the Congressional Budget Office (CBO) that it will probably be $199 billion for fiscal year 2004, which means it will probably be revised up in the next few months to beyond $200 billion.* That is on top of the approximately $157 billion deficit that we had for fiscal year 2003, which when you extract the Social Security monies that are going into the budget is well beyond $300 billion as a deficit for the operating budget of the federal government for fiscal year 2003.

In addition, it will certainly cost more than half a trillion dollars to do anything on prescription drugs. And you have all heard your doctors and hospitals saying how much they need relief. Medicare reform will cost us several tens of billions of dollars.

At some point we will address the growing divide within Social Security as a result of demography. That will cost us trillions. Those tax cuts that were passed in 2001 and proposed in 2003 will not immediately stimulate the economy. When you talk to most economists they will tell you those are long-term injections into the economy, if they have any measurable effect at all.

To stimulate the economy you need something that acts right away. As for the dividends tax cut proposal, I do not know how much stock you own, but I do not own very much any more. What I used to own has greatly diminished over the last two years. I do not know how many of you have thousands of dollars in stock dividends, where as a result you are going to have a lot of tax savings from no taxation on dividends. Certainly it does save folks a lot of money, but that is extremely skewed toward very wealthy individuals.

You have to do the math at some point and add up our costs. The war in Iraq has estimated costs of $200 or $300 billion. That does not include the rebuilding of Iraq or peacekeeping. It also does not include potential efforts with North Korea and all the rest.

It adds up, and I do not see any way to balance the books. Even though we are now hearing from the administration that budget deficits are not bad, I think the reality is that budget deficits are antigrowth, and unless we deal with them we will have real trouble. The biggest tax cut we can give any American—at least middle-class Americans—is not in dividends tax relief; it is not in marriage penalty relief. It is in keeping the interest rates low throughout America so that every middle-class family that owns a home will

---

*By March the CBO had increased this projected deficit to $246 billion for 2003 and $200 billion for 2004. By August the projections were for deficits of $401 billion in 2003 and $480 billion in 2004. The CBO's baseline projections for deficits between 2003 and 2013 add up to $1.397 trillion.

continue to pay low rates on the mortgage. It is in assuring that every middle-class American who does not get the benefits of grants and scholarships for low-income people and does not earn enough to pay the full cost of an education at our good colleges and universities throughout this nation can get low-cost student loans, That is the best break we can give to middle-class America.

But, if you start spending money here and there, you will not be able to do some things, and that includes, of course, Social Security into the long term.

So the budget picture, I believe, is shaky. The president says we have now pulled out of a recession. I go home and people tell me they have not seen us pull out of it. I believe that we are going to find it will be very difficult to add up the numbers, including simple things like the president's proposal to increase AIDS money in Africa by $10 billion.

QUESTION: I care very much about the Latino community. I hope that you are going to have some input into this totalization agreement that we are trying to work out with Mexico. I think that we have done a great disservice to some of our foreign workers, particularly Mexicans. I did not like the 1983 anti-immigrant provisions on Social Security. I want Mexicans who have worked in this country, and people of other nationalities who have worked here, to get a fair return on their dollar.

As you say, we are living off their earnings and cutting them off, and particularly cutting off any spouses unless you lived here at least five years and can prove it. Some of these stipulations are just ungodly.

I want you to have input because I think you can do it.

REP. BECERRA: We are trying to see if there is an opportunity to work on resolving that issue and coming up with a treaty with Mexico. I believe that this was one of the proposals that came forward, along with immigration reform, when President Fox met with President Bush and the administrations talked to each other.

Unfortunately, I think that right now other matters are consuming President Bush's attention. As you saw, Jorge Castañeda, who was the foreign minister for Mexico, resigned recently, complaining for the most part that many of his initiatives, principally that of immigration reform with the United States, faltered. One of the issues that they have been trying to address is the fact that so many migrants from Mexico work in the United States and, whether documented or undocumented, oftentimes when they return to Mexico they return with no stability for their retirement.

At some point we will address it, but there are dollars involved, and it goes both ways. We do have Americans who go to work in Mexico; it is a far smaller number, but it does go both ways.

QUESTION: Do you see AIDS assistance going to El Salvador, Guatemala, and Honduras—those countries in the Americas that are almost as devastated as Africa?

REP. BECERRA: We have to fight to get what the president said with regard to Africa because right now if we cannot get it for Africa, where things are dire when it comes to HIV and AIDS, we are never going to get it into places like Central America, where it is becoming a growing problem.

We have to first succeed in passing what the president proposed when it comes to AIDS/HIV. Given the numbers in Africa, this is still a drop in the bucket, and that's scary to say, $10 billion additional to the $5 billion already earmarked.

QUESTION: I'd like to ask you about one of the common things that is argued about the so-called unaffordability of Social Security, which is that the aging of the population, of course, increases the number of people who will require benefits. A common proposal made by many people has been that the retirement age be raised.

And from the standpoint of diversity, in particular, of one's work history, that is a potential problem because the people who are working at the jobs you are talking about are not likely to be able to work to the age of sixty-eight, sixty-nine, or seventy as easily as other people.

One thing that is also true of them is that they generally started work at eighteen or nineteen, say, whereas the people who make the recommendations about raising their time and age may have only gone full time into the work force at twenty-five or, in the case of someone who took a long time on the Ph.D., like myself, even later.

But that suggests that if you are concerned about diversity, about the kind of work people do, and about the difference between blue-collar and white-collar jobs, you might consider changing the basis of entitlement for Social Security to not just age based, but a mix of age and years in the work force. If you made it a mix of age and years in the work force, then your terms could be such that a blue-collar person could retire at sixty-five with full benefits, and a person who got a J.D. or Ph.D. would have to go to sixty-eight or seventy.

What do you think about the issue itself? You might not have any thoughts on that proposal itself, but what about the basic issue of how raising the retirement age affects diversity concerns?

REP. BECERRA: I was hoping I'd get to escape having to answer what are the solutions to Social Security, but raising the age has to be among the proposals considered simply because of the realities of America's demography. I don't think you can take anything off the table, given that we are getting closer and closer to the time when everyone will understand that Social Security needs to be supported.

I agree with you that if we are shortsighted enough to just say that we can increase the age of retirement because we are all living longer, you again will ignore my parents. My father has had operations on both hands over the years because his tendons have fused and it is difficult for him to open his hand. That is principally because for the first twenty years of his life he used a pick and shovel eight to ten hours a day, and then after that it became the jackhammer.

He has had one knee operation, and he should have had a second, but he does not like the results of the first, and he has always had chronic back problems. I won't tell you about the scars on his back. I won't tell you about the chunks of skin that are missing from his body, but he is one of those individuals who for years used his physical abilities, his body, to construct America.

To believe that people like my father should continue to work—my father is now in his early seventies—is outrageous.

I hope that we recognize that, while the numbers say that we are living longer, we should go beyond the numbers. That is why I try to say that diversity is more than skin deep. You have to analyze what diversity means. There are a lot of folks who have been in this country a long time working the same type of work physically, especially places in the South, where for the longest time that was the only type of work available to people of color, where we have for generations denied them an opportunity to have more for the next generation, and so we have exacerbated a problem.

To just all of a sudden increase the retirement age because we need to resolve Social Security's dilemmas, we have said to a whole lot of folks that we will not respect the physical labor that have given this country. We will not acknowledge the impediments to getting educated and becoming more prosperous.

I hope that what we will do is to think about the men and women in America who look a little bit different from most of those who get to make the policy and recognize that it is a lot more difficult when you go beyond skin to resolve the problem.

We will have many options to deal with Social Security's imbalance, but if we go toward something like increasing the retirement age, I hope we accommodate the realities of work life, especially for women, because they do not have an opportunity even today, even with the change in society, to put in the same number of years of work that a man does. A woman's work life, on average, is about fourteen years less because of the days caring for family.

3

Equity and Social Insurance

Samuel L. Myers Jr.

Current debate about the fairness or equity of alternative policy options for reform of social insurance is marred by confusion about what constitutes fairness or equity. In particular, when race and ethnicity enter the equation, notions of equity or fairness change. The conventional public finance dichotomy between vertical and horizontal equity fails to convey the complexity of contemporary conceptualizations of fairness. In this chapter an illustration is offered from the literature on affirmative action in public sector labor markets to underscore the competing ideas surrounding fairness when race and ethnicity are added to the mix. Future directions in evaluating the racial impacts of alternative social insurance proposals must make more explicit the measurement of fairness adopted.

Context

Public administrators need explicit guidelines for implementing social programs. This is true whether the implementation goals are to encompass cost-effectiveness and efficiency or fairness and equity. While explicit criteria and guidelines exist for measuring efficiency and cost-effectiveness, there is much ambiguity in the profession about how to measure fairness. There is an equal amount of ambiguity in the general population as to what constitutes fairness.

The National Academy of Public Administration has recognized this dilemma and in response has created a social equity committee to review measurement issues. The committee aims to propose a set of criteria that will help public administrators assess the equity impacts of policies. Specifically, the committee was created to:

1. review and evaluate developments in public administration, including existing and emerging issues and problems, new ideas and current opinions,

significant research and research needs, institutional development, and critical matters in social equity and governance in need of attention

2. provide general guidance and evaluation of related problem-solving project activities of the academy relating to social equity and governance

3. inform the academy membership of important developments in social equity and governance

4. initiate or sponsor educational meetings to communicate with a wider portion of the public administration community

5. prepare papers on social equity and governance for public release, when judged appropriate

6. serve as a forum where interested fellows can interact with each other to learn about issues and developments in social equity and governance

7. serve as a means of identifying ideas, issues, and projects in social equity and governance

8. provide or recommend witnesses, and/or draft or review testimony, for congressional hearings related to social equity and governance.[1]

In creating this committee, the National Academy of Public Administration acknowledged that the profession lacks specific guidelines and standards for *implementing* equity. Why is there such a lack? And, what is, or what should be, the basis for making equity judgments in the public sector? Part of the answer lies in developments within the field of public finance.

What Is Fairness or Equity?

Equality of treatment is a widely held notion of fairness among public finance scholars. Richard Musgrave, writing in the first edition of his widely heralded treatise on public finance, wrote:

> Perhaps the most widely held accepted principle of equity in taxation is that people in equal positions should be treated equally. This principle of equality, or *horizontal equity,* is fundamental to the ability-to-pay approach, which requires equal taxation of people with equal ability and unequal taxation of people with unequal ability.[2]

This notion of fairness can be expanded to mean equal treatment of those who are in all relevant senses identical. Anthony B. Atkinson and Joseph E. Stiglitz, however, point out that in implementation this definition raises more questions than it answers. What do we mean by "relevant"? Is marital status a relevant factor? What do we mean by "equal treatment"? Do we mean equal treatment at birth or equal treatment after the fact?[3] While extensive literature exists detailing how to deal with these implementation issues, not everyone agrees that the most important measure of fairness is horizontal equity.[4] Pitted against horizontal equity is the notion of vertical equity, which roughly assures unequal treatment. C. Eugene Steuerle defines vertical equity this way:

> Vertical equity, for its part, generally requires that those with less ability be treated favorably relative to those with greater ability.[5]

The idea is that a given tax payment burdens someone with a small income more than someone with a large income. The attractiveness of vertical equity is that it may solve the *social welfare maximization* problem, wherein those with the highest incomes receive lower extra utility or satisfaction from an extra dollar than those with the lowest incomes. Equality of treatment (horizontal equity) may fail to achieve social optimization.

Unfortunately, additional measurement problems are introduced by the vertical equity solution. How can we gauge people's ability to pay? Could people distort their ability to pay in order to benefit from the lower marginal tax rates for low-income people? Does the higher tax rate on high-income people reduce their work effort or their incentives in ways that harm efficiency?

Equality of Outcomes and Opportunity

Two other notions of fairness commonly found in the social justice literature include equality of outcomes and equality of opportunity. Equality of outcomes requires a standard for outcomes. The standard might be income, satisfaction, admission to college, or job application success rates. The equality of outcomes measure is often used in measuring *the fairness of public processes.*

Consider the problem of public procurement and contracting. Billions of dollars a year are spent by state and local governments on construction projects and on purchases of goods and services. As does the federal government, many state and local governments procure goods and services from the private sector. One way to determine whether women- and minority-owned business enterprises receive a "fair share" of government contracts is to compare their share of contracts to their share of the number of businesses. If 15 percent of all business enterprises are women- and minority-owned, then the equality of outcomes would dictate that 15 percent of government contracts—or of government contract and procurement dollars—should go to women- and minority-owned firms. Of course, the premise here is that the 15 percent of business firms found in the general population are willing, able, and qualified to bid on government contracts. While it may be necessary to make appropriate adjustments to the base numbers of business firms in order to derive the "willing, able, and qualified" sample, the resulting computation is clear: equal outcomes for equally qualified firms.

Pitted against the concept of equality of outcomes is the notion of equality of opportunity. Herein the idea is that all firms should be lined up at the starting gate with the same initial endowments. Account may be taken of unequal endowments by appropriate compensatory efforts, but once equality of opportunity is achieved, no special effort should be made to mandate or create specific outcomes.

What is interesting about the distinction between equality of outcomes and equality of opportunity is that it parallels, in many respects, the distinction between horizontal equity and vertical equity. Although it may surprise many who hear this claim, the "equal treatment" dictum of horizontal equity really is about equality of outcomes. The reasoning is simple. If two persons with identical incomes (or other relevant characteristics) are to be treated equally, then they must pay the same tax. But what is the equal treatment in this instance? The equality of treatment is nothing more than the equality of observed outcomes from tax payments. Equal treatment means equal outcomes for identically situated individuals.

Thus we see that this commonly adopted measure of fairness—horizontal equity—is analogous to equality of outcomes. Many conservative economists and political thinkers who reject normative judgments that underlie arguments for vertical equity in taxation fiercely cherish the concept of horizontal equity. As soon as the topic turns to racial admissions policies or diversity in employment, however, the same thinkers characteristically embrace the idea of equality of opportunity while rejecting the idea of equality of outcomes.

There are other competing measures of equality, such as individual equality,[6] equality of groups, and equality of identically situated segments of individuals. But equality is not the only measure of fairness or equity. Compensatory equity captures the idea that in order for one group (or individual) to be equal today, compensation for past inequalities must be made. For example, consider the fact of unequal homeownership rates. Many white families in the current generation own homes as a result of gifts or transfers from parents or grandparents. Their parents or grandparents often benefited from federal policies that significantly advantaged white Americans while no comparable advantage was given to nonwhites. The legacy of home ownership among white families in the post-World War II era also conferred upon whites benefits in the credit market. The patterns and practices that help consumers signal to lenders that they are good credit risks are significantly related to home ownership. After generations of not owning homes, African Americans, in particular, are often viewed as poor credit risks and thus have high loan-denial rates. Therefore, even though racial gaps in homeownership have narrowed, signaling a decline in historic housing market disadvantages, racial minority groups still lag behind whites in their ability to obtain loans.[7] Policy efforts to compensate for these prior inequalities necessitate unequal treatment of whites and nonwhites. Compensatory equity is unequal by design.

Social justice scholars also point to another type of inequality as fairness. *Procedural fairness* dictates only that all persons confront the same set of rules and that those rules be applied consistently and transparently.[8] The rules themselves may not produce equality. The only thing equal in this instance is the application of the rules.

Another notion of fairness that deviates from the dictum of equality is Rawlsian fairness.[9] This familiar concept argues for maximizing the position of the worst-off person. Unequal distributions are inevitable. What matters is where one falls within the distribution. The least well-off person is as well off as possible in the Rawlsian world. Simple equality is neither necessary nor sufficient for this type of fairness.[10]

Baumolian-Varian fairness represents another attempt to codify and rationalize measures of equity. This concept may be illustrated by the phrase "I cut, you choose." The idea is that a distribution is considered fair if it does not generate envy.[11] It is an individualistic measure of fairness that shares many of the virtues of conventional rational-choice analysis, which places great emphasis on the preferences of consumers.[12] The Baumolian-Varian fairness measure asks, "Would I prefer the slice of the pie that the other person gets or my own slice of the pie?" Although the Baumolian-Varian approach has not received the same amount of attention as other approaches to equity, it clearly has revolutionary implications for understanding why there is so much hostility to affirmative action and other public policies designed to compensate for previous inequalities. An example will suffice to indicate these dramatic implications.

An Illustration

Suppose that the municipal fire department has one midlevel slot to fill. Suppose that this slot is desirable because it confers on the holder prestige, improved salary and benefits, and perhaps even increased self-esteem or self-worth.[13]

Scenario one. There are two criteria for promotion to this desirable position: merit, as measured by a test score, and managerial ability. Managerial ability is determined through a subjective assessment. Now, suppose there are

100 applicants, all of whom are white males. One person is selected. This person has the tenth highest test score but the highest rating on the managerial ability assessment. How many people think this is unfair?

Scenario two. The criteria are the same as above. There are 100 applicants; 99 white males and 1 white female. The white female is selected for promotion. She has the highest score on the managerial assessment and the tenth highest test score. How many people think this is unfair?

Scenario three. A public body announces that diversity is a new criterion for promotion. There are 100 applicants: 99 white males and 1 white female. The white female is selected. She has the tenth highest test score, the tenth highest managerial ability, but highest contribution to diversity. How many people think this is unfair?

These three scenarios capture something specific about real affirmative action hiring and promotion plans. The plans often build on existing concepts of merit. In scenarios one and two there are "objective" and "subjective" measures of merit that have long-standing acceptance within the profession. The third scenario adopts an additional measure of merit, which is contested in many circles.

In dozens of presentations before professional audiences (including firefighters, police officers, and private security officials, but also with social workers, public administrators, and corporate executives), I discovered that the point about alternative measures of fairness was completely lost if in the second scenario I substituted "black" for "white female." Even in my graduate-level classes, for some reason my students become uncomfortable and sufficiently enraged by the prospect of a "quota" or other "unfair" promotion scheme so as to be unable to grasp the point I wish to make. Thus to avoid the distraction of race, I focus on gender in this example.

In my experience, few people feel that scenario one is unfair, although many point out that, at most, nine firefighters might consider the outcome unfair. These are the nine firefighters who received higher scores than the firefighter who was promoted. Since only one person can be promoted, the other ninety firefighters must be content with knowing that a more qualified candidate got the job.

Reactions to scenario two vary by gender. The vast majority of women participants in my seminars think that ninety-nine men would see the process as unfair. These women report that not only do the nine men with better scores feel there is unfairness, but that the ninety men with lower test scores also feel unfairness. The women respondents report that somehow men do not believe that the real reason for the selection was managerial ability, which after all is measured subjectively.

How can ninety-nine men feel that scenario two is unfair when at most nine men would feel that scenario number one is unfair? The outcome is essentially the same. One person got the job and the person who got the job had the highest managerial score and the tenth highest test score. Nothing is different except the gender composition of the pool and the gender of the winner. I ask men in my audience whether, in this scenario, they would prefer to be a woman and the winner or a man and the loser. Most would prefer to be a man. "I cut, you choose" reveals that this outcome is not necessarily unfair, despite initial protests to the contrary.

Scenario three opens everyone's eyes. Even some women mention that the low scores on two of the other criteria make the ultimate selection suspect. Yet, is affirmative action the cause of the discontent with the *outcome* in scenario three? Opposition to affirmative action as unfair requires that we compare the distribution in scenario two with that in scenario three and conclude that someone is worse off. But, who is worse off? There may be at most eighteen white men who feel this result is unfair (assuming no overlap among the nine who received higher test scores and the nine who received higher managerial scores). In the limiting case where the managerial score *is* the diversity measure, there is no difference between the two scenarios, despite the heavy reaction among many males to the "unfair" introduction of diversity to the evaluation process.

Now, in a way, the existing evaluation criteria *privilege* those who have historically held the job. The introduction of compensatory criteria must by necessity create inequality. The "best qualified" candidate as measured by the old criteria is not offered the promotion. Privileged applicants will view the revised process as being unfair under equality measures. But Baumolian-Varian fairness does not mandate equality. Instead, it asks, "Would white male firefighters prefer to be females—who historically have been excluded from firefighting as a profession—and receive the added bonus that comes from the diversity criterion or would they prefer to be males?"[14] One way to convince those who are privileged by the prevailing notion of fairness (for example, equality of outcomes) is to invite them to explore alternative notions of fairness.

Application to Disability Insurance and Social Security

Consider two hypothetical systems. One is neutral with respect to race, although it differentiates between individuals based on life expectancy and marital status. The first system, while race-neutral on its face, rewards persons with longer life expectancies and those who are married. African Americans have shorter life expectancies and are less likely to be married. Thus the criteria for rewards have a differential impact on African Americans, despite the seeming neutrality of the criteria.

Now consider a second hypothetical system. This system contains progressivity. The benefit formula provides proportionately higher benefits to lower earners. Moreover, those who are disabled receive their benefits sooner and thus obtain higher rates of return than those who live to the same retirement age. African Americans have lower earnings and are more likely than whites to become disabled at early ages, thus they are advantaged in this system.

There are racially unequal rates of return in both systems. In the first, African Americans are disadvantaged, even though everyone in principle is treated the same. In the second, not everyone is treated the same; those with low ability to work receive high benefits.[15]

Suppose that a policy change is proposed that will *equalize* the rates of return in these two hypothetical systems. The change envisioned compensates blacks for their higher mortality rates by paying them more. The change would reduce disability benefits, penalizing blacks for their higher accident rates. For the sake of argument, let us suppose that the net effect of this equalization is to increase the overall rate of return to the blacks as a group. Is this system fair?

Would whites prefer to be black and thereby benefit from a race-based remedy or would they prefer to be white with their existing advantages?[16]

What is wrong with this picture?

Does anyone seriously believe that Social Security or disability insurance should be adjusted by race? Shouldn't the process be "fair" by making it race-neutral? Why is this picture so germane to the current discussions about social security reform?

In many respects the current discussions acknowledge that there are racially unequal outcomes but seek to remedy these inequities without directly confronting their historically significant antecedents.[17] The question, then, is why are race-based solutions not a part of the larger policy discussion? In policy discussions about racial gaps in labor markets, housing markets, public contracting and procurement, and education, race-conscious remedies are among the most frequently identified solutions. Why, then, are race-based solutions not also in the forefront of discussions of unequal rates of return within the Social Security and disability insurance systems?

The Problem of Shifting Measures of Fairness

The current social security system arguably provides unequal benefits across races. It also seeks to provide equality of benefits across the three main components of the system: survivors' insurance, disability insurance, and retirement funds. It presumes equal outcomes for individuals of identical circumstances. But, because African Americans are more likely than whites to receive disability and survivor's benefits, *as a group* blacks appear to be favored by this aspect of the system. Because they earn less over shorter periods, blacks appear to be disfavored in the retirement component of the system. Many argue that on balance the current system favors African Americans. Nevertheless, the system does appear to meet the standard of horizontal equity, wherein there are equal outcomes for those who are in all relevant senses identical. If there were no difference in benefits by race, there probably would be little dispute over the fairness of the system. But, precisely because of the uneven distribution of benefits by race, the idea of fairness is challenged. In this instance, the unfairness is unwittingly registered because of the apparent benefits that one racial group receives relative to others.

Those who argue that there ought not be any racial favoritism in the system but that there ought to be equality of rates of return both across programs and between groups are in effect arguing that beneficiaries of the system—such as African Americans—derive their benefits from an inherent unfairness of equating benefits levels rather than equating rates of return. Put differently, proposals to reform Social Security by assuring *equality of rates of return* adopt a principle of fairness that is color-blind. Unfortunately, this color-blindness could adversely affect African Americans. If disability and survivor's benefits—that disproportionately benefit blacks—were to be cut to assure equality of rates of return across components of the social security system, blacks as a group might lose (depending on how they fare with respect to retirement benefits).

The color-blind notion of fairness deviates from the horizontal equity dictum that there ought to be equality of treatment of "those who are in all relevant senses identical." The operable term in this conventional definition of horizontal equity is *relevant*. Few analysts are willing to concede—at least until recently—that race is a relevant factor in assessing what is "identical." Ignoring race—as one attempts to do when constructing color-blind policies— ignores the historic forces that contribute to unequal life circumstances based on race. Equal treatment of identically situated individuals—where race is a relevant factor in assessing one's circumstances or situation—is no longer "fair" in the color-blind scenario. From a distance, it looks like the notion of fairness has shifted as soon as the reality of race enters the equation.

Precisely because of the apparently shifting evaluation criterion when discussions of race emerge, I argue for adopting multiple measures of fairness that are made explicit at the outset. Just as conventional policy analysis offers multiple measures of effectiveness, appropriateness, political feasibility, and the like, in the analysis of social insurance programs there should be multiple measures of fairness.[18] We need to make more explicit the possibility that differing standards of fairness may apply for race or ethnicity considerations than to income or ability to pay considerations. It would be particularly helpful to acknowledge that many fairness criteria are in conflict with one another and that race and ethnicity considerations frequently expose these conflicts.

Notes

1. National Academy of Public Administration, *Standing Panel on Social Equity in Governance: Panel Charter*, 2001 (www.napawash.org/aa_social_equity/panel_charter.html [accessed April 21, 2003]).

2. Richard Musgrave, *The Theory of Public Finance: A Study in Public Economy* (McGraw-Hill, 1959), p. 160.

3. Anthony B. Atkinson and Joseph E. Stiglitz, *Lectures on Public Economics* (McGraw-Hill, 1980), p. 353.

4. Alan. J. Auerbach and Kevin A. Hassett, "A New Measure of Horizontal Equity," *American Economic Review* 12, no. 4 (2002), pp. 1116–25; Udo Ebert and Peter J. Lambert, "Horizontal Equity and Progression When Equivalence Scales Are Not Constant," Discussion Paper, Department of Economics and Related Studies, University of York, United Kingdom, 2002; Dale W. Jorgenson, "Aggregate Consumer Behavior and the Measurement of Social Welfare," *Econometrica* 58, no. 5 (1990), pp. 1007–40; Mervyn A. King, "An Index of Inequality: With Applications to Horizontal Equity and Social Mobility," *Econometrica* 51, no. 1 (1983), pp. 99–115; Harvey S. Rosen, "An Approach to the Study of Income, Utility, and Horizontal Equity," *Quarterly Journal of Economics* 92, no. 2 (1978), pp. 307–22.

5. C. Eugene Steuerle, "And Equal (Tax) Justice for All?" Urban Institute, 2002 (www.urban.org/url.cfm?ID=900579 [accessed April 25, 2003]).

6. Steuerle, "And Equal (Tax) Justice for All?"

7. Sheila D. Ards and Samuel L. Myers Jr., "The Color of Money: Bad Credit, Wealth, and Race," *American Behavioral Scientist* 45, no. 2 (2001), pp. 223–39.

8. E. Allan Lind and Tom R. Tyler, *The Social Psychology of Procedural Justice* (Plenum Press, 1988).

9. John Rawls, *A Theory of Justice*, rev. ed. (Harvard University Press, 1999).

10. John Rawls, "Some Reasons for the Maximum Criterion," *American Economic Review* 64, no. 2 (1974), pp. 141–46.

11. William J. Baumol, "Applied Fairness Theory and Rationing Policy," *American Economic Review* 72, no. 4 (1982), pp. 639–51; William. J. Baumol, "Applied Fairness Theory: Reply," *American Economic Review* 73, no. 5 (1983), pp. 1161–62; William J. Baumol, *Superfairness: Applications and Theory* (MIT Press, 1986).

12. An early representation of this perspective is found in Alan M. Feldman and Alan Kirman, "Fairness and Envy," *American Economic Review* 64, no. 6 (1974), pp. 995–1005.

13. I make this assumption based on responses from firefighters and police officers in various seminars and presentations who argue that some midlevel managerial (or

office) jobs are not necessarily preferred by frontline personnel who may gain nonpecuniary benefits from fighting fires or catching criminals.

14. These examples are motivated by actual court-mandated hiring and promotion plans in the Minneapolis and St. Paul fire departments in response to allegations of racial discrimination. See *Robert Mems, Nathaniel Khalif, Philip Webb, Thurman Smith, and Byron Brown* v. *The City of St. Paul–Department of Fire and Safety Services*, 224 F. 3d 735 (8th Cir. 2000).

15. These two simple scenarios abstract from the more complex factors underlying social security benefits and disability insurance. For details on the racial disparities inherent in both, see U.S. General Accounting Office, *Social Security and Minorities: Earnings, Disability Incidence, and Mortality Are Key Factors That Influence Taxes Paid and Benefits Received,* GAO–03–387 (2003); Daniel M. Garrett, "The Effects of Differential Mortality Rates on the Progressivity of Social Security," *Economic Inquiry* 33, no. 3 (1995), pp. 457–75; John R. Grist, "Social Security Reform: How Do Minorities Fare under Social Security? A Response to Two Heritage Foundation Reports," AARP, 1998 (research.aarp.org/econ/ib34_ssmindd_1.html [accessed April 25, 2003]).

16. One question that I do not pursue here is: Would blacks prefer race-based equalization rather than some social scheme that reduced their accident rates and increased their life expectancies?

17. The current system uses one benefit formula, ensuring that everyone receives the same benefit whether it is from the disability, survivors, or old age pool. But, the same benefit amount means different rates of return. If the rates of return were made equal, inequality in benefit amounts would result. Some argue that the net result is more racially equal because of the structure of survivors' benefits and the significant disparity in black/white mortality rates in early midlife. Note, for example, the historically low social welfare benefits to African Americans. See Frances Fox Piven and Richard A. Cloward, *Regulating the Poor: The Functions of Public Welfare* (Vantage Books, 1993); Robert C. Lieberman, "Diversity in the U.S. Social Insurance: A Historical Overview," chapter 4 of this volume; and Jill Quadagno, "How Medicare Integrated Southern Hospitals," chapter 5 of this volume.

18. For a modern catalogue of criteria for evaluating policy recommendations, see William N. Dunn, *Public Policy Analysis: An Introduction* (Prentice-Hall, 1994).

4

Diversity in U.S. Social Insurance: A Historical Overview

Robert C. Lieberman

The beginnings of the Social Security system were inauspicious for diversity. As noted by Charles Hamilton Houston—a pioneering African American attorney representing the National Association for the Advancement of Colored People—in his 1935 testimony before the Senate Finance Committee: "From the Negro's point of view, [the Social Security Act] looks like a sieve with the holes just big enough for the majority of Negroes to fall through."[1]

Houston was referring to a number of characteristics of the Social Security Act, not the least of which were a set of critical exclusions from social insurance coverage. These were key occupational categories—groups of workers who were explicitly excluded from Old Age Insurance coverage; they were not required to pay payroll taxes and were not eligible to receive benefits.

Among the categories of workers excluded at the outset were farm laborers and domestic workers. These occupational exclusions had important and immediate racial consequences because they accounted for approximately 50 percent of the African Americans in the work force in the 1930s and 1940s. In the South, where most African Americans still lived at the time, these categories accounted for approximately 60 percent of African Americans in the labor force. So, from the founding moment of social insurance in the United States, at least half of the African American workers in the country were excluded from Social Security by the terms of the Social Security Act.[2]

Despite this unpromising start for diversity in American social insurance, a number of forces supported and enhanced the possibility for minority inclusion, particularly of African Americans, in Social Security over time. Since the 1940s the history of Social Security has been one of growing inclusion for minorities under the social insurance umbrella. As a result, these pressures have impelled social insurance in the United States toward a more broadly racially and ethnically inclusive set of programs.

There are two major forces driving this inclusiveness: the expansion of coverage and the growth of benefits. The primary method for expanding coverage was bringing in new workers. Originally there were numerous categories of workers who were excluded from Social Security coverage—not only agricultural and domestic workers but also farmers, self-employed people, government employees, and a number of smaller groups. Over time, however, political and fiscal pressures to expand the scope of Social Security helped to bring in these previously excluded categories of workers.

Politically, Social Security grew to be an extremely popular program, to the point where it was politically irresistible even for many of its erstwhile opponents. This dynamic became apparent in the 1950s when Dwight Eisenhower became president. Eisenhower entered office in 1953 with Republican majorities in both houses of Congress. Many Republicans expected that he would take advantage of this opportunity to repeal New Deal policies, such as Social Security, that Republicans had long opposed.

Eisenhower, however, had different ideas. In 1954 he wrote to his right-wing brother, Edgar, about the movement within his own party to repeal Social Security among other things. "Should any party attempt to abolish Social Security," he wrote, "you would not hear of that party again in our political history." He added that "there is a tiny splinter group, of course, that believes you can do these things . . . but their number is negligible and they are stupid."[3] This moment, in many ways, represents the political maturity of Social Security. Even the Republican Party, whose members in Congress had been railing against Social Security for twenty years, recognized by the mid-1950s that, due to its broad public acceptance and popularity, the program was here to stay and that it would be impossible to eliminate it or fundamentally to alter its contours.

Fiscal pressure for expansion derived from the program's contributory financing structure. As long as there were uncovered workers in the labor force, bringing them into the system provided an immediate fiscal bonus. The system would begin collecting payroll taxes from newly covered workers immediately without incurring obligations to pay benefits until later, because people must work for enough time to build up wage credits before becoming eligible to receive benefits when they retire. Expanding Social Security coverage thus became attractive to members of Congress because they could offer more voters the protection of an increasingly popular social program and thereby ensure a growing stream of revenue that allowed them to increase benefits, postpone tax increases, and delay the challenges of a mature social insurance system. For election-minded members of Congress, these proved to be irresistible benefits.

Except for a few instances in the early years when very small groups of workers who had originally been included were excluded, this is a story of steadily growing coverage. In the 1930s seamen and bank employees were admitted, but agricultural processing workers were excluded. In the 1940 news and magazine vendors were also excluded. But in the 1950s the expansion was most dramatic. Two key categories—farm workers and domestic employees—were brought into the system, in a series of congressional acts in 1950 and 1954.*

The pressure for growing benefits was the second inclusionary force the program encountered. This force had two characteristics. The first was the shift from equity—benefits related to the amount of contributions people pay into the system—toward adequacy—benefits related to earnings and aimed at making up some percentage of a what a worker earned during his or her working life. Over time, beginning in the 1950s, Congress regularly raised Social Security benefits and adjusted the benefits formula to move in this direction.

Benefits grew over time from 1940 (the first year the system paid benefits). Until 1950 benefits remained the same, and due to inflation their purchasing power deteriorated. Beginning in 1950 Congress increased benefits. Benefit levels hit a plateau in the mid-1950s at 15–20 percent above the original value of benefits, and they remained at this level through the 1960s. In the late 1960s and early 1970s Congress again raised benefits significantly until 1974, when Congress indexed benefit increases to inflation so that they rise automatically with the cost of living each year. Thus the real value of benefits today remains approximately what it was in the mid-1970s, somewhere between 40 and 50 percent above the level of benefits in the early years of the program.

The second characteristic is that benefits are progressive. Under the formula that converts wages to Social Security benefits, the benefits of low-income workers are increased to meet a certain minimum level, while the benefits of high-income workers are constrained by a ceiling on benefits. Consequently, the growing inclusion of low-income workers, among whom minorities are disproportionately represented, has enhanced the modestly redistributive character of Social Security benefits.

Figures 4-1 through 4-3 show a general picture of the growing inclusion of nonwhites in the Social Security program over time. These figures compare

*Self-employed professionals were also added during this time, and state and local government employees and the clergy were offered voluntary membership. Doctors were added to the program in the 1960s, and nonprofit employees, including federal government employees, entered during the 1970s. State and local government employees were offered full membership in the 1980s.

Figure 4-1. *Social Security Retirement Beneficiaries by Race, 1940–2000*

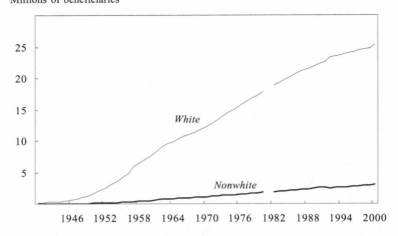

Millions of beneficiaries

Source: *Social Security Bulletin, Annual Statistical Supplement*, various years.

benefits for white and nonwhite retirees from 1940 through 2000. They show data for whites and nonwhites rather than more precise racial categories because this was the way the Social Security Administration and its predecessor, the Social Security Board, reported this information until the 1970s. The gap in 1981 in each figure is the result of data that were evidently lost by the Social Security Administration and hence not reported.

Figure 4-1 shows the number of retirees receiving benefits over time by race. For both whites and nonwhites, this is a picture of a steadily growing beneficiary population. Figure 4-2 shows average monthly benefit levels (in constant dollars) by race. Nonwhite benefits are, on average, consistently lower than white benefits because benefits are related to earnings and nonwhite workers have consistently had lower earnings than whites. Again, this is a picture of benefits growth across the board.

The key question is whether the position of nonwhites in the Social Security system has improved *relative to that of whites* over time, and figure 4-3 answers this question. The solid line shows nonwhite beneficiaries as a percentage of white beneficiaries and the dotted line represents nonwhite benefit levels as a percentage of white benefit levels. This picture shows clearly that the position of nonwhite beneficiaries in the Social Security system has, in fact, steadily improved over time. Nonwhite beneficiaries make up a growing share of Social Security beneficiaries, and their benefits are moving toward parity with those of white beneficiaries.

Figure 4-2.   *Social Security Retirement Beneficiaries by Race, 1940–2000*

Average monthly benefit (in 2000 dollars)

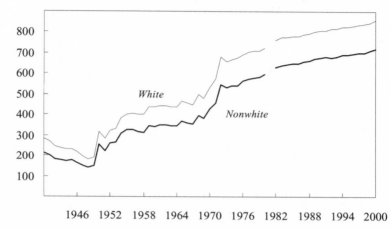

Source: *Social Security Bulletin, Annual Statistical Supplement,* various years.

There are three points that are essential for understanding the changing role of diversity in social insurance. First, Social Security is as close to a color-blind program as there has been in the American welfare state. The history and the data suggest that social insurance principles and programs in the United States have served a diverse society well.

Second, the Social Security system and social insurance more generally have promoted social citizenship, through the secure, rights-based attachment of individuals to a national welfare state.[4] This attachment has been a key part of the creation, solidification, and reproduction of an African American middle class in the United States.

Finally, political coalitions underlying social insurance benefits are important. Coalition building is the key to the development of any social welfare policy. The construction and maintenance of strong, cross-class, cross-racial, and cross-ethnic coalitions in support of social insurance have been critical to the success of Social Security in American politics. African Americans and other minorities have been successful in American social policy when the coalitions that underlie and sustain programs have been inclusive, reaching across lines of race as well as class, and when African Americans and other minorities have been included in social benefits as honorable beneficiaries on equal terms.[5] The key to understanding and promoting the evolution of diversity in American social insurance lies in uncovering the political condi-

Figure 4-3. *Nonwhite Social Security Beneficiaries and Benefits as a Percentage of White Beneficiaries, 1940–2000*

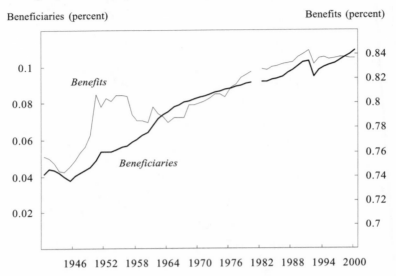

Source: *Social Security Bulletin, Annual Statistical Supplement*, various years.

tions that have allowed the building of coalitions that bridge racial and ethnic divides in American political life.

Notes

1. Senate Committee on Finance, *Economic Security Act,* 74 Cong. 1 sess. (Government Printing Office, 1935), p. 641.

2. Robert C. Lieberman, *Shifting the Color Line: Race and the American Welfare State* (Harvard University Press, 1998), pp. 43–48. The agricultural workers category includes only wage workers on farms and not sharecroppers or tenant farmers, who were also excluded from Social Security coverage because they were not legally considered "employees" under the act's terms. Consequently, these figures probably underestimate the extent of black exclusion.

3. Quoted in Fred I. Greenstein, *The Hidden-Hand Presidency: Eisenhower as Leader* (Basic Books, 1982), p. 50.

4. T. H. Marshall, ed., "Citizenship and Social Class," in *Class, Citizenship, and Social Development* (Garden City, N.Y.: Doubleday, 1964).

5. Theda Skocpol, "African Americans in U.S. Social Policy," in Paul E. Peterson, ed., *Classifying by Race* (Princeton University Press, 1995), pp. 129–55.

5

How Medicare Integrated Southern Hospitals

Jill Quadagno

In the 1960s racial discrimination was as pervasive in the health care system as in other U.S. social institutions. Many hospitals maintained white and colored floors, labeled equipment by race, and reserved a certain number of beds for patients of each race. Throughout the South black doctors were refused staff privileges, and black students were excluded from nurse training programs. Fourteen southern states constructed entire hospital systems based on the principle of separate but equal. The problem was not confined to the South. In northern cities, too, many hospitals segregated black patients from white patients and discriminated against black health care workers.

Yet, unlike integration efforts in education or employment, desegregation in the health care system proceeded rapidly and smoothly. Within the six-month period between July and December 1966, nearly every hospital in the country began admitting patients regardless of race, most racially segregated wards were dismantled, and hospitals began granting staff privileges to black physicians. Why did hospitals eliminate racial barriers with minimal resistance?

To answer this question, I conducted archival research in the National Archives in College Park, Maryland, and the Library of Congress. The main data sources are the records of the Department of Health, Education, and Welfare (HEW) and the Social Security Administration (SSA). I supplemented the archival data with personal interviews with federal officials and physicians who were involved in the effort to integrate hospitals and who provided information on issues that were not fully elucidated in the archival records.

This chapter is a summary of the key points from a previously published article, Jill Quadagno, "Promoting Civil Rights through the Welfare State: How Medicare Integrated Southern Hospitals," *Social Problems* 47 (2000), pp. 68–89.

Racial Segregation in the Health Care System

From 1946 until 1965 the Hill-Burton Act—a federal program that provided funds for hospital construction—supported health care segregation. Segregated practices were protected by the principle that the hospital was a private institution beyond the regulatory authority of the government.

The 1954 *Brown* v. *Board of Education of Topeka* Supreme Court decision, however, provided a new political resource for civil rights advocates who could now challenge the constitutionality of racial segregation in health care. Until 1963 court decisions continued to uphold the principle that the Equal Protection Clause of the Fourteenth Amendment did not apply to private institutions. In 1963 the U.S. Court of Appeals in *Simpkins* v. *Moses H. Cone Memorial Hospital* finally overturned these claims, ruling that, because the hospital received federal funds, it was not a private entity but an arm of the state and thus subject to Fourteenth Amendment prohibitions. The court decision prohibited internal segregation in any facility on the basis of race, creed, or color; banned hospitals or other health care facilities from denying staff privileges on the basis of race; and asserted that all benefits associated with staff privileges must be available without discrimination.

Yet like *Brown* and other landmark decisions, the *Simpkins* decision had little immediate impact on southern hospitals because segregationists defied the ruling. Although HEW issued new Hill-Burton regulations that prohibited hospitals from discriminating in admissions, denying physicians hospital privileges on the basis of race, and segregating patients by ward or room, HEW had limited authority to enforce compliance. These regulations only applied to *pending* applications, not to hospitals that had received Hill-Burton funds in the past.

Title VI of the Civil Rights Act of 1964 prohibited discrimination in any organization that received federal funds. Title VI went into effect in January 1965. It applied to more than 400 federal programs administered by 33 agencies. It was the only title of the Civil Rights Act not delegated to the courts but to the federal bureaucracy.

Implementing Title VI through the Welfare State

The Public Health Service was given responsibility for desegregating 20,000 hospitals, 2,000 nursing homes, and more than 1,000 home health agencies through a newly created Office of Equal Health Opportunities. Although Title VI applied to all hospitals that currently received Hill-Burton funds, hospitals that had completed construction projects remained untouchable, beyond the enforcement power of federal authorities. Not surprisingly, one year after passage of the Civil Rights Act virtually no progress had been made in desegregating southern hospitals. Federal authorities now had the legal mandate but no institutional capacity to enforce that mandate. By 1965 health rights advocates had the courts, the law, and the weight of public opinion on their side. Yet these gains were insufficient to change hospital practices. By historical accident the capacity to implement the law came through the new Medicare program.

To become eligible for federal funds, hospitals applying for Medicare certification now also had to prove they were not engaging in racial discrimination. Unlike Hill-Burton funds, which were provided for a one-time project, Medicare increased federal regulatory authority by providing a continuous flow of federal dollars and thus a continuous enforcement capacity over hospitals. If hospitals refused to comply, they would be ineligible to receive Medicare payments.

To initiate the process all hospital administrators received a letter informing them that they could not receive Medicare funds unless they could certify that the hospital did not discriminate in patient admissions, room assignments, or staff assignments. Next, a staff of nearly 500 people was hastily assembled, including several hundred temporarily assigned from other HEW programs, medical students on summer internships, and some outside consultants. After a three-week crash training program in civil rights, they were sent south to inspect hospitals and review their compliance reports for evidence of discrimination. According to one physician involved in the effort, southern hospital administrators most feared investigators who were also white southerners because these investigators knew what they were looking for. When deceitful tactics were used to cover up discriminatory practices, these investigators sniffed it out.

By May 30, 1966, the SSA had a list of all institutions that were in compliance with Title VI. On July 1, 1966, Medicare was put into operation. By July 21, 1966, fewer than 0.5 percent of hospitals were not certified for Medicare eligibility.

Some southern hospitals found a way to avoid complying with Title VI and still receive reimbursement from Medicare by billing the government under an emergency treatment provision, which was initially allowed. Gradually, this flexibility was eliminated. Others did the "HEW shuffle" during on-site inspections, moving white and black patients into new beds in new rooms and wards for the study team's visit.

The threat of withholding Medicare funding provided enormous leverage, and by October 1966 only twelve southern hospitals still were not certified.

Most hospital authorities quietly signed nondiscrimination assurances, and most hospitals took steps to comply with Title VI. Some wrote to black physicians inviting them to apply for staff privileges. A few hospitals held out longer by rejecting Medicare patients, but in the long run the financial viability of all hospitals depended on the continuous receipt of this stream of federal funds. Yet one of the unintended and perverse consequences of the integration of white hospitals was the closing of many small, black hospitals in the South.

Medicare funds proved to be a powerful mechanism to undermine resistance and promote compliance with equal opportunity initiatives because funds were payable to all hospitals and the flow of dollars was continuous. In the 1960s the route to equality of health care access was through racial integration. Although the formal barriers to racial equality have been removed, more than three decades later racial discrepancies in access to care remain.

PART TWO

Exploring the Implications
of Growing Diversity

Race, ethnicity, gender, class, age, marital status, and health status are a few variables that inform the distribution of social insurance benefits. Many accounts indicate that the rapid expansion of racial and ethnic diversity in America will have substantial implications for social insurance policy. The three chapters and two comments in Part II provide an in-depth analysis of demographic trends that will likely influence the scope and depth of future programs.

Offering a rich array of data, the authors highlight demographic and labor force data to describe how public policy, private sector employers, and society at large have been affected by changing trends. Nancy M. Gordon, associate director for demographic programs at the U.S. Census Bureau, shared information from the 2000 Census that showed significant population shifts over the past decade. J. Lee Hargraves, senior health researcher at the Center for the Study of Health Systems Change, discusses disparities in life expectancy and mortality rates among diverse populations. Cecilia Conrad of Pomona College examines income disparities among racial and ethnic groups and by gender. The statistical portrait painted by each of these authors sets a rich context for subsequent chapters focusing on how these variables interface with different aspects of social insurance policy.

Final comments by Jerry Mashaw of Yale University and Donna Chifriller and Audrietta Izlar, corporate managers for Verizon, provide a philosophical and practical context for interpreting contemporary data trends.

6

What Are the Implications of Growing Diversity? Background Data from Census 2000

Nancy M. Gordon

Census 2000 showed us that we are becoming more diverse in many ways: by race, by ethnicity, and by age. These demographic trends interact with many social and policy issues and may present challenges for individuals and organizations dealing with our aging population.

Population Growth

The United States grew a lot in the 1990s. Census 2000 counted 281 million people (figure 6-1). The increase of 33 million people from 1990 was the largest census-to-census increase in population in our country's history. The growth rate for the 1990s (13.2 percent) was the highest in three decades, but it was less than the growth rate of every decade from 1790 until 1930. Of course, the population was much smaller during these earlier decades.

During the 1990s the population increased in every state, and growth was concentrated in the South and the West.

Racial and Ethnic Diversity

One way to measure diversity is to look at the opposite—the "nondiverse" population. When one considers racial and ethnic diversity, the nondiverse population is non-Hispanic whites. (In the federal statistical system, being Hispanic is not a racial identity but a separate concept of ethnicity, so Hispanics may be of any race.)

Nationally the proportion of non-Hispanic whites decreased from 76 percent to 69 percent of the population. Moreover, declines occurred in every state. In California, which is a bellwether for many demographic issues, the proportion of non-Hispanic whites dropped from 57 percent to 47 percent of the population.

Figure 6-1. *U.S. Population Growth, 1800–2000*

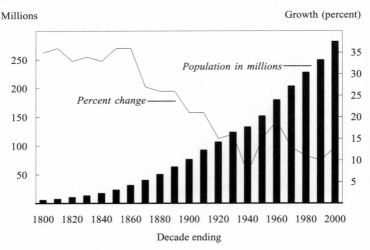

Source: Decennial censuses.

Non-Hispanic whites remained the largest segment of the population in 2000, but for the first time in our history the black and Hispanic populations were roughly the same size.

The large number of non-Hispanic whites in 2000 stands in sharp contrast to their growth rate during the 1990s, which was far lower than for any other group. The fastest growing groups were Hispanics and Asians. As a result, the United States is expected to be even more diverse in the future than it is now.

Age Distribution

The age distribution of the population has a large bulge in the middle from the baby boom generation (defined as those born between 1946 and 1964), who are now ages thirty-eight to fifty-six (figure 6-2). Between 1990 and 2000 the largest percentage change in the population occurred as the youngest baby boomers joined the first "boomers" in full adulthood.

The next largest increases occurred in two of the smallest groups—those aged seventy-five to eighty-four, and those eighty-five and older.

The over-sixty-five population is less diverse than the overall population and has a relatively high percentage of non-Hispanic whites. Another way of thinking about it is that the largest racial group, non-Hispanic whites, is also the "oldest."

Figure 6-2.   *Change in Population by Age Group, 1990–2000*

Change (percent)

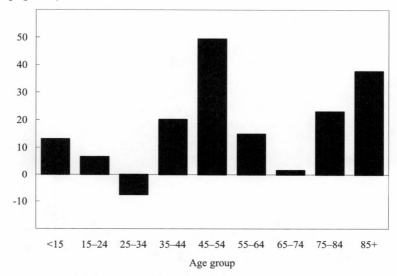

Source: 1990 and 2000 censuses.

The over-sixty-five population will remain less diverse than the overall population as the baby boom enters its senior years because a relatively high percentage of non-Hispanic whites are age forty-five or older.

The Foreign-Born

Another type of diversity is place of birth. The number of foreign-born grew tremendously over recent decades, increasing 40 percent during the 1970s, nearly 50 percent in the 1980s, and more than 50 percent again during the 1990s (figure 6-3). However, despite these huge numerical increases, the percentage of the population that was foreign-born in 2000 is still relatively low—11 percent in 2000 compared with 14 percent early in the decade.

The foreign-born come from different countries now. At the beginning of the century, immigrants came mainly from European countries. At the end of the century, most immigrants had come from Latin America and Asia.

Language Diversity

One by-product of diversity is that people speak many different languages. The challenge is that some of the foreign-born are not fluent in English and

Figure 6-3.   *Total Population and Percent Foreign-Born, 1900–2000*

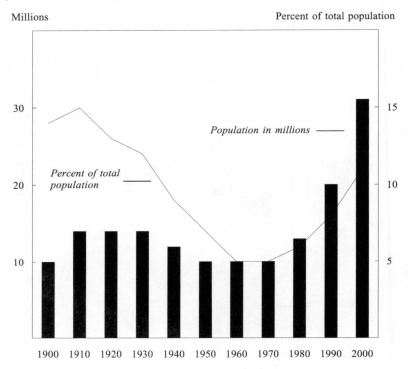

Millions   Percent of total population

Source: Decennial census.

some of them do not speak English at all. More than 11 million people live in households where no one speaks English well, which complicates the provision of social services and other interactions with the public. Besides these people, who are considered to live in linguistically isolated households, in 2000 an additional 21 million people spoke English less than very well. The majority of these people, more than 15 million, are eighteen to sixty-four years old.

Senior Citizens

Considering senior citizens, the highest proportions of people over age sixty-five are not evenly distributed throughout the country but clustered in the center, in Florida, and in some sections of the West. As a result, the need for social services (such as those to enable the elderly to live at home) will be much greater in some areas than others.

Figure 6-4.   *One-Person Householders Age Sixty-Five and over, by Sex of Householder, 1960–2000*

Millions

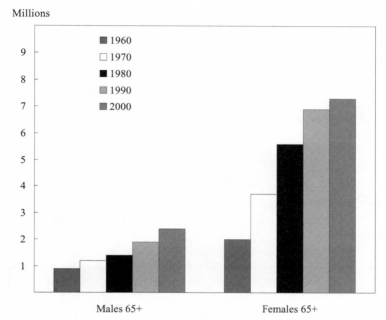

Source: Decennial census.

Living Arrangements

Living arrangements have changed considerably since 1950. The number of married-couple households has remained fairly steady over the last few decades, while the number of people living alone (one-person households) and the number of single-parent families (other family households) have increased dramatically.

Growth in the number of people who live alone was strong among those age sixty-five and over (figure 6-4), and it is particularly evident among older women. In 2000 nearly one-third of the population over age sixty-five lived alone, and the number of men over age sixty-five who were living alone increased by almost 25 percent from 1990 to 2000.

This phenomenon of living alone will also place more demands on social institutions, especially in areas with high proportions of their population over age sixty-five.

Diversity Will Continue to Increase

Projections indicate that diversity will continue to grow. In essence, the non-Hispanic white population will hardly grow at all between now and 2025. Almost all the increase will be in the black and Asian populations, and among Hispanics.

Even beyond 2025 we are likely to see continued increase in diversity, because diversity among the school-age population in 2025 will be even greater than for the total population. In short, some aspects of our country are likely to be vastly different by 2050 than they are today.

Census Bureau Resources

The wealth of Census Bureau data is one of the best-kept secrets in the country, or so people keep telling us. Census 2000 products are available in a variety of formats, including CD-ROM, DVD, on the Internet, and even some on paper.

The Census Bureau also conducts ongoing surveys, such as the Current Population Survey and the Survey of Income and Program Participation. Microdata are available from the Census Bureau website or on CD-ROM.

To keep the country informed, the Census Bureau plans to collect data every year, using the American Community Survey, rather than waiting for data from another long-form census in 2010 that would not be available until 2012 and 2013. Eliminating the long form will also allow us to simplify the census in 2010.

This innovative approach will enable us to provide updated information every year and will help improve the accuracy of the count in 2010. Information about current circumstances that is necessary for good decisionmaking and for allocating federal funds accurately will be available every year, and we will have a more accurate census in 2010 without the use of statistical methods. These are some of the main aspects of what Census 2000 has shown us about demographic and economic characteristics of the country and the great changes that are under way.

7

Racial and Ethnic Diversity in Health Care and Health

J. Lee Hargraves

As I was preparing my text about race, ethnicity, and health, my son was preparing his first presentation in the third grade. One of the great rewards in helping your children and teaching is that sometimes you learn more than they do. He was talking about Jackie Robinson. I remember from school, Jackie Robinson in 1947 was the first African American to play major league baseball. What I did not know was that Jackie Robinson died at the age of fifty-three. He had heart disease and diabetes. He was going blind at that point in his life.

What was striking is that it has been eighty years since Jackie Robinson was born, but some of the same trends in life expectancy that one would observe then are present today. If Jackie Robinson had been born in 1999, he would have had a life expectancy of about sixty-eight years.[1] Figure 7-1 shows life expectancies at birth by ethnicity and race, with data for men on the left and for women on the right. Men typically do not live as long as women do, and there is a marked difference in life expectancy by race. Asian males live much longer than African American males, and non-Latino whites and Latinos are somewhere in the middle. For all ethnic groups, women live on average about five years longer.

For health researchers like myself, these disparities in health are fairly well known, and they are caused by a multitude of reasons, including socioeconomic status, life-style, and employment. The different kinds of jobs that people have also affect life expectancy. These disparities in health shape the research that we see today.

Ethnic and Racial Disparities in Health

For example, if one looks at mortality rates, one sees a mirror image of life expectancy data. Mortality rates, that is, death rates, differ significantly among

Figure 7-1.   *Life Expectancy at Birth, by Ethnicity, Race, and Gender, 1999*

Years

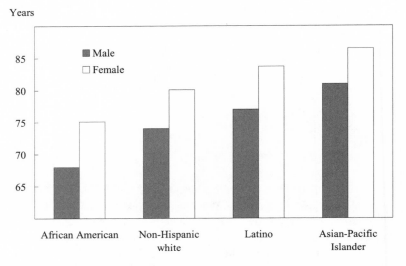

Source: National Projections Program, Population Division, U.S. Census Bureau, 2000 (www.census.gov/population/projections/nation/summary/np-t7-b.pdf).

racial and ethnic groups. Mortality rates for 1990 and 1998 show that African Americans have the highest age-adjusted death rates for both years, followed by rates for whites, Latinos, and Asian Americans.[2]

When these data were released, the big headline was that we are all getting healthier—death rates are dropping. But one point that was missed in a lot of the discussion is that the gaps in mortality rates really are not changing. They are the same today as they were ten years ago.

These data, of course, are adjusted for age. Such statistical adjustments are necessary for using data that compare different ethnic groups. One trend of note is that Asian Americans and Latinos are doing much better healthwise.

Then one can look at other population-based data and find that there are differences in the percentage of people living with chronic illness. For example, one frightening trend appears for diabetes. The prevalence of diabetes in the U.S. population is so striking that many observers talk about it as an epidemic. In researching this, I observed that the same categories of ethnic and racial groups are not reported in all research. For example, data on the prevalence of diabetes among Native Americans and Asian Americans are hard to find.

The age-adjusted prevalence rates for diabetes among Americans over age twenty shows that approximately 19 percent of Native Americans are afflicted, followed by African Americans at 15 percent, Latinos at 14 percent, and non-Latino whites at 6 percent.[3] Beyond the data on life expectancy and mortality, this pattern is alarming because the complications of diabetes are fairly well known and very serious. For example, complications of diabetes include blindness, amputation, heart disease, and stroke. So this pattern of illness, perhaps, tells us something about what may be coming ahead as far as the health of the nation is concerned.

So we find that disparities exist in health and also in health care. *Health* really shows our status as individuals and how we are doing with regard to mental and physical health, whereas *health care* refers to interactions with the health care system, that is, seeing physicians, getting treatment and procedures, and so forth. The message here is that health disparities are persistent over time, and even though we are getting better as a nation, ethnic and racial disparities in health are not changing.[4]

Many of the racial and ethnic disparities in health and health care cannot be totally explained by income, socioeconomic status, and other characteristics. Most researchers who look at these data, controlling as best they can for background characteristics of different ethnic and racial groups, find unexplained differences.

Ethnic and Racial Disparities in Quality of Care

One transition in the discussion of ethnic disparities in health care has happened in the last couple of years. This mixes two lines of research, racial and ethnic disparities in health care and quality of health care.

Disparities research has shifted somewhat to being considered as a quality of care problem. In 2002 the Institute of Medicine (IOM) released a report by B. D. Smedley and others called *Unequal Treatment.*[5] What was striking about that report was that the IOM was tasked by Congress to look at disparities in health care, particularly disparities in treatment that could not be explained by access to health care and differences in health plans.

In many ways, this was a landmark report that says that there are disparities in health care quality that cannot be explained by access, insurance, and other socioeconomic characteristics of people from different ethnic and racial groups. And then, of course, that provides a rationale for researchers to try to explain the remaining differences. Some of the more recent research examines things like bias, clinical uncertainty, discrimination, stereotyping, and other issues.

The IOM also released *Crossing the Quality Chasm,* a study that begins the process of thinking of racial and ethnic disparities in health and health care as a quality problem.[6]

We know that African Americans and Latinos are much less likely to have health insurance. As I will discuss a little bit later, health insurance eases access to health care and reduces disparities in care.

Another piece of the puzzle related to understanding racial and ethnic disparities in health care is the type of health plans that ethnic minorities join. We know from prior research that privately insured African Americans and Latinos are much more likely to join health plans that have cost controls.[7]

Ethnic and Racial Disparities in Access to Care

As was documented in the "Quality Chasm" report, members of certain racial and ethnic groups are much less likely to get certain procedures and treatment. If we think that America has the greatest health care system around, many observers believe that having equal access to treatment and procedures would be part of that system.

The lack of health insurance among nonelderly adults is shown in figure 7-2, which charts the uninsured rate over time. Latinos are the top three data points, and non-Latino whites are the bottom data points, with uninsured rates for African Americans in the middle. The data come from the Community Tracking Study's Household Survey, a biannual, nationally representative survey of more than 60,000 Americans.[8]

Between 1997 and 2001, the gaps in having health insurance between Latinos, African Americans, and whites were large and relatively unchanging. If you recall, this five-year period was a great time of economic prosperity. One would have thought that the percentage of nonelderly adults lacking health insurance would be dropping, but it did not. Lack of health insurance and the gaps between ethnic groups appear to be a stable phenomenon. Among working-age adults, one in ten whites lacked health insurance compared to two in five African Americans and one in three Latinos, and this is not changing.[9]

As I mentioned earlier, there are differences in the type of insurance programs that people are getting based on their racial and ethnic background. The good news is that managed care was more likely offering a lower cost product. So that is why you will find that, over time, African Americans and Latinos were much more likely to be in a managed care plan with gatekeeping.

The percentage of people who were in plans that required primary care physicians (PCPs) and needed referrals—in other words, plans with more controls—has increased for whites from 42 percent in 1997 to 49 percent in 2001. The percentage of African Americans in such plans also increased over the same periods, with levels of 48 and 57 percent. Latino percentages fluctuated from 58 percent in 1997, to 61 percent in 1999, and down to 57

Figure 7-2. *Rates of Uninsured Nonelderly Americans, by Ethnicity and Race*

Percent

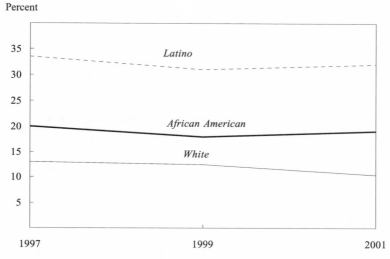

Source: Community Tracking Study Household Surveys, 1997–2001.

percent in 2001. For many people having a health plan with more controls is part of a trade-off between cost and choice. So the good news is that if these plans with gatekeeping requirements were not available, uninsured rates might be higher. However, it does lead many people to be concerned about the ability to access care.

We looked deeper into these data and compared the gap in access among members of plans with gatekeeping controls and members in the plans without such controls.[10] The bottom line from our analysis was that the racial and ethnic gaps in access to care in managed care plans were similar to the gaps in non–managed care plans.

Gaps in Access to Care among Insured and Uninsured Americans

Figure 7-3 examines the percentage of insured and uninsured Americans with a regular health care provider. Having a regular provider, in this usage, refers to people who have a place to go where they see the same provider every time. This point is important because people who have a regular health care provider are connected to the system and have better access to and coordination of care.[11] For this analysis, it does not matter whether the provider is a physician, nurse practitioner, or physician's assistant.

Figure 7-3.   *Insured and Uninsured Americans with*
a Regular Health Care Provider

Percent

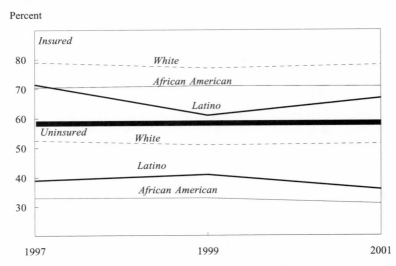

Source: Community Tracking Study Household Surveys, 1997–2001.

The percentage of uninsured Americans who lack a regular health care provider is quite high.[12] The point that I want to make here, very strongly, is that among the uninsured over time, non-Latino whites are much more likely to be connected to the health care system than both African Americans and Latinos (with a gap of 16.6 percentage points in 1997). In other words, white Americans are more likely than others to have a place to go and see the same provider.

So the gaps between ethnic and racial groups are wide among the uninsured. If we make a similar comparison of people *with* health insurance, one trend is that these gaps are much narrower (7.3 percent in 1997). The racial-ethnic disparities or differences are small among people with health insurance compared to the uninsured, and that general trend persists year after year.

I have talked about health insurance in general. However, health insurance may be too broad as an analytic category. So, now I will break it up. Figure 7-4 compares the rates of having a health care provider among the uninsured, those on Medicare, those on Medicaid, and finally the privately insured. What one should notice is that non-Latino whites are much more likely to have a health care provider among the uninsured, and there is much less variation among Medicaid, Medicare, and the privately insured.

One point that could be made is that a lot of these differences might be due to variations in age and health status among the racial and ethnic groups in

Figure 7-4. *Variation in Having a Regular Health Care Provider*

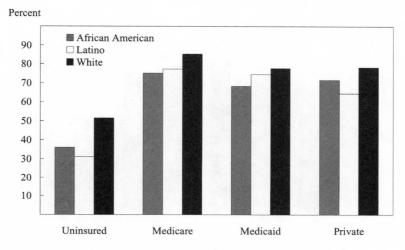

Percent

Source: Community Tracking Study Household Survey, 2001.

different health insurance groups. As part of this analysis I controlled for age and health status and got the same exact picture. Some totals may have shifted by one percentage point. The age and health status distribution is somewhat similar within those categories of insurance and so the racial and ethnic patterns persisted. The gaps in access to care for uninsured African Americans and Latinos were wider than the gaps between both insured African Americans and Latinos and whites.

So, if people have a place to go, do they ever go and see a health care provider? Figure 7-5 presents the percentage of the American population that has seen a doctor in the last twelve months. This assessment of access to care is key because people typically cannot get preventive care and other medical care unless they actually walk into a doctor's office. Although you can sometimes get preventive care, such as a blood pressure check at a drugstore, you get very uneven care outside of health care providers' offices.

Seeing a doctor is one of the access measures that researchers typically examine. The picture for seeing physicians is similar to the picture we saw for access to a regular health care provider. Among the uninsured, three out of ten Latinos actually saw a doctor in the last year, compared to five out of ten non-Latino whites. There is a wide gap there, which is narrower among the insured, and it does not really matter what type of insurance. In other words, the ethnic

Figure 7-5. *Variation in Having a Doctor Visit in the Last Twelve Months*

Percent

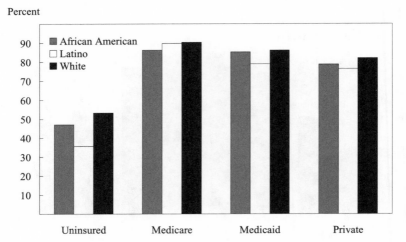

Source: Community Tracking Study Household Survey, 2001.

and racial gaps in access are narrower among Medicaid, Medicare, or private insurance than among the uninsured.

The message that I am trying to deliver is that health insurance matters, and others have said that before. Uninsured persons of all racial and ethnic backgrounds have lower access to health care than people with insurance. In any measure that you look at, the uninsured fare worse.

Summary and Conclusions

The additional message that I have is that gaps in access to care persist over time between different racial and ethnic groups, and my final point is that the gaps are much wider among the uninsured than the gaps in access to care among the insured.

So what does this mean? If one wants to eliminate racial and ethnic disparities in health, I do not believe that this problem can be dealt with without solving the problem of the uninsured or the lack of health insurance.

In fact, it is because of the importance of health insurance coverage in the United States that we see policymakers lining up to propose ways to increase health insurance coverage. Having some information to suggest that increasing insurance coverage will reduce some of the disparities in access to care—that is a message worth delivering.

There are a wide variety of activities that are going on to eliminate racial and ethnic disparities in health. Healthy People 2010 aims to reduce disparities in health. Many of the philanthropic foundations are putting a lot of effort into reducing disparities in health and health care.

For many disparities—for example, diabetes—life-style plays an important role. So efforts are being made to educate patients and consumers of health care. However, one of the barriers in that education process is related to the diversity of the United States. If we have a diverse population, then we need to tailor information so that a diverse population can understand it.

We know that the American population is changing. If some of these disparities are not addressed now, the ethnic and racial disparities in health and health care are going to get worse over time.

Notes

1. National Projections Program, Population Division, U.S. Census Bureau, 2000 (www.census.gov/population/projections/nation/summary/np-t7-b.pdf [accessed March 31, 2003]).

2. K. G. Keppel, J. N. Pearcy, and D. K. Wagener, "Trends in Racial and Ethnic-Specific Rates for the Health Status Indicators: United States, 1990–98," *Healthy People Statistical Notes*, no. 23 (Hyattsville, Md.: National Center for Health Statistics, 2002).

3. Centers for Disease Control and Prevention, *National Diabetes Fact Sheet: General Information and National Estimates on Diabetes in the United States, 2000* (Atlanta: U.S. Department of Health and Human Services, Centers for Disease Control and Prevention, 2002).

4. Keppel, Pearcy, and Wagener, "Trends in Racial and Ethnic-Specific Rates for the Health Status Indicators."

5. B. D. Smedley, A. Y. Stith, and A. R. Nelson, eds., *Unequal Treatment: Confronting Racial and Ethnic Disparities in Health Care* (Washington: National Academy Press, 2002).

6. Institute of Medicine, *Crossing the Quality Chasm: A New Health System for the 21st Century* (Washington: National Academy Press, 2001).

7. J. L. Hargraves, P. J. Cunningham, and R. G. Hughes, "Racial and Ethnic Differences in Access to Medical Care in Managed Care Plans," *Health Services Research* 36, no. 5 (2001), pp. 853–68.

8. Community Tracking Study Household Surveys, 1997–2001 (www.hschange.org/index.cgi?data=01 [accessed March 31, 2003]); P. D. Kemper Blumenthal, J. M. Corrigan, P. J. Cunningham, S. M. Felt, J. M. Grossman, L. T. Kohn, C. E. Metcalf, R. F. St. Peter, R. C. Strouse, and P. B. Ginsburg, "The Design of the Community Tracking Study: A Longitudinal Study of Health System Change and Its Effects on People," *Inquiry* 33, no. 2 (1996), pp. 195–206.

9. J. L. Hargraves, "The Insurance Gap and Minority Health Care," Tracking Report no. 2, Center for Studying Health System Change, Washington, June 2002.

10. Hargraves, Cunningham, and Hughes, "Racial and Ethnic Differences in Access to Medical Care," pp. 853–68.

11. P. J. Cunningham and S. Trude, "Does Managed Care Enable More Low-Income Persons to Identify a Usual Source of Care? Implications for Access to Care," *Medical Care* 39, no. 7 (2001), pp. 716–26.

12. Hargraves, "The Insurance Gap and Minority Health Care."

8

The Economic Vulnerability of Blacks and Hispanics, 1980–2001

Cecilia Conrad

Blacks and Hispanics are among the most vulnerable participants in the United States economy.[1] Three factors contribute to their vulnerability. First, and most obvious, is their low income. By almost every measure, black and Hispanic incomes are lower than the incomes of whites. Over the past two decades the incomes of African American families have increased relative to those of white families, but the relative incomes of Hispanic families have deteriorated.

A second factor contributing to the economic vulnerability of blacks and Hispanics is their marginal position in the labor force. For blacks, this marginality is experienced as an inability to find jobs. Latinos have greater success maintaining employment than blacks, but they more frequently occupy jobs without health insurance or pension benefits. In part as a response to their marginal position in the labor force, black and Hispanic households tend to be configured differently from the households of the non-Hispanic white population and tend to derive income from different sources. The high proportion of African American families maintained by women increases the proportion of households with zero or one earner and, thus, increases economic vulnerability. A relatively high proportion of Hispanic households have three or more earners, but those earners generate less income than a white household with only two earners.

Finally, because African Americans derive a high percentage of income from public sources (government employment, transfer programs, and so forth), their incomes are especially vulnerable to budget cuts.

The obvious manifestation of the economic vulnerability of blacks and Hispanics is the high proportion of their children who live in poverty. Figure 8-1 reports the proportion of persons under eighteen and over sixty-five living in households with incomes below the poverty line by race and ethnicity from 1981 to 2001. The poverty rate for black children has declined since 1993 and

Figure 8-1. *Poverty Rates by Age and Race, 1981–2001*

Percent below poverty threshold

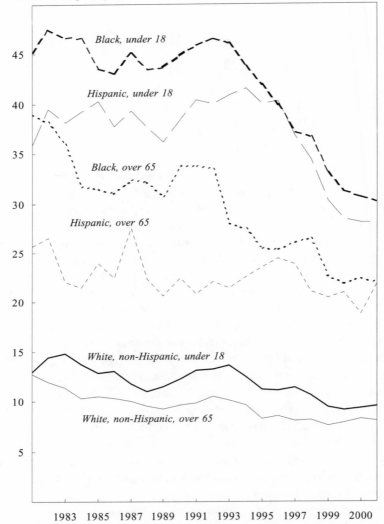

Source: U.S. Bureau of the Census, table 3 (www.census.gov/hhes/poverty/histpov/hstpov3.html [accessed January 2003]).

for Hispanic children since 1996. Yet the poverty rates for both black and Hispanic children remain more than three times that for non-Hispanic white children. At the other end of the life cycle, poverty rates have also fallen for black adults over sixty-five, but again the poverty rate of older blacks is nearly three times that for older non-Hispanic whites. The poverty rate of older Hispanics declined slightly in the late 1990s, but it is also nearly three times that of older non-Hispanic whites.

This chapter examines racial trends in family income, labor market status, and living arrangements over the last two decades that might be relevant to the provision of social and private insurance. The principal findings are:

—Black family incomes are growing both in absolute and in relative terms. Hispanic family incomes grew but at a much slower pace than the incomes of either black or white families (table 8-1).

—The upper quintile of income distribution experienced the greatest growth in income for all racial groups, but racial income disparity increased among the very rich (table 8-2).

—A decrease in the proportion of black families headed by women and a narrowing of the income disparity between black and white families headed by women (table 8-3) contributed to the growth in black family income relative to white family income.

—Hispanic families are more likely to have multiple earners than are black or white families (table 8-4).

—Although the wage gap between black and white men narrowed, the wage gap between black and white women increased (table 8-5).

—Blacks continue to have higher unemployment rates and lower employment rates than either whites or Hispanics.

—Hispanic workers are less likely to be covered by a pension plan or have employer provided health coverage than either blacks or whites (table 8-6).

—Blacks derive a greater percentage of income from government sources than do whites (table 8-7).

Trends in Family Income

In the 1960s median family income rose especially rapidly for African Americans. In 1960 the median income for black families was $14,709 (in 2001 dollars). Over the next decade median black family income increased to $24,295, an increase of nearly 40 percent. White median family income also grew, but at a slower rate. White median family incomes increased from $28,475 in 1958 to $39,663 in 1969, an increase of 28 percent. Consequently, the income gap between black families and white families narrowed. The ratio of black to white median family incomes increased from 0.52 to 0.61.

Since the economic gains achieved by African Americans in the 1960s and the subsequent stagnation in the 1970s and 1980s have been the subject of considerable study,[2] this chapter focuses on trends since the 1980s, using the

Table 8-1. *Median Family Income Ratios at Peaks of Business Cycle*

Type of family	Median income (2001 constant dollars)			Average percentage change		Percentage change
	1981	1990	2000	1981–90	1990–2000	1981–2000
Black	24,131	27,506	34,192	1.5	2.2	34.5
Hispanic	29,834	30,085	35,054	0.1	1.5	16.1
Non-Hispanic white	43,751	49,098	56,442	1.3	1.4	25.3
Black to non-Hispanic white ratio	0.55	0.56	0.61	0.8	0.8	9.4
Hispanic to non-Hispanic white ratio	0.68	0.61	0.62	0.5	0.1	−9.3

Source: U.S. Census Bureau, Table F-5 (www.census.gov/income/ftp/histinc/CPI-U-RS/family/f05.1st [accessed January 2003]).

years 1981, 1990, and 2000 as points of comparison because these years represent similar stages in a business cycle.[3] Table 8-1 reports median family incomes and income ratios for these three years. The growth in median income of black families has slightly outpaced that of whites, especially in the 1990s. Hence, the black/white income ratio has increased.

Hispanics have experienced slower growth in median family income than either blacks or whites. Indeed, Hispanic median family income decreased from 1981 to 1990. However, the slower growth in Hispanic median family income is likely to reflect the continual entry of new immigrants rather than a deterioration in the status of native-born and long-term residents. According to a Census Bureau report, 39.1 percent of the Hispanic population was foreign-born in 2000, and 72 percent of this group entered the United States in the 1980s and 1990s.[4] Arturo Gonzalez has analyzed Mexican American median family incomes by generation using data from the 1999 Current Population Survey.[5] In his data the median family income of second-generation Mexican American families was $30,800 and of third-generation families $34,000. The median family income for all Mexican American families was $27,600, confirming that the inclusion of recent immigrants does lower the median for the group.

The data in table 8-1 describe what has happened to the middle of the income distribution for each group but reveal little of what has happened at either tail. Table 8-2 reports mean family income for the bottom and top quintiles for 1981, 1990, and 2000. The mean incomes of the poorest blacks and Latinos increased over the past two decades but at an uneven pace. Mean

Table 8-2.   *Mean Family Income for Bottom and Top Quintiles at Peaks of Business Cycles*

Type of family	Mean income (2001 constant dollars)			Average percentage change		Percentage change
	1981	1990	2000	1981–90	1990–2000	1981–2000
Bottom quintile						
Black	6,503	5,949	8,473	−0.1	3.5	26.3
Hispanic	8,904	8,279	10,181	−0.8	2.1	13.4
White	14,263	14,914	16,302	0.4	0.9	13.3
Top quintile						
Black	69,126	85,522	112,455	2.4	2.7	47.7
Hispanic	76,672	88,004	104,706	1.5	1.7	30.9
White	95,393	117,536	150,374	2.5	2.6	47.3

Source: U.S. Census Bureau, Table F3A-D (www.census.gov/hhes/income/histinc/ineqtoc. html [accessed January 2003]).

incomes of the bottom quintile decreased for both groups from 1981 to 1990 and then increased from 1990 to 2000. Mean income for the poorest whites showed more consistent improvement, increasing from 1981 to 1990 and from 1990 to 2000, but the overall increase was small.[6] The net effect was a decrease in racial income disparity among the poorest families. In contrast, mean incomes for the top quintiles increased for whites, blacks, and Hispanics over the entire two decades, but the highest growth rate was enjoyed by the richest 20 percent of white families.

Differences in Family Structure

One of the dynamics underlying trends in family income is family structure. A higher proportion of black families are maintained by women than either Hispanic or white families. In 2000 women maintained 55 percent of black families, 28 percent of Hispanic families, and 21 percent of white families. Families maintained by women have lower family income on average than do married couple families regardless of race. For example, the 2001 median family income of a non-Hispanic white family maintained by a woman is $30,062 and the mean is $38,718. The 2001 median family income of a white married couple family is $63,862 and the mean is $80,222. Thus, even if there were no racial difference in income for families of the same type, the racial difference in family structure would lead to a racial difference in family incomes. If black married couple families had the same mean income as white married couple families and black female-headed families had the same income as white female-headed families, and so forth, mean family income would increase from $44,964 to $55,894 but would still be only 84 percent of white mean family income.[7]

Women maintain a higher proportion of black families than of white families, but since 1995 black and white family structures have become more similar. In 1981 women maintained 47 percent of black families and 14 percent of white families.[8] In 1990 this percentage was 51 percent for black families and 16 percent for white families. The percentage of families maintained by women continued to increase for all racial and ethnic groups until 1995. Between 1995 and 2000 the percentage of black families maintained by women decreased from 53 percent to 50 percent while the percentage of white families maintained by women remained at 17 percent. In addition, the incomes of families headed by black women have grown more rapidly than the incomes of similarly situated white families. Table 8-3 reports the median income by family type for 1981, 1990, and 2000. The median income of black female-headed family households increased by nearly 40 percent from 1981 to 2000, while the median income of white female-headed family households increased by 22 percent. Both the decrease in the proportion of black families headed by women and the greater parity among female-headed families have contributed to the narrowing of racial differences in family income.

Hispanics also experienced a decrease in the proportion of families headed by women and an increase in the Hispanic/white income ratio for female-headed families. Between 1995 and 2000 the percentage of Hispanic families maintained by women fell from 26 percent to 24 percent. The Hispanic/white income ratio for female-headed families increased from 0.62 in 1990 to 0.71 in 2000. However, these trends were offset by the slow growth in median income of Hispanic married couple families. In contrast with blacks, among Hispanics the greater income disparity with whites occurs for married couple families. As a result, a decrease in the proportion of Hispanic families headed by women has the opposite effect on the income ratio than does a decrease in the proportion of black families headed by women. One source of income disparity between Hispanic and white married couple families is the difference in female labor force participation rates. Labor force participation rates are lower for Hispanic married women than for blacks and whites. Among husband-wife Hispanic families, 49 percent fit the traditional model of a husband who works year round, full time and a wife who does not work for pay. Only 38 percent of black husband-wife couples and 44 percent of white husband-wife couples fit this model. The proportion of husband-wife families with two year-round, full-time workers grew between 1981 and 2000 for both blacks and whites but

Table 8-3. *Median Family Income by Family Type*

Type of family	Median income (2001 constant dollars)			Average percentage change		Percentage change
	1981	*1990*	*2000*	*1981–90*	*1990–2000*	*1981–2000*
Male householder, no spouse present						
White	37,146	39,251	37,488	0.61	0.1	6.0
Black	26,356	28,052	31,268	0.69	1.1	17.1
Hispanic	26,909	29,203	32,864	0.91	1.2	19.9
Non-Hispanic white	n.a.	40,915	41,315	n.a.	0.1	n.a.
Black to white ratio	0.71	0.72	0.79	0.1	1.0	11.1
Hispanic to white ratio	0.72	0.74	0.83	0.3	1.1	14.0
Female householder, no spouse present						
White	22,752	25,073	28,379	1.1	1.2	22.0
Black	13,654	15,568	20,405	1.5	2.7	39.6
Hispanic	13,799	15,297	21,013	1.1	3.2	41.5
Non-Hispanic white	n.a.	26,838	30,236	n.a.	3.0	n.a.
Black to white ratio	0.60	0.62	0.72	0.4	1.5	18.0
Hispanic to white ratio	0.59	0.62	0.71	0.5	1.3	17.7
Married couple family households						
White	46,388	51,784	59,952	1.2	1.5	25.6
Black	35,697	43,378	50,722	2.2	1.6	34.8
Hispanic	35,160	35,946	40,630	0.3	1.2	14.4
Non-Hispanic white	n.a.	53,074	62,046	n.a.	1.6	n.a.
Black to white ratio	0.77	0.84	0.85	0.9	0.1	9.4
Hispanic to white ratio	0.76	0.69	0.68	−1.0	−0.2	−11.3

Source: U.S. Census Bureau, Table F-5 (www.census.gov/hhes/income/histinc/f05.html [accessed January 2003]).

n.a. = Not available.

declined slightly for Hispanics. The proportion of black husband-wife families with two year-round, full-time workers grew from 0.25 in 1981 to 0.41 in 2000.[9] The proportion of white husband-wife families with two year-round, full-time workers grew from 0.19 in 1981 to 0.31 in 2000.[10] In contrast, the proportion of Hispanic husband-wife families with two year-round, full-time workers decreased from 0.36 in 1981 to 0.33 in 2000.

Although Hispanic married couple families are less likely to have both husband and wife as full-time, year-round workers, Hispanic family households are more likely to have multiple earners than are black or white households. Fifty-two percent of Hispanic households had multiple earners in 2001 compared with 44 percent of non-Hispanic white households and 35 percent of black households. Table 8-4 compares median income and the proportion of families by number of earners for the years 1990 and 2000. (Data for 1981 were not readily available.) As the data in table 8-4 reveal, the ratio of Hispanic to white median household incomes increases once the number of earners is held constant. Hispanic households with three earners have incomes below that of white households with only two. Only with four or more earners does the ratio climb to 0.76.

Consistent with the higher proportion of black families maintained by women, a higher percentage of black families (65 percent) have zero or one earner than white (55 percent) or Hispanic households (49 percent). The ratio of black median household income to white median household income increases as the number of earners increases.

Between 1990 and 2000 the proportion of one-earner households increased slightly for all groups, while the proportion of other household types decreased. Almost all households experienced a growth in income. Consistent with the growth in income of black female-headed families reported above, median income for black households with zero or one earner increased by a greater percentage than the median incomes of other households.

Marginality in the Labor Market

Both black and Hispanic workers occupy marginal positions in the labor market, but this marginality manifests itself differently for the two groups. Both groups have lower earnings than white workers. Black men have the lowest employment to population ratios and the highest unemployment rates. Surveys of employer attitudes show that employers rank African American men at the bottom of their list of preferred workers.[11] Employers tend to have more positive attitudes about Hispanic workers, especially recent immigrants. Employment rates for Hispanic men tend to be higher and unemployment rates lower than those of black men. On the other hand, Hispanics, more so than blacks, tend to be employed in jobs that offer few benefits.

Table 8-5 reports the earnings of full-time, year-round workers by sex, race, and Hispanic origin for 1981, 1990, and 2000. Earnings of Hispanic men deceased between 1981 and 1990 and continued to decrease until 1996. The overall trend in earnings has been positive for all other groups of men. Indeed,

Table 8-4. *Households by Number of Earners*

Type of household	Median income (2001 constant dollars)			Proportion of households			Ratio to white income		
	1990	*2000*	*% Change*	*1990*	*2000*	*Change*	*1990*	*2000*	*Change*
All households									
White	41,016	45,467	10.3	1.00	1.00		1.0	1.0	
Black	24,527	31,285	24.2	1.00	1.00		0.60	0.69	0.09
Hispanic	29,326	34,389	15.9	1.00	1.00		0.71	0.76	0.04
No earners									
White	16,278	16,578	1.8	0.21	0.20	-0.01	1.0	1.0	
Black	7,709	9,491	20.7	0.24	0.20	-0.04	0.47	0.57	0.10
Hispanic	9,256	10,169	9.4	0.16	0.12	-0.04	0.57	0.61	0.04
One earner									
White	33,884	35,830	5.6	0.33	0.34	0.01	1.0	1.0	
Black	22,379	26,131	15.5	0.39	0.43	0.04	0.66	0.73	0.07
Hispanic	22,557	24,307	7.5	0.34	0.35	0.01	0.67	0.68	0.01
Two earners									
White	55,812	65,198	15.5	0.36	0.36	-0.01	1.0	1.0	
Black	44,202	53,210	18.5	0.28	0.29	-0.04	0.79	0.82	0.02
Hispanic	39,697	44,160	10.6	0.35	0.37	-0.04	0.71	0.68	-0.03
Three earners									
White	71,265	77,895	8.9	0.08	0.07	-0.01	1.0	1.0	
Black	56,336	66,897	17.1	0.06	0.07	-0.04	0.79	0.86	0.07
Hispanic	50,230	56,780	12.2	0.10	0.11	-0.04	0.70	0.73	0.02
Four or more earners									
White	87,828	93,428	6.2	0.03	0.03	-0.01			
Black	79,222	78,428	-1.0	0.02	0.01	-0.04	0.90	0.84	-0.06
Hispanic	66,859	71,416	6.6	0.05	0.05	-0.04	0.76	0.76	0.00

Source: U.S. Bureau of the Census, Tables H12a-d (www.census.gov/hhes/income/histinc/inchdet.html [accessed January 2003]).

Table 8-5. *Earnings of Year-Round, Full-Time Workers, by Race and Sex*

2001 constant dollars, except as indicated

Type of worker	1981	1990	2000
Men			
White	38,514	37,939	39,955
Black	27,393	27,393	30,941
Hispanic	27,380	25,131	24,442
Non-Hispanic white	n.a.	39,674	42,389
Black to white ratio	0.71	0.73	0.78
Hispanic to white ratio	0.71	0.66	0.62
Women			
White	22,521	26,329	29,031
Black	20,830	23,693	25,789
Hispanic	19,956	20,582	21,236
Non-Hispanic white	n.a.	25,735	30,670
Black to white ratio	0.93	0.90	0.89
Hispanic to white ratio	0.89	0.78	0.73
White female to white male ratio	0.59	0.69	0.73
Black female to white male ratio	0.54	0.65	0.65
Hispanic female to white male ratio	0.52	0.54	0.53

Source: U.S. Census Bureau, Tables P37 A-E (www.census.gov/hhes/income/histinc/incperdet.html [accessed January 2003]).

n.a. = Not available.

the ratio of earnings of black male to white male workers increased between 1990 and 2000. Women's earnings exhibited a different pattern. Earnings of Hispanic women were relatively stable, while the earnings of other racial and ethnic groups increased. Black women's earnings eroded relative to those of white women but not relative to those of white men.

Black workers are more than twice as likely as white workers to be unemployed, and this ratio has been remarkably stable over the past twenty years.[12] For example, in 2000—near the peak of the Clinton expansion—the unemployment rate averaged 7 percent for black men and 6.3 percent for black women, ages twenty and older.[13] In comparison, the unemployment rate was 2.8 percent for white men and 3.1 percent for white women. In addition to higher rates of unemployment, black men consistently have lower employment rates and lower participation rates than white men. In 2000 the employment rate for white men was 74.8 percent but only 67.6 percent for black men, ages twenty and older.

Hispanics have higher employment rates than blacks but a greater probability of employment in jobs with few benefits. Table 8-6 reports the percentage of workers eligible for employer pensions and with employer-provided health coverage by sex, race, and Hispanic origin. Hispanic men and women have

Table 8-6.   *Eligibility for Employer Pension Plan and Availability of Employer-Provided Health Insurance, 1995*

Percent

Type of worker	Pension plan		Employer-provided health insurance	
	Men	*Women*	*Men*	*Women*
All workers				
White	43.6	38.9	58.3	47.5
Black	42.2	40.3	50.3	51.3
Hispanic	24.5	26.0	41.2	38.7
Poor workers				
White	7.3	5.9	16.6	14.9
Black	8.4	9.1	13.1	18.9
Hispanic	5.1	3.5	13.9	10.2

Source: U.S. Census Bureau (http://ferret.bls.census.gov/macro/031996/noncash/6_000.htm and http://ferret.bls.census.gov/macro/031996/noncash/8_000.htm [accessed January 2003]).

lower rates of both types of coverage than do blacks or whites. Particularly striking is the low incidence of coverage for poor Hispanic workers as compared with poor black workers. These differences are not readily explained by a greater incidence of part-time work or self-employment for Hispanics or by differences in age.[14]

Sources of Income

Blacks derive a greater percentage of their income from government sources than do other groups. Government income sources include earnings from federal, state, or local employment, social security, supplemental social insurance, public assistance, and veteran's benefits. In 2000 black men fifteen years of age and older with work experience had 20 percent of earnings derived from government employment as compared with 11 percent for all races.[15] For black women, 28 percent of earnings were derived from government employment. Table 8-7 reports the percentage of total income derived from different sources for persons twenty-five and older and sixty-five and older.[16] Twenty-five percent of aggregate income for African American males twenty-five and older and 33 percent of aggregate income for black women twenty-five and older derive from government sources, without including retirement and pension income other than Social Security.

Among persons sixty-five and older, blacks and Hispanics rely more heavily on social security than do whites. Social security is the source of 53 percent of the income earned by older black women and 62 percent of the

Table 8-7.   *Proportion of Income from Each Source, 2000*
Percent

Type of worker	Government employment	Social Security	Other government transfers	Property	Retirement and pension
Men, 25 and older					
Non-Hispanic white	8.1	5.0	1.0	5.0	9.3
Black	17.4	5.2	2.2	2.1	7.4
Hispanic	10.2	3.4	1.3	1.6	3.1
Women, 25 and older					
Non-Hispanic white	12.8	9.1	23.0	8.1	6.4
Black	22.9	6.9	32.8	2.3	6.3
Hispanic	16.6	5.3	24.9	1.7	1.2
Men, 65 and older					
Non-Hispanic white	2.5	33.9	2.0	14.6	45.9
Black	5.1	42.2	3.3	6.6	41.4
Hispanic	3.0	45.9	0	7.6	18.2
Women, 65 and older					
Non-Hispanic white	2.2	49.0	0.6	20.9	26.4
Black	4.3	52.8	0	6.6	34.6
Hispanic	2.9	62.0	0	6.3	14.8

Source: U.S. Census Bureau (http://ferrett.bls.census.gov/macro/032002/perinc/new08_000.htm and http://ferret.bls.census.gov/macro/032002/perinc/new07_000.htm [accessed January 2003]) and author's calculations

income received by older Hispanic women. By contrast, social security provides 49 percent of income received by older white women. A similar racial disparity exists for men. Black and Hispanic older persons derive less income from property. Consistent with their lower rates of pensions coverage, older Hispanics derive less income from pensions than either blacks or whites.

Concluding Observations

The status of blacks and Hispanics has not changed dramatically over the past twenty years. By some indicators, the status of blacks has improved, especially during the expansion of the 1990s. Family income and the wages of black men with jobs have increased both in absolute and relative terms. However, a high proportion of black men still remain without jobs, and the wages of black women workers have declined relative to those of white women. Furthermore, blacks are more dependent than other groups on the public sector as a source of employment.

At first glance, Hispanics appear to have lost some ground during the 1980s and 1990s. Family income decreased during the 1980s and grew at a slower rate than white and black family incomes during the 1990s. Median earnings of year-round, full-time workers were lower in 2000 than in 1981 for men and essentially unchanged for women over the same period. However, a final assessment of changes in the economic status of Hispanics will require a separate analysis of U.S.-born and long-term residents.

Two interesting questions emerge for future research. The first is how to reconcile the increase in the relative income of black female-headed families with the decline in relative earnings of black women. A likely explanation is a change in the composition of black female-headed families. For example, if the rate of formation of new black female-headed households decreased, then the average age of female household heads might increase. An increase in the average age of female household heads is likely to lead to an increase in incomes. The racial and ethnic differences in access to pensions and employer-provided health insurance are also puzzling. Black and Latino workers occupy low-paying jobs, but blacks are more likely to have health insurance and pension coverage. These differences merit further study.

Notes

1. American Indians are probably the most vulnerable, but because of data limitations, they will not be explicitly discussed in this chapter.

2. Some recent examples are James P. Smith, "Race and Ethnicity in the Labor Market; Trends over the Short and Long Term," in Neil J. Smelser, William Julius Wilson, and Faith Mitchell, eds., *America Becoming: Racial Trends and Their Consequences,* vol. 2 (Washington: National Academy Press, 2001), pp. 52–97; Harry J. Holzer, "Racial Differences in Labor Market Outcomes among Men," in Smelser, Wilson, and Mitchell, eds., *America Becoming,* pp. 98–123; Cecilia A. Conrad, "Racial Trends in Labor Market Access and Wages: Women," in Smelser, Wilson, and Mitchell, eds., *America Becoming,* pp. 124–51; William A. Darity Jr. and Samuel L. Myers Jr., *Persistent Disparity: Race and Economic Inequality in the United States since 1945* (Northampton: Elgar, 1998).

3. There were business cycle peaks in the third quarters of 1981 and 1990 and the first quarter of 2001.

4. Melissa Therrien and Roberto R. Ramirez, *The Hispanic Population in the United States: March 2000,* Current Population Reports, P20–535, U.S. Census Bureau, 2000.

5. Arturo González, *Mexican Americans & the U.S. Economy: Quest for Buenas Dias* (University of Arizona Press, 2002).

6. These data are for all whites, regardless of Hispanic origin. The mean income of the bottom quintile of whites increases if Hispanics are excluded. In 2001 the mean income of the poorest white, non-Hispanics was $11,463.

7. Author's tabulations are available on request.

8. Data on family structure obtained from U.S. Census Bureau (www.census.gov/population/socdemo/hh-fam/tabFM-2.xls [accessed January 2003]).

9. Data on the number of workers in husband-wife families was obtained from U.S. Bureau of the Census, Tables H12a-d (www.census.gov/hhes/income/histinc/inchhdet.html [accessed January 2003]).

10. A separate statistic for non-Hispanic whites is not available for 1981. In 2000 the proportion of non-Hispanic white husband-wife families with two year-round, full-time workers was 0.32.

11. For examples, see Philip Moss and Chris Tilly, *Stories Employers Tell: Race, Skill, and Hiring in America* (Russell Sage Foundation, 2001).

12. The persistence of this 2:1 ratio is discussed in William Spriggs and Rhonda Williams, "What Do We Need to Explain about African American Unemployment?" in Robert Cherry and William M. Rodgers III, *Prosperity for All? The Economic Boom and African Americans* (Russell Sage Foundation, 2000), pp. 188–207. Several other articles in the same volume investigate the sources of racial disparity in employment and unemployment rates.

13. Data on employment status by race and gender were obtained from U.S. Department of Labor, Bureau of Labor Statistics (www.bls.gov [accessed January 2003]).

14. Marianne Ferber and Jane Waldfogel, "The Effects of Part-Time and Self-Employment on Wages and Benefits: Differences by Race/Ethnicity and Gender," in Françoise Carré, Marianne Ferber, Lonnie Golden, and Stephen A. Herzenberg, eds., *Nonstandard Work: The Nature and Challenges of Changing Employment Arrangements* (Champaign: Industrial Relations Research Association, 2000), pp. 213–34. The data in Table 8-6 would look similar even if reported separately by age of workers.

15. Author's calculations using data from http://ferret.bls.census.gov/macro/032001/perinc/new07_000.htm.

16. I have estimated the percentage of earnings derived from government employment using the percentages determined for persons fifteen and older.

Commentary on Part Two

Comment by Donna Chiffriller and Audrietta Izlar

As a large employer, Verizon provides health insurance coverage for about 1 million people. That includes our employees, retirees, and their dependents. There are some states that do not even have a population of 1 million people. We feel that, as a larger employer, we can either on our own or with other employers do things to help solve or help work toward solutions of some social issues.

We have a goal of trying to continue to raise awareness of the issue of disparate health care treatment, and we want to raise awareness both internally at Verizon and externally and to partner with other employers and with our health plans to try to affect this issue.

First we will describe Verizon's commitment to diversity, because that is the foundation for what has really piqued our interest in this area. We will also discuss why health care disparate treatment is very relevant to us, how we became aware of this issue, how and why we got involved, and, finally, how we think we can play a role in effecting change.

Verizon is one of those companies out there selling DSL lines and wireless phones. In fact, we are the company that was formed by the merger of Bell Atlantic and GTE. We are the largest telecommunications provider in the United States, and we have employees in every state.[1]

For many years both former companies have recognized that there are many implications associated with growing diversity in our society. We do have growing diversity and that diversity of our society will continue—that is, our society will continue to become more diverse.

The foundation that we operated on is that the make-up of the employee base that serves our customers is just as important as the make-up of our customer base. While it is fairly obvious and clear to see that you have to maintain products and services that reflect the needs and wants of a diverse customer base, the same holds true for our employees.

Our diversity commitment is to establish and foster a workplace culture that values individual differences and provides a workplace environment for all employees to grow, participate, and contribute.

We do not often think about health benefits or the package that we offer being part of what contributes to the workplace environment that helps keep employees productive and at work. At Verizon more than 28 percent of our population consists of minority employees.[2] And that is why we need health care that takes into account cultural diversity in medical treatment.

There have been many studies done that show that marked disparities exist between Caucasians and minorities in certain aspects of the health care system. There is no doubt that there is a gulf between whites and people of color with regard to socioeconomic status and access to adequate health providers and insurance.

All these elements play a role in the current political debates around universal health coverage, expansion of Medicaid, and prescription drug coverage for Medicare.

What really surprised us as an employer is that there is research that shows that even when you control for economic status and health insurance status, there are still differences that appear in the diagnosis and treatment of specific health conditions.[3]

There are differences in how preventive services are utilized, and there are differences in health outcomes.

Some key facts really caught our attention. For example, African Americans suffer much higher rates of end-stage renal disease, while Caucasians are twice as likely to receive life-saving kidney transplants.[4]

Another fact is that Native Americans have a diabetes rate that is nearly three times the rate of Caucasians, and the Hispanic rate is nearly double that of Caucasians.[5]

Women of Vietnamese origin in the United States suffer from cervical cancer at nearly five times the rate of Caucasian women,[6] and African-American women are 28 percent more likely to die from breast cancer, although the incidence of breast cancer is greater in Caucasian women.[7]

Now that you are aware of some of the existing disparities, I want to share with you some of the factors that influence the presence of disparities. What is the reason behind some of the gulf that we see?

Some of the research shows that geographic access is a problem, not only with regard to primary care physicians but also with regard to access to specialists.[8] Are there practices in or near neighborhoods that are primarily of one ethnic or racial group?

What about transportation?[9] If the specialists are across town, how can minorities get to those specialists?

Education, literacy,[10] and language barriers are common problems. For example, there is no Vietnamese equivalent for the word *cervix*. So how do you communicate what the issues are with this area of the body?

Health beliefs, which could be religious, generational, or cultural, are also factors.[11] I have firsthand knowledge of a prime example—my father. Being from the previous generation, he did not believe in going to doctors. He believed in home remedies: "We'll just take care of it with a little mixture of this and that before we have to worry the doctor."

Racial concordance or agreement between provider and patient is another factor to consider.[12] How many available doctors look like me or are familiar with my culture?

I recently saw the results of a survey conducted by the Bureau of Health Professions based on some 1990 data that showed 84 percent of U.S. physicians are white, which leaves about 7 percent who are African American or Hispanic and about 9 percent who are Asian or Pacific Islander.[13]

Provider bias, stereotypes and prejudices may be unintentional and perhaps a matter of ignorance of a particular culture, yet they still exist.[14]

Patient attitudes and preferences also are factors.[15] Patients may have prejudices about providers and may be noncompliant with particular treatment recommendations.

And the last factor on the list is something that we all can attest to—competing demands, including work and child care.[16] Can I take time off to go to the doctor or to follow a treatment plan? What do I do with my child if I have to go to radiology?

Of course, this factor can apply to anyone, but it is particularly of interest with regard to minority groups.

So how did Verizon become aware of the issues and the facts? As a member company of the Washington Business Group on Health (WBGH), Verizon was first made aware of the issue early in 2001 in a leadership forum provided by the WBGH. That forum included presentations by experts on the health disparities and cultural competence theories among the insured.

In 2002 we were invited to attend a press conference where the WBGH was announcing a pilot project in cooperation with Pfizer Pharmaceuticals to address health care disparities in a culturally diverse work force. That particular project came on the heels of the release by the Institute of Medicine (IOM) of their study, *Unequal Treatment: Confronting Racial and Ethnic Disparities in Health Care,* as Lee Hargraves alluded to in chapter 7. This study was really the first comprehensive look at racial disparities in health care among people who actually have insurance.

Matthew Guidry from the U.S. Department of Health and Human Services spoke at that conference and announced that the two main goals of the Healthy People 2010 initiative would be increasing the quality and years of healthy life and eliminating health disparities by the year 2010—not just reducing them.

Since Health and Human Services believes that one of the ways they can eliminate disparities is through strong partnerships with the private sector—with companies like Verizon—Guidry charged the private sector at that conference to exert influence with health plans to address health in a diverse way. In other words, purchasers like Verizon and other companies need to hold their health care delivery system accountable to address disparity. Therefore, we have devised a two-part action plan for reaching that goal: hold health plans accountable and raise awareness internally at Verizon.

As an initial step in holding the health care delivery system accountable, at some of our face-to-face renewal meetings last year (preparing for contract year 2003) we took the opportunity to ask some of our health plans a couple questions.

1. Are you familiar with the IOM study made public in March 2002 on unequal treatment?

2. If you are aware of it, what exactly is your health plan doing to address it?

Of the seven plans we surveyed, five were aware of the study and the issue. Three plans were doing something about the issue, and there was one out of those seven plans that stood out as a champion for addressing the issue with existing programs. They had been looking at the issue far before the study was released.

One consistent problem that we heard from the health plans is that they do not collect racial and ethnicity data. This noncollection includes employers like Verizon, which does not provide the data, and health plans that do not ask for it voluntarily from their members.

One of the tools that the Washington Business Group on Health is developing to help employers address disparities will include a summary of some of the laws and standards surrounding the collection and sharing of racial and ethnicity data, especially in light of the new Health Insurance Portability and Accountability Act regulations that are now in effect.

Another tool being researched by the WBGH is a set of national standards for health care organizations, providers, and health care executives to use as a measure to ensure that health services are culturally and linguistically appropriate.

While that and other tools are being developed for employers to use, health plans now are discovering that employers really do care about this issue, and they are expecting some type of action from health plans.

Verizon does not want to only engage our external providers in addressing diversity in health care; we also want to include some internal actions that will make our employees and retirees aware of the issues.

Each of the ethnic populations that are represented by Verizon, whether they are African American, Hispanic, Asian, Pacific Islander, or Native American, are represented within Verizon by what we call Employee Resource Groups. Their purpose is to promote the personal and professional growth of employees, enhance career advancement, and provide a stronger sense of community within the company.[17]

A few of those groups have health topics as one or more of their annual agenda items. We in the Verizon health care management group partner with those groups to help target health issues in general, but particularly ones that are key for their particular culture.

We asked the question earlier: What are the implications of a growing diversity? When you are responsible for delivering quality medical care to your beneficiaries and your beneficiaries can no longer be characterized by any one particular flavor, you are also responsible for ensuring that all of your flavors have the best unique ingredients to keep them performing and serving at their best. That is Verizon's mission.

Comment by Jerry Mashaw

I do not do numbers. I did a book once that had a lot of numbers in it, and I promised I would never do it again. It is much too hard. My comments will, therefore, not engage data directly. I want, instead, to focus on the challenges and opportunities that seem to me to come with talking about diversity in connection with social insurance.

Let me suggest first a few tensions or challenges that emerge from a concentration on diversity, meaning ethnic or racial or population diversity, and social insurance. The first is ideological. Social insurance ideology is riveted on the notion that we are all alike, that we are all in the same boat, that we owe obligations to each other because of our common humanity, and that we should forget about the differences between or among us. This notion of universality has been extremely important in promoting and protecting social insurance programs.

Diversity is not necessarily destructive of that ideology, but it looks in a different direction. It asks us to think about different situations, differences in perspective, and, at least potentially, things that might divide as well as unite us. We have to pay attention to that as we think about diversity and social insurance.

Second, people who do policy analysis about social insurance normally think about diversity in different ways than how diversity is addressed in this volume. Social insurance analysts tend to think about diversity in terms of categories like age, attachment to the work force, or health status. From this perspective equity in relation to groups in the population means groups characterized in these ways—ways that seem policy-relevant for social insurance provision.

These differences in perspective create a potential political danger. When one maps diversity, taken as racial and ethnic diversity, onto programs of social insurance and looks at the outputs of those programs, one inevitably finds that some groups are doing better and some are doing worse in terms of the effectiveness of their social insurance protections. This is obviously an important insight into the functioning of social insurance programs. But it also permits people who do not have a commitment to either social insurance or to the use of diversity as a unifying rather than divisive factor, to engage in forms of wedge politics that can divide social insurance supporters.

This sort of argument is particularly easy to make if the analyst focuses only on one social group, one social insurance program, and one measure of benefit or protection. Indeed, it is child's play as we have all seen already in relation to African Americans and Social Security retirement pensions. I do not need to recount this sordid history here. The question is what to do about it.

So the question is how to think about diversity and social insurance in ways that are productive, both in recognizing, indeed, celebrating the diversity that we have in our population and the strengths that it gives us, while at the same time understanding how diversity interacts with social insurance, can strengthen it, and can promote revisions that will strengthen it still further. The first thing to recognize is that social insurance is a large collection of programs, not one or two. To be sure, it is a system that is oriented toward a core series of risks, that is, the risks to income security that we run as members of a market economy when for various reasons we are cut off from wage income. Those risks include age, whether youth or old age, unemployment, disability, and illness.

We are all susceptible to these common risks. But our public policies do not, indeed cannot, respond to our common interest in income security in a single comprehensive program. Public policy has responded to that simple goal in a marvelously diverse set of programs. It is just not the case that Old Age Survivors and Disability Insurance and Medicare and Medicaid, unemployment insurance, worker's compensation, the earned income tax credit, tax subsidies for private insurance, and so on are similar programs. They are aimed at similar goals, but some of these programs are state run, while others are federal. Some are funded by earmarked taxes; some by general revenues. Some are non–means tested; others are means tested.

Thus, while all these programs are a part of the safety net that helps to build income security for Americans, they are almost certain to relate to different groups in different ways. In a general sense this is as it should be. Differently situated populations have differing risks—or at least differing degrees of exposure to the common risks that social insurance seeks to cushion.

Hence, in thinking about the adequacy of social insurance protections for our diverse polity, we need to take a holistic perspective. Put slightly differently, we should try to think about these problems like the people who wrote about social insurance back in the 1920s and early 1930s, before program-specific analysis dominated the social insurance literature. We should try to think about social insurance as pursuing a unitary goal that necessarily must be pursued through diverse means. But, in the end, it is meant to add up to equal and adequate protections for all Americans.

That is a big challenge. Almost all of our contemporary discourse is programmatic—we tend to talk about Medicaid or Social Security pensions or Medicare or unemployment insurance. But, if we keep that focus, we will not actually grasp the promise of thinking about the way diversity affects social insurance and the way diverse social insurance programs can provide adequate protection for all of us.

Notes

1. Verizon website(http://investor.verizon.com/profile/index.html [accessed January 30, 2003]).

2. Verizon data warehouse, September 2002.

3. B. Kearney and C. Arberg, "Minorities More Likely to Receive Lower-Quality Health Care, Regardless of Income and Insurance Coverage," National Academies press release, March 20, 2002 (www4.nationalacademies.org/news.nsf/(ByDocID)/ 019EBFFF2620394885256B82005 [accessed March 26, 2002]).

4. J. Z. Ayanian, P. D. Cleary, J. S. Weissman, and A. M. Epstein, "The Effects of Patients' Preferences on Racial Differences in Access to Renal Transplantation," *New England Journal of Medicine*, 341, no. 22 (November 25, 1999). Presented at Aetna's Academic Medicine and Managed Care Forum, Washington, D.C., May 2001.

5. E. Cohen and T. D. Goode, "Rationale for Cultural Competence in Primary Health Care," National Center for Cultural Competence, Georgetown University, Child Development Center, Washington, D.C., Winter 1999. Presented at Aetna's Academic Medicine and Managed Care Forum, Washington, D.C., May 2001.

6. B. A. Miller, L. N. Kolonel, L. Bernstein, J. L. Young Jr., G. M. Swanson, D. West, C. R. Key, J. M. Liff, C. S. Glover, G. A. Alexander et al., eds., "Racial/Ethnic Patterns of Cancer in the United States, 1988–1992," National Cancer Institute, NIH Pub. No. 96-4104, Bethesda, Md., 1996. Presented at Aetna's Academic Medicine and Managed Care Forum, Washington, D.C., May 2001.

7. *Health, United States, 1995 Chartbook,* U.S. Dept. of Health and Human Services, Centers for Disease Control and Prevention, National Center for Health Statistics, May 1996. Presented at Aetna's Academic Medicine and Managed Care Forum, Washington, D.C., May 2001.

8. N. Lurie and B. Malone, "Racial and Ethnic Health Disparities: An Overview," Promoting Health for a Culturally Diverse Workforce: The Impact of Racial & Ethnic Health Disparities on Employee Health and Productivity, a WBGH Employer Leadership Forum, Washington, D.C., 2001, p. 6.

9. Lurie and Malone, "Racial and Ethnic Health Disparities," p. 6.

10. Lurie and Malone, "Racial and Ethnic Health Disparities," p. 6.

11. Lurie and Malone, "Racial and Ethnic Health Disparities," p. 6.

12. Lurie and Malone, "Racial and Ethnic Health Disparities," p. 6.

13. K. Collins, A. Hall, and C. Neuhaus, "U.S. Minority Health: A Chartbook," The Commonwealth Fund, New York, May 1999, p. 139

14. Lurie and Malone, "Racial and Ethnic Health Disparities," p. 6.

15. Lurie and Malone, "Racial and Ethnic Health Disparities," p. 6.

16. Lurie and Malone, "Racial and Ethnic Health Disparities," p. 6.

17. Verizon Intranet (http://hr.verizon.com/div_comp/ergs.shtml [accessed September 2002]).

PART THREE

Social Security in a Diverse America

In this section, presenters focused on how components of the Old Age Survivors and Disability Insurance (OASDI) program, also known as Social Security, affect diverse populations. From disability and domestic workers to privatization's impact on African Americans, the articles discuss a range of issues pertinent to the role, function, and future of Social Security in the United States.

Margaret Simms of the Joint Center for Political and Economic Studies moderated the conference discussion and asked the audience to question the intent versus the impact in looking at discrimination within Social Security. She observed that a system on the face may be neutral or may appear to be neutral, but the impact may be quite different, both during people's working years and later in their retirement years.

Chapter 9, written by Lee Cohen, an economist at the Social Security Administration, with coauthors Eugene Steuerle and Adam Carasso from the Urban Institute, examines the progressive nature of the current Social Security program using newly available data from the Model of Income in the Near Term simulation model. In chapter 10, Pamela Herd, a Robert Wood Johnson Foundation scholar in health and health policy at the University of Michigan, presents a possible remedy to benefit disparities experienced by caregivers. Kilolo Kijakazi, a senior policy analyst at the Center on Budget and Policy Priorities, examines the impact of unreported earnings in the domestic and agricultural industries in chapter 11.

Kim Hildred, Republican staff director for the Subcommittee on Social Security of the House Committee on Ways and Means, and Kathyrn Olson, Democratic staff director, close the section with commentary and some words of advice for researchers who want policymakers to draw on their research.

9

Redistribution under OASDI: How Much and to Whom?

Lee Cohen, Eugene Steuerle, and Adam Carasso

This chapter presents the results from a study of redistribution in the Social Security program under current law provisions. The focus is on differences in the redistributional effects between the Old Age and Survivors Insurance (OASI) and the Disability Insurance (DI) programs and how these effects are rolled up into the Old Age Survivors and Disability Insurance (OASDI) program.

The basic findings are presented first, followed by a discussion of the sources of redistribution in Social Security, the data and analytic measures, and the methodology for generating the lifetime earnings upon which payroll taxes and Social Security benefits are based. The results are discussed in detail, looking first at gender, then earnings, education, and finally race/ethnicity, as follows:

—Old Age and Survivors Insurance is progressive in the sense that persons with high lifetime earnings receive lower rates of return than do persons with low lifetime earnings.

—The disability insurance program is even more progressive than the OASI program, but DI is a relatively small program, so that the combined OASDI program is only moderately more progressive than OASI.

—The groups who benefit most when the DI program is added to the OASI program are men, workers in the bottom earnings quintile, high school dropouts, and minorities.

In this chapter *redistribution* is the transfer of Social Security–related monies from one group to another. The main sources of redistribution in Social Security are:

1. *The progressive benefit formula.* This formula provides higher returns for the first dollar contributed than for the last. Payroll taxes are a fixed percent of taxable earnings, but benefits are progressive. Persons with low average monthly earnings receive benefits equal to 90 percent of their monthly earn-

ings, while persons with high monthly earnings receive benefits that replace less than 30 percent of their monthly earnings. This effect is seen when one analyzes the data by quintiles of lifetime earnings.

2. *Forced annuitization.* For most people Social Security benefits are like an annuity. Most beneficiaries receive Social Security benefits until they die. All else being equal, the people who live longer receive more benefits. The influence of lifespan differences is seen when one analyzes redistribution by education since longevity is correlated with education.

3. *Spousal and survivor benefits.* The Social Security benefit formula gives benefits to the beneficiary's qualifying spouse and survivors without additional contributions. Thus Social Security redistributes income to qualified spouses, divorced spouses, and survivors. This effect provides a partial explanation for differences in redistrubution by gender and education.

4. *Disability insurance.* All covered workers pay for DI, but only the disabled and their dependents get DI benefits. Thus DI redistributes income to the disabled. DI benefits relative to taxes are more generous than OASI benefits because disabled workers are credited with a full work career.

The Modeling Income in the Near Term (MINT) simulation model is used for this study. It was developed jointly by the RAND Corporation, the Urban Institute, and the Social Security Administration (SSA). MINT starts with respondents in the 1990–93 Survey of Income and Program Participation (SIPP) panels, with matched earnings histories from the SSA. MINT projects future earnings based on the earnings history. The earnings histories are adequate for this purpose only for birth cohorts 1931–64, so this analysis is restricted to those birth cohorts. A preliminary data set that became available in the summer of 2002 is used, and the study is based on 65,369 observations.

Two measures are used to look at redistribution: internal rates of return (IRRs) and lifetime net benefits. The IRR is similar to a return on investment, where the investment is payroll taxes and the revenue stream is Social Security benefits. It is tricky to compute IRRs for individuals because many have erratic work and benefit histories. Therefore the payroll taxes and benefits were first aggregated according to our analysis groups. Even so, it was not possible to compute an IRR for every group in the DI program, so we defined the rate of return in DI to be the difference in rates of return between OASDI and OASI.

The second measure used to evaluate redistribution is the lifetime net benefit. This is the lifetime benefit less the lifetime payroll tax for each individual, with the mean or median evaluated for each analysis group. Unlike the IRR, there were no methodological difficulties with the net benefits.

The IRR and net benefits are measures of equity, not adequacy. High IRRs can be consistent with poverty, but that is a topic for subsequent research.

Table 9-1. *Social Security Equity across Programs: From OASI to OASDI*

Redistribution by	OASI	DI	OASDI
Gender	Women lead men in all categories	Negligible; DI does not change the redistributive pattern	Women continue to lead men in all categories
Lifetime earnings	Progressive; lower income quintiles lead higher quintiles in all cases	Progressive; more for men than for women	Progressive; more progressive than OASI across all cohorts
Education	Not progressive for men; college men lead high school graduated men, who in turn lead high school dropout men in all cohorts	Progressive; DI transforms increasing returns for men to decreasing returns	Progressive; high school dropouts lead high school graduates, who in turn lead college graduates
Race and ethnicity	Very similar; Hispanics lead whites	Very similar; black men and women gain, as do Hispanic men	Very similar; Hispanics and blacks lead whites

In Social Security, a worker's record can generate benefits for the worker and for various current and former family members. A beneficiary's benefits can come from his or her own record and other people's records. To account for as much of the taxes and benefits as possible in the MINT model, a notion of "shared" payroll taxes and benefits is used. These are, for each person, his or her own taxes and benefits when single and half the combined taxes and benefits when married. Thus, the "shared" measure takes the family context into account. Finally, there are beneficiary populations not included in MINT, notably children and elderly parents. These populations receive about 12 percent of the total benefits, so to keep the payroll taxes consistent with the benefits they purchase, the payroll taxes are reduced by about 12 percent.

This study is not based on stylized earnings patterns but rather on actual earnings histories from SSA records covering 1951–99 for most respondents. Some earnings histories had to be imputed, such as for former spouses. For the earnings projection time period (2000–31), earnings up to age fifty, or if disabled up to age sixty-seven, were spliced onto each record in five-year increments from donors who were five years older. If earnings after age fifty were not observed, a trajectory was made based on prior earnings, and a retirement model then applied. Earnings after retirement were also projected. The resulting redistributions, accounting for both earnings and benefits, are summarized in table 9-1.

Figure 9-1.   *Real Internal Rates of Return, by Gender and Birth Cohort*

Percent

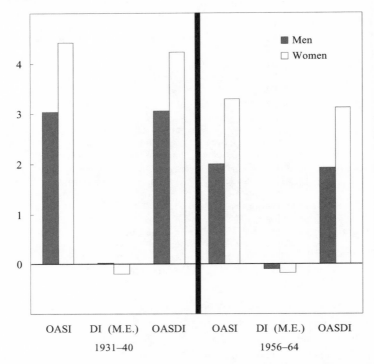

OASI	DI (M.E.)	OASDI	OASI	DI (M.E.)	OASDI
	1931–40			1956–64	

Note: M.E. stands for the "marginal effect" of the DI program on this benefit measure.

When one looks at Social Security by gender, in OASI women lead men in rates of return and in net benefits (figure 9-1). If DI is added into the mix, almost no difference is found. That is, DI does not appear to change the redistributive pattern between men and women. In OASDI women continue to have higher IRRs and net benefits than do men.

The left side of figure 9-1 is the Depression cohort born 1931–40, and the right side is the late baby boom cohort born 1956–64. Three programs are charted within each cohort: OASI, DI, and OASDI. The IRRs are declining across cohorts, but that generalization does not hold true for all subgroups, as will be shown later.

Women do better than men in OASI and in OASDI in both cohorts, and it appears that women fare worse than men in DI. But why? Men in general have higher lifetime earnings than do women, so we would expect men to have lower returns in both OASI and DI on account of the benefit formula progressivity. Men have a higher DI take-up rate than do women, which more than offsets the progressive effect of higher earnings relative to women. Sixteen percent of Depression-cohort males are DI beneficiaries, compared to 10 percent of females. The gap narrows over time to 17 percent male DI take-up, compared to 14 percent female DI take-up in the late baby boom cohort. The net result is that men do better than women in DI. The gender differences in DI are smaller in the late baby boom cohort than in the Depression cohort.

The next category is lifetime earnings (figure 9-2 for men and figure 9-3 for women). Real IRRs are shown in the upper graph for the OASI program, by birth cohort for the lowest quintile (Q1), the middle quintile (Q3), and the highest quintile (Q5) of lifetime earners. OASDI is on the lower graph. As expected from the benefit formula, Q1 has higher returns than Q3, and Q3 has higher returns than Q5, so OASI is progressive in lifetime earnings. DI adds to this progressivity, so OASDI is more progressive than OASI across all cohorts. Thus, Social Security is progressive for men.

The lines for men in figure 9-2 are close in OASI and more spread out when DI is added. This increased difference in returns between the lowest and highest quintiles means that DI is boosting progressivity in each cohort. The lowest to highest quintile divergence also increases across cohorts, so OASDI (and perhaps OASI also) are becoming more progressive over time.

Returns in OASI for Q1, the lowest quintile, seem to have stabilized for persons born after 1941, while in OASDI the returns are increasing. Why is this? In OASI the percent of men in the lowest quintile who are fully insured for benefits has been rising from 70 percent in the Depression cohort to 84 percent in the early baby boom cohort, although it dropped again for the late baby boom cohort. Thus higher proportions of Q1 men from recent cohorts will be getting benefits than Q1 men from earlier cohorts. Similarly, in DI the benefit take-up rates for Q1 men increased from 8 percent in the Depression cohorts to 22 percent in the late baby boom cohorts, so higher proportions of Q1 men from recent cohorts are getting DI benefits than Q1 men from earlier cohorts. In general, higher benefit take-up rates appear to explain the increasing return over time in the lowest earnings quintile for men.

The story for women is simpler. Both OASI and OASDI are progressive, but they look very similar. DI does not appear to change the progressivity between OASI and OASDI (figure 9-3).

In looking at education, just as men had a curious outcome by earnings quintiles, there is also an unexpected outcome by education (figure 9-4). For women the redistribution is as would be expected, but for men the returns in OASI do not decrease as education increases. College men lead high school

Figure 9-2. *Real Internal Rates of Return for Men's Shared Benefits,*
by Earnings Quintile and Birth Cohort

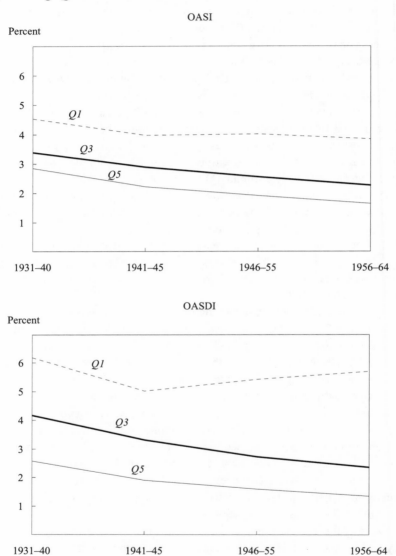

Figure 9-3. *Real Internal Rates of Return for Women's Shared Benefits, by Earnings Quintile and Birth Cohort*

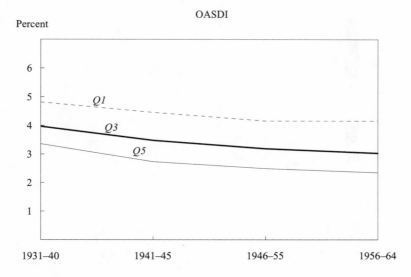

Source: Authors' calculations (January 2003).

Figure 9-4. *Real Internal Rates of Return for Shared Benefits,*
by Education, Gender, and Birth Cohort

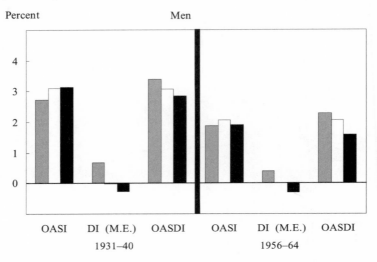

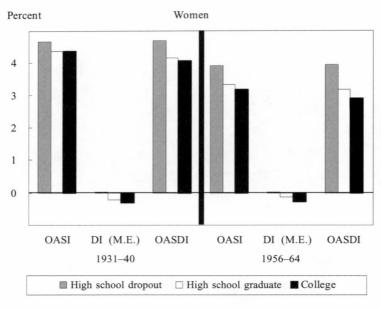

Source: Authors' calculations (January 2003).
Note: M.E. stands for the "marginal effect" of the DI program on this benefit measure.

graduate men, who in turn lead high school dropout men in all cohorts. The effect of DI, though, is to transform OASI for men into an OASDI program that has the expected "progressivity" by education.

Among women, OASI is mildly progressive in education for the Depression cohort, and DI reduces the returns as education increases, so that OASDI is more progressive than OASI. The effect of DI is similar in the late baby boom cohort of women.

But what causes this non-intuitive OASI pattern for men? It would be expected that the lower earnings for high school dropouts would generate the highest returns in the benefit formula. The answer, we think, is that less educated men do not live as long as more educated men. High school dropouts typically die three to five years younger than high school graduates and five to seven years younger than college graduates. The regressive effect of mortality differentials outweighs the progressive effect of the benefit formula.

High school dropout women also have relatively short life spans, and a pattern similar to men might have been expected, where returns decline in relation to educational advancement in OASI. But spousal benefits make up a larger portion of benefits among high school dropout women than among more educated women. These extra benefits raise the returns of high school dropouts above those of more educated women.

Figure 9-5 focuses on rates of return from the perspective of race and ethnicity. In OASI Hispanics lead non-Hispanic whites. In DI non-Hispanic black men and women gain, as do Hispanic men, so that in OASDI minorities lead non-Hispanic whites in rates of return.

In this perspective the differentials between minorities are less substantial. Perhaps this reflects a limitation of the MINT model while race and Hispanicity are not used consistently in all the demographic projections. Initial mortality projections in MINT use race but not Hispanic ethnicity as predictors of mortality. The earnings splicing that is used to project earnings for some people in MINT also splices mortality, in which case the nearest-neighbor match accounts for Hispanic ethnicity. But a further adjustment to mortality among the disabled does not account for race or Hispanic ethnicity. The bottom line is to not overinterpret these results. Hispanics lead non-Hispanic whites, and non-Hispanic blacks usually do also. DI raises returns for minorities, more so for men than for women. DI also lowers returns for non-Hispanic whites, more so for women than for men.

Why does DI favor minorities? There are two reasons:

1. Minorities are more likely to be in lower earnings quintiles than non-Hispanic whites.

Figure 9-5.   *Real Internal Rates of Return for Shared Benefits, by Race/ Ethnicity, Gender, and Birth Cohort*

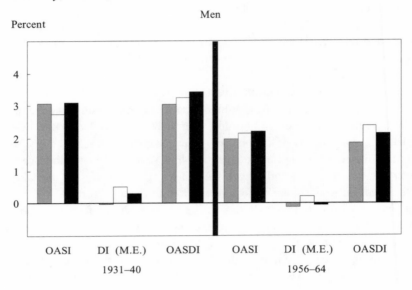

Men

Percent

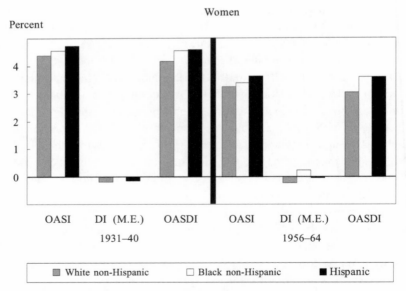

Women

Percent

Source: Authors' calculations (January 2003).
Note: M.E. stands for the "marginal effect" of the DI program on this benefit measure.

2. The DI take-up rate among minorities is higher than among nonminorities. The differences in rates of return between minorities and nonminorities are probably significant, but among minorities the differences are probably not significant.

In summary, we arrived at these principal findings:

1. DI increases overall progressivity modestly, primarily because DI is small relative to OASI.

2. DI boosts IRRs for select lower-return groups, making them the highest return groups in each cohort: men, workers in the bottom earnings quintile, high school dropouts, and minorities.

10

Reforming Social Security Family Benefits: Balancing Equity and Adequacy

Pamela Herd

Women are almost twice as likely to be poor in old age compared to men, and the disparities are even worse among minority and unmarried women. More than 25 percent of older black and Hispanic women are poor compared to 11 percent of white women. Further, the poverty rate for unmarried women is almost six times higher than that for married women.[1] While Social Security, the largest income support program for the elderly, keeps many elderly women's incomes secure, it clearly is not adequately protecting all older women. One of the explanations for this failure is that Social Security does not compensate women for raising children. Women face large reductions in their earnings after having children, which ultimately reduces their Social Security benefits.[2] Further, the women who fare best under the current structure—married women in single-earner households—are a declining proportion of the population. Since the late 1970s these facts have pushed policymakers and scholars to suggest that Social Security should credit the time women spend raising children to improve women's benefits.

A major policy problem is that, despite the calls to create care credits, there has been little study of how to structure them. I address this problem by using the 1992 Health and Retirement Study to examine how three different care credit proposals—substitute, drop low years, and drop zeros, all of which compensate individuals for raising children through their Social Security benefits—affect Social Security's primary goals: benefit adequacy (protecting the neediest beneficiaries) and benefit equity (maintaining a close relationship between what individuals contribute to the system and what they ultimately receive in benefits). Although most reforms entail a tradeoff between these goals, I show how implementing care credits can actually meet both goals.

The Problem with Current Family Benefits

Although most people think of Social Security as retirement benefits distributed to workers, in fact 40 percent of new beneficiaries in 2000 were family members.[3] Family benefits were created under the 1939 Social Security Amendments. Along with the worker benefit, based upon a worker's highest thirty-five earnings years, individuals are also eligible for spousal and widow benefits. Intended to buffer family retirement incomes in traditional one-earner, married couple households, the spousal benefit is one-half of the worker's benefit. When the worker dies, the widow(er) is eligible for 100 percent of the worker benefit. Divorced women can qualify for spousal and widow benefits, but they must have a minimum ten-year marriage. More than 98 percent of those drawing on spousal and widow benefits are women, even though benefit eligibility is gender blind.[4]

Spousal and widow benefits have gradually failed to meet both goals of benefit adequacy and benefit equity. Social Security was designed to meet the economic needs of a traditional one-earner, married couple household. A breadwinning man went off to work while his wife minded the household. Social Security subsidized this arrangement by tying noncontributory benefit eligibility to marriage. These women (and their husbands) could count on retirement benefits above and beyond the original worker benefit, and when he died she could count on receiving his worker benefit. But over the last fifty years there has been a massive "retreat from marriage" that threatens the program's ability to provide adequate benefits. More people are divorcing, never marrying, and having children outside of marriage. From 1970 to 2000 the percentage of married women dropped from 60 percent to 52 percent, while the percentage of divorced women more than doubled, from 6 percent to 13 percent. The percentage of families headed by single mothers rose from 12 percent in 1970 to 26 percent in 2000.[5] Many of these women will be ineligible for the noncontributory benefits that could keep them secure in old age. Indeed, overall poverty projections for older women are not expected to fall over the next twenty years largely due to the increase in never-married and divorced women.[6]

One of the most significant problems with marital status benefits is the resulting race inequities in consequent access to these benefits. As shown in figure 10-1, the proportion of black married women relative to white women has been steadily dropping since 1970. Between 1970 and 2000 the percent of black married women as a percent of white married women fell from around 85 percent to less than 60 percent.[7] Moreover, white unmarried women are more likely to be divorced, while unmarried black women are more likely to be never

Figure 10-1. *Black Married Women as a Percentage of White Married Women, by Age, Various Years, 1970–2000*

Percent

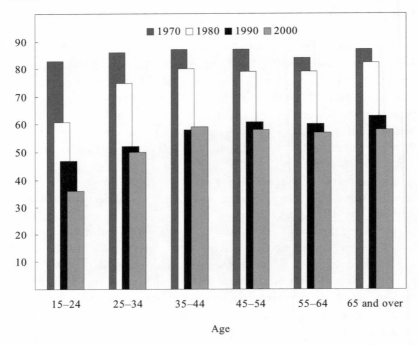

Age

Source: Madonna Harrington Meyer, "Race, Declining Marital Rates, and Changing Eligibility for Social Security," presentation at the Gerontological Society of America meetings, Chicago, 2001, based on Bureau of Census data. 1970: U.S. Bureau of the Census, 1973, table 2003, pp. 6543–643, married; 1980: U.S. Bureau of the Census, 1984, table 264, pp. 70–72, married; 1990: U.S. Bureau of the Census, 1992, table 34, pp. 45–46, married except separated; 2000: U.S. Bureau of the Census, 2000, table A1.

married.[8] This is problematic for black women because divorced women can receive spousal and widow benefits if they had a minimum ten-year marriage, but never-married women are not eligible. Given that poverty rates among black women are three to four times those of white women, this further challenges the ability of spousal and widow benefits to meet benefit adequacy goals.

Differences in single parenthood between black and white women also raise some adequacy issues. Single mothers head 21 percent of white families with children compared to 55 percent of black families.[9] Unmarried mothers face greater income difficulties throughout their life course as compared with consistently married women, but they do not have access to spousal and widow benefits as would married mothers or even married women without children.[10] Thus, while some have argued that spousal and widow benefits are an indirect way to reward women's work raising children, increasing numbers of single mothers who will not have access to these benefits in old age make it clear that these benefits simply reward marriage, not raising children.[11]

While the retreat from marriage has further undermined the ability of spousal and widow benefits to meet adequacy goals, this has always been problematic. Both black women and women from low-income households benefit far less from noncontributory spousal and widow benefits than do white, upper-class women, despite their higher labor force participation rates. A woman with no children who never did paid work but had a high-earner spouse would receive a higher benefit than a low-income woman with four children who worked a low-paid, part-time job. On average, black women's spousal and widow benefits are one-quarter of white women's because of differences in earning between black and white men.[12] Spousal and widow benefits stand in stark contrast to the progressive worker benefit, which replaces a higher percentage of average lifetime income for low earners than high earners. In essence, while 99 percent of men receive progressive worker benefits, almost two-thirds of women receive regressive spousal and widow benefits.[13]

Aside from adequacy issues, there have always been equity problems with spousal and widow benefits. Many low-income working women, both single and married, are subsidizing the noncontributory benefits of many middle- and upper-class married women. Black and low-income women have benefited less from spousal and widow benefits because of their greater likelihood to participate in paid labor. These women would not be able to make ends meet if they left work to raise their children. Historically, black married women have had labor force participation rates two and three times that of white married women,[14] and black women continue to have higher labor force participation rates than do white women, 65 percent versus 60 percent, respectively.[15] Eight out of ten black women, compared to seven out of ten white women, work full time, which is defined here as at least thirty-five hours a week.[16]

This variation in black and white women's labor force participation has also specifically put *married* black women at a disadvantage in regard to spousal and widow benefits.[17] Single-earner couples receive more from their contributions than do dual-earner couples. In comparable retired couples who had earned an average $50,000 annually, the dual-earner couple would receive $23,808 in annual benefits, while the single-earner couple would receive $26,604. This is exacerbated more heavily with widow benefits. A hypothetical widow from a one-earner family receives a benefit based upon her husband's $60,000 annual earnings. A woman from the two-earner couple receives a benefit in widowhood based upon her $30,000 annual earnings; her late husband's earnings are disregarded in her benefit calculation. The widow who had never done paid work would receive a $14,400 benefit, while the widow who had worked would receive a $9,636 benefit.[18] Black women fare particularly poorly from this effect because their incomes make up a greater percentage of household income than those of white women. In 1997 black women's earnings made up 44 percent of black married couples' combined earnings compared to 36 percent for white women.[19] Couples with equivalent earnings fare the worst from this programmatic quirk.

Although many see spousal and widow benefits as a way to reward women for raising children, they actually reward women for simply getting married. Many mothers will not have access to these benefits because they either did not get married or stay married long enough. Moreover, many working mothers will receive nothing from these noncontributory benefits. As the opportunities for women in the workplace increase, the effect of having children on women's wages has become strikingly clear. Women continue to have lower labor force participation rates and earnings than men mainly due to women's disproportionate responsibility for raising children and caring for the elderly. The labor force participation rate among married parents in 1998 was 70 percent for mothers, compared to 95 percent for fathers.[20] There also is a pay gap between mothers and nonmothers that reflects how children affect women's earnings. In 1995 mothers earned 75 cents compared to one dollar for men, while nonmothers earned 83 cents.[21] As women's general paid labor force participation has increased, the impact of women's unpaid care responsibilities on their participation and wages in paid labor has become more evident.[22] Years of unpaid care work ultimately take a toll on most women's Social Security benefits.[23]

It is important to note that, despite these problems, Social Security has proved a vital source of income for all older women. Three out of five people lifted out of poverty by Social Security are women.[24] The average replacement rate for the median female retiree is 54 percent of lifetime earnings compared to 41 percent for the median male.[25] Women's longer lives do not lead to their benefits being discounted as they would if buying a private annuity. Black women, with their higher participation in low-wage jobs, have benefited significantly from the progressive worker benefit. Moreover, because black men on average die younger than white men, black women have been more likely to benefit from survivor benefits, which are benefits directed toward the widows and children of someone who dies before retirement.

Nonetheless, many older women are poor, and future projections show little hope for improvement. While 7 percent of men aged sixty-five and over live in poverty, 12 percent of women in this age group have incomes at or below the poverty level.[26] The disparities are even sharper between black and white women. Eleven percent of white women are living in poverty, compared to 26 percent of black women (USBC 2001). Moreover, the proportion of older women in poverty is not expected to drop.[27]

Possible Reforms

Discussions about how to improve benefits for women have centered on adjusting family benefits. One oft-cited and popular proposal is the introduction of care credits. Care credits would reward women's disproportionate burden for raising children and caring for the elderly, although I only analyze credits for raising children. Implementing care credits moves away from marital status as an eligibility criterion and shifts women onto benefits that are contributory in nature. That is, care credits would reflect the societal value of women's unpaid care work. If the unpaid care work provided mainly by women within families were assigned an overall monetary value, it would total $1 trillion—or 44 percent of U.S. gross national product in 1990.[28] Women would no longer receive benefits simply for marrying but would receive benefits based upon both their labor force participation and their unpaid care work.

I evaluate how adding care credits to Social Security would affect women's benefits, while paying close attention to how different groups of women would fare. Care credits, which move away from marital status as an eligibility criterion, should have a positive impact on black women's benefits because they are less likely to be married and more likely to be single mothers compared to white women.

Three care credit proposals are analyzed because the details of a policy have an enormous impact on the policy's outcomes. Each proposal contains specifics on how they would alter the present benefit calculation:

—*Substitute:* Earnings below half of median wage are substituted with half of median wage in a person's thirty-five highest earnings years for up to five years for one child and up to nine years for more than one child. Spousal benefits are eliminated, but widow benefits are kept.

—*Drop low years:* Persons with one child drop five low-earnings years within their thirty-five highest earnings years, while persons with more than one child drop nine low-earnings years within their highest thirty-five earnings years. Spousal benefits are eliminated, but widow benefits are kept.

—*Drop zeros:* Persons with one child drop up to five zero-earnings years in their highest thirty-five earnings years, while persons with more than one child can drop up to nine zero-earnings years within their highest thirty-five earnings years. Spousal benefits are eliminated, but widow benefits are kept.

Spousal benefits are eliminated with all three of these proposals, but widow benefits maintain. Consequently, widows would not have benefit cuts but could have benefit increases if their worker benefits combined with the care credits are higher than their deceased spouses' benefits. The "drop zeros" proposal, which has received the most discussion, would allow individuals to remove the zero-earnings years from their benefit calculation. Most women have zero-earnings years that are calculated into their benefit, thus substantially lowering their benefit. For example, 60 percent of women born between 1925 and 1945 had six or more zero-earnings years in their thirty-five highest years of earnings. Women in later cohorts, however, are expected to have fewer zero-earnings years. For example, less than one-quarter of baby-boomer women are expected to have six or more zero-earnings years.[29] The argument for allowing women to remove these years is that their zero-earnings years are due to years spent out of the paid labor force raising children.

There are two concerns, however, about this approach. The first is that the women most likely to have zero-earnings years are actually those who can afford not to work. Both black and low-income married women are more likely to participate in paid labor compared to upper-income, white married women. The second concern, related to the first, is that this approach only rewards women's care labor when they do not participate in paid labor. In fact, most mothers now combine paid work and unpaid care work, and the studies are clear that mothers in paid labor have lower earnings than women who are not mothers.[30]

The "drop low years" approach to care credits would drop additional low-earnings years from the benefit calculation. Presently, workers can drop five low-earnings years between the ages of twenty-two and sixty-two, leaving them with thirty-five earnings years. This care credit proposal would allow individuals to drop additional low-earnings years on top of the five already allowed. They would not have to be zero-earnings years. This type of care credit would reward women who combine work and caregiving, as well as those who do not.

The disadvantage to this approach is that the rewards for caregiving would be directly tied to women's earnings histories. That is, women with high earnings would fare better under this proposal than women with low earnings. Consequently, these women's care work would be valued differentially based upon their paid work experience. Social Security would reward a highly paid executive's care work more than it would a day care worker's. Moreover, the wage gap between white and black women has been growing despite black women's high labor force participation rates. Between 1979 and 1988 white women's earnings increased at twice the rate of black women's earnings. White women presently earn 17 percent more than black women.[31]

The "substitute" method to structure care credits would actually place a value on care. Care credits would be a set amount of earnings, which would substitute for a certain number of years of earnings that are below this level. For example, a care credit could be set at $15,000. If a woman, within her highest thirty-five years of earnings, had two years where she earned $7,000, she would be credited with an additional $8,000 for those years.

Unlike the drop earnings proposal, a well-paid lawyer would not receive more credit than a day care worker. At the same time, women who do paid work as well as those who do not could be eligible for these benefits. The disadvantage is that those with higher earnings, who may well be balancing care responsibilities with their paid work, may not benefit.

How Do Care Credits Affect Benefit Adequacy and Equity?

So how would women fare if spousal benefits were eliminated and replaced with care credits? Would care credits increase Social Security's adequacy? There are large statistical differences as to the extent of each proposal's ability to meet adequacy goals. Overall, it appears that the substitute proposal would be a more progressive way to distribute benefits than the current rules. This approach would move women onto the worker benefit, while buffering their low earnings by valuing their unpaid care work. Nonetheless, while most low-income and black women would fare best under the substitute proposal, there are some women from low-asset households who would take a cut in benefits. This is of particular concern when these women are not married and thus do not have a partner's benefit to supplement their own.

Most women generally would fare best if wages are substituted for low-earnings years; women would fare worst if zero-earnings years are dropped. Just 30 percent of women would have an increase in benefit under this proposal, compared to 48 percent of women when income is substituted into low-earnings years. Ironically, dropping zero-earnings years is the care credit option that has received the most attention.

In regard to the size of benefit increases, on average women fare best when low-earnings years are dropped. Average benefit increases when low-earnings years are dropped is $102 a month, compared to about $80 when earnings are substituted for low-earnings years and when zero-earnings years are dropped.

This, however, is not a dramatic difference. Because these proposals entail eliminating spousal benefits (albeit not widow benefits), women's average benefits do not rise. Benefits are simply redistributed among women.

Overall, black women would fare well under these proposals, but they would fare best when half of median wage is substituted into low-earnings years. They would be more likely than white women to either experience an increase in benefit or no change in benefit than suffer a cut under all three proposals. Black women would fare particularly well, compared to white women, if half of median wage is substituted for years of earnings below the median wage, as opposed to if low-earnings or zero-earnings years are dropped. Almost double the percentage of black women would receive benefit increases compared to white women when half of median wage was substituted instead of dropping zero-earnings years. Fewer black women would receive benefit decreases under the substitution proposal compared to the proposals that dropped low- or zero-earnings years. While black women would receive smaller benefit increases than white women under the proposals that drop low- or zero- earnings years, black women would receive about a 20 percent higher benefit increase than white women under the substitution proposal.

Unmarried women who have a lower benefit under current rules would also be more likely to receive an increase in benefits compared to married women with high benefits under the current rules. A never-married, black mother with a $500 current benefit has a 94 percent probability of receiving an increase in benefit, compared to a 76 percent probability for a married woman with a $1,000 current benefit under the substitute proposal. In regard to the size of benefit increases, if half of median wage were substituted in low-earnings years, never-married mothers with a benefit increase would have an additional $141 a month in their benefit. This would lift their annual benefit above the poverty line. Moreover, divorced mothers would receive a greater than $900 annual improvement in their benefit.

Yet these reforms would also hurt some women. Although neither never married nor widowed women would risk a cut in their benefits, some divorced and married women could have benefit cuts even under the most progressive option where wages are substituted for low-earnings years. But, while married women make up 85 percent of those who have a benefit cut under this proposal, only 14 percent of married women with a benefit cut are in the lowest asset quartile. Divorced women, however, do not fare as well. One-quarter of divorced mothers would see their average benefit fall from $662 to $479 a month. In fact, divorced women would make up a disproportionate share of those in the bottom quartile of household assets who suffer a benefit loss. On average, however, these are women whose husbands had maximum earnings under Social Security benefit calculations. In contrast, if these women had been married to men who were average earners (giving the men about a $1,000 benefit), most of them would not have experienced such a large decline in their benefit.

While the substitute proposal was clearly most effective at improving benefit adequacy, all three proposals tightened the link between women's contributions to Social Security and their eventual benefits by transferring women to the more progressive worker benefit from the regressive spousal benefit. Consequently the women who fared best under all three reforms had at least some paid work experience. The probabilities for receiving a benefit increase were four to ten times higher for women with significant earnings histories compared to those with very limited work years. Women who worked the most and *earned the most* fared the best under the proposal in which women could drop additional low-earnings years. But women who worked the most and *earned the least* fared best under the substitute proposal.

Conclusion: Thoughts on the Politics of Social Security Reform

Moving women off noncontributory spousal benefits and onto contributory worker benefits, while still buffering their lower wages with care credits, improves the adequacy and equity of benefits distributed among women. Care credits substituting half of the median wage for low-earnings years would do more good than harm, while dropping low- or zero-earnings years would likely do more harm than good. Of all three care credit options, black women and low-income women fare best when half of median wage is substituted in low-earnings years. Dropping zero-earnings years appears to preference upper-income women, more often white women. But, more important, fewer women are going to have zero-earnings years in their benefit calculation in the coming years. Dropping low-earnings years also preferences upper-income women by placing a value on care that is dependent upon a person's paid labor force participation. The growing wage gap between black and white women also works against black women when care credits are based upon their earnings. These analyses of care credit reforms highlight the importance of recognizing race and class differences among women when asking the more general question of how to improve Social Security benefits for women.

Eliminating spousal benefits is not a prerequisite to implementing care credits. The results from this study can still provide information for the policy debates whether or not spousal benefits are eliminated. Under my analyses those who received increases would still receive increases whether or not spousal benefits were phased out. Ultimately, the neediest older women would still fare best under the substitute proposal.

Because Social Security has provided enormous income security, ultimately lowering the poverty rate among women by 40 percent, some have shied away from critiquing it for fear of provoking changes that would both hurt the program and women who receive its benefits. In some ways debates over implementing individual accounts helped show how critiques of family benefits could be used to support changes to the program that many think would be harmful for women. For example, some argued that family benefits undermined Social Security's redistributive goals to such a degree that individual accounts would not actually affect the program's progressivity. But what a study like this makes clear is that there are other ways to improve an already strong Social Security system without resorting to drastic changes. Care credits, unlike individual accounts, would reward those who suffer significant cuts in their earnings because of the work associated with raising children. Finally, because spousal benefits would be eliminated to implement care credits, my preliminary cost estimates show that this reform would likely not cost any more money. Proponents of privatization surely cannot make the same case.

While these proposals may not be adopted any time in the near future, it is imperative that we continue to research how to alter family benefits in ways that improve the program's ability to protect older women. It is not the job of academic policy researchers to do research based on their interpretation of the political climate and political viability of policy proposals. It is, however, the job of policy researchers to carefully consider social problems and the possible policy solutions to them. Current political climates are not necessarily indicative of future political climates. A rather prescient example is the current stay on executions in the state of Illinois put in place by a Republican governor. He announced his decision at Northwestern University, where scholars had spent decades documenting extreme inequities and errors in the use of the death penalty. He specifically cited this work, and in fact made his announcement at Northwestern precisely because of it. Imagine if these scholars, in the early 1980s, had decided that the political climate was not appropriate for this kind of research? While family benefits are not a matter of life and death, they will shape the economic security for millions of older women in the coming decades. Those benefits need to be reformed and we need considerably more research on how to do it.

Notes

1. Bernadette Proctor and Joseph Dalaker, "Poverty in the United States," *Current Population Reports,* P60–219, 2002.

2. Eric Kingson and Regina O'Grady-LeShane, "The Effects of Caregiving on Women's Social Security Benefits," *Gerontologist* 33, no. 2 (1993), pp. 230–39.

3. Social Security Administration, *Fast Facts and Figures about Social Security*, 2000 (www.ssa.gov/statistics/fast_facts/2001/ff2001.pdf [accessed January 10, 2003]).

4. Madonna Harrington Meyer, "Making Claims as Workers or Wives: The Distribution of Social Security Benefits," *American Sociological Review* 61, no. 3 (1996), p. 451.

5. U.S. Census Bureau, "America's Family and Living Arrangements: Population Characteristics," *Current Population Reports*, pp. 20–537, 2000.

6. Timothy Smeeding, Carroll Estes, and Lou Glasse, "Social Security Reform and Older Women: Improving the System," Center for Policy Research Income Security Policy Series, paper no. 22, The Maxwell School, Syracuse University, 1999.

7. Madonna Harrington Meyer, "Race, Declining Marital Rates, and Changing Eligibility for Social Security," presentation at the Gerontological Society of America Meetings, Chicago, 2001.

8. U.S. Census Bureau, "America's Family and Living Arrangements," p. 8.

9. U.S. Census Bureau, "America's Family and Living Arrangements," p. 8–9.

10. Suzanne M. Bianchi, "Feminization and Juvenilization of Poverty: Trends, Relative Risks, Causes and Consequences," *Annual Review of Sociology* 25 (1999), pp. 307–33; D. Pearce, "The Feminization of Poverty: Update," in Alison Jaggor and Paul Rotherbery, eds., *Feminist Frameworks,* 3d ed. (McGraw-Hill, 1993), pp. 290–96.

11. Harrington Meyer, "Making Claims as Workers or Wives," pp. 449–65.

12. Harrington Meyer, "Making Claims as Workers or Wives," p. 460.

13. Harrington Meyer, "Making Claims as Workers or Wives," p. 462.

14. Claudia Goldin, "Female Labor Force Participation: The Origin of Black and White Differences, 1870 and 1880," *Journal of Economic History* 37, no. 1 (1997), pp. 87–108.

15. U.S. Bureau of Labor Statistics, "Labor Force Participation Rate." *Statistics from the Current Population Survey*, Public Data Query, 2001 (http://data.bls.gov [accessed January 10, 2003]).

16. U.S. Department of Labor, "Facts on Working Women: Black Women in the Labor Force, 1997" (www.dol.gov./dol/wb/public/wb_pubs/bwlf97.html [accessed January 10, 2002]).

17. Pamela Herd, "Crediting Care, Citizenship, or Marriage: Gender, Race, Class and Social Security Reform," doctoral dissertation, Syracuse University, 2002.

18. Richard Burkhauser and Timothy Smeeding, "A Budget-Neutral Approach to Reducing Older Women's Disproportionate Risk of Poverty," Policy Brief no. 2, Center for Policy Research, Syracuse University, 1994.

19. Ida Castro, "Equal Pay: A Thirty-Five Year Perspective," U.S. Department of Labor, 1998 (www.dol.gov/dol/wb/ [accessed January 10, 2003]).

20. U.S. Bureau of Labor Statistics, "Labor Force Participation Rate." *Statistics from the Current Population Survey,* Public Data Query (http://data.bls.gov [accessed January 10, 2003]).

21. Susan Harkness and Jane Waldfogel, "The Family Gap in Pay," Luxembourg Income Study, working paper no. 219, Maxwell School, Syracuse University, 1999, p. 32.

22. Martha Riche, "Demographic Changes and the Destiny of the Working-Age Population," in O. Mitchell, ed., *As the Workforce Ages* (New York: ILR Press, 1993), pp. 19–37.

23. Kingson and O'Grady-LeShane, "The Effects of Caregiving on Women's Social Security Benefits," pp. 230–39.

24. Kathryn Porter, Kathy Larin, and Wendell Primus, *Social Security and Poverty among the Elderly: A National and State Perspective* (Washington, D.C.: Center on Budget and Policy Priorities, 1999), p. ix.

25. National Economic Council, "Women and Retirement Security," Interagency Working Group on Social Security, National Economic Council, Washington, D.C., 1998.

26. Proctor and Dalaker, "Poverty in the United States."

27. Smeeding, Estes, and Glasse, "Social Security Reform and Older Women," p. 5.

28. Brian Strong and Christine DeVault, *The Marriage and Family Experience* (St. Paul, Minn.: West Publishing Company, 1992), p. 409.

29. Social Security Administration, "Distribution of Zero-Earnings Years by Gender, Birth Cohort, and Level of Lifetime Earnings," *Research and Statistics Note*, no. 2000–02, 2000.

30. Harkness and Waldfogel, "The Family Gap in Pay."

31. Mary Bowler, "Women's Earnings: An Overview," *Monthly Labor Review,* December 1999, pp. 13–21.

The research reported herein was supported (in part) by the Center for Retirement Research at Boston College pursuant to a grant from the U.S. Social Security Administration funded as part of the Retirement Research Consortium. The opinions and conclusions are solely those of the author and should not be construed as representing the opinions or policy of the Social Security Administration or any agency of the federal government or the Center for Retirement Research at Boston College. An alternate version of this paper appeared in the *Public Policy and Aging Report,* vol. 12, no.3.

11

Impact of Unreported Social Security Earnings on Women and People of Color

Kilolo Kijakazi

This chapter focuses on those unheard voices in the social insurance system: workers who are vulnerable to unreported earnings.

To be fully insured for Social Security benefits a worker must have forty quarters of reported earnings. Some individuals who have worked hard do not qualify for benefits or qualify for relatively low benefits because some or much of their earnings were not reported by their employers, and payroll tax contributions were not made.

Social Security benefits are determined not only by the level of wages a worker earns but also by the amount of wages actually reported by an employer. Women and people of color represent a disproportionate share of private household workers and farm workers, two groups of workers who may be susceptible to employers' failing to report wages fully.[1] Failure to report these wages can leave some workers unable to qualify for Social Security benefits. Even workers who are able to qualify will likely receive lower monthly benefits than if all their earnings had been reported.

When Social Security was enacted in 1935 the program covered only employees who worked in private industry and commerce.[2] It was not until the 1950s that coverage was expanded to include domestic and farm workers. Prior to 1994 employers were required to report earnings for domestic employees if the workers' earnings exceeded $50 per calendar quarter.[3] This is the "cash-pay test." In 1994 the threshold was raised to $1,000 per calendar year and adjusted in successive years based on changes in average wages. In 2002 the threshold was $1,300.[4]

The 1994 provisions facilitated reporting requirements for employers but made it more difficult for some domestic workers to have their earnings reported and thus to earn quarters of Social Security coverage. Currently an employer does not have to report the earnings of a domestic worker unless they reach the $1,300 a year threshold.[5] This requirement is easier for employers to meet than the previous $50 in a quarter standard, but this change makes it harder for some workers to have their earnings reported. For example, workers who have several employers but receive less than $1,300 per year from each of them may not have any of their earnings reported to Social Security that year. This makes it harder for these workers to qualify for Social Security benefits and also affects the level of benefits the worker will receive if he or she does qualify.[6]

Women and People of Color as Domestic and Farm Workers

Table 11-1 provides the distribution of domestic (private household) workers and farm workers by gender, race, and ethnicity in 2001. Women dominated domestic occupations. Latinos were overrepresented among domestic workers and farm workers. African Americans were not overrepresented among domestic and farm workers in 2001, but this has not been the case historically. (In 1999 African Americans made up 17.6 percent of cleaners and other servants.) Record low rates in unemployment levels for African Americans over the last several years may have enabled some domestic workers to obtain better paying jobs. However, African Americans likely make up a disproportionate share of workers nearing retirement whose career work histories include substantial amounts of work in private households.

Unreported Earnings for Domestic and Farm Workers

Individuals employed as private household workers and farm workers appear to be more likely than other workers not to have had their earnings reported for Social Security purposes. This assessment is supported, at least with regard to domestic workers, by a 1965 study by Ella J. Polinsky that analyzed Social Security Administration (SSA) data collected on women household workers' earnings from 1951 to 1961, the decade after household workers received Social Security coverage.[7] Polinsky compared the SSA statistics against data from the Bureau of Labor Statistics (BLS) and the U.S. Census Bureau. According to BLS data, 11 percent of women who were gainfully employed in 1962 held jobs as household workers. Similarly, the 1960 Census data indicated that 10 percent of women earning wages and salaries were in household employment. However, only 5 percent of the women with reported wages in the SSA database for 1961 were household workers. Polinsky concluded:

Table 11-1. *Distribution of Domestic and Farm Occupations, 2001*
Percent

Occupation	Women	Hispanic	African American
Service occupation	60.4	16.3	17.9
Private household	96.2	32.8	12.1
Child care workers	97.0	18.8	8.1
Cleaners and servants	96.1	39.5	13.5
Farming, forestry, fishing	20.8	21.5	5.0
Farm workers	20.7	42.3	3.7
Proportion of labor market	46.6	10.9	11.3

Source: U.S. Department of Labor, Bureau of Labor Statistics, *Employment and Earnings*, January 2000, table 11, pp. 178–83, and table 39, pp. 213–18; *Employment and Earnings*, January 2002, table 11, pp. 176–81, and table 39, p. 215.

The limited coverage under OASDI and deficiencies in the reporting of covered household employment by employers are chiefly responsible for the large difference between the OASDI proportion and those of the BLS and the Bureau of the Census. . . . [T]he requirements for reporting are probably less widely understood by household workers and employers and are less easily enforced for household employment than for most other types of covered employment.[8]

The workers examined by this study are now part of the elderly population, and unreported earnings may have left them with insufficient quarters of coverage to receive Social Security benefits (or to receive more than a low level of benefits). The 1994 legislation was intended to simplify the reporting process for employers, with the expectation that more employers would understand and adhere to the reporting requirements regarding household workers. To date no study has been undertaken by the SSA to determine how effective this legislative change has been or to gauge the level of nonreporting that still exists for domestic workers.

Information on reporting compliance for farm workers is even more sparse. Most types of agricultural labor are covered by Social Security, but only if one of two cash-pay tests is met.[9] Wages are supposed to be reported if cash payments (of any amount) are made by an employer whose total agricultural labor costs are $2,500 or more annually. Alternatively, an employer who has less than $2,500 in farm labor expenditures must report wages for a given employee if cash payments by the employer to that employee equal at least $150 per calendar year. (However, Social Security does not provide coverage for agricultural work performed by any foreign-born individual who is lawfully admitted to the United States on a temporary basis for the purpose of doing agricultural work.)

The rules for reporting wages for farm workers are complex, and the extent to which employers of farm workers understand and comply with these rules is not clear. There is a limited amount of research in this area. Consequently it is difficult to determine the magnitude of the problem. Evidence of substantial nonreporting of earnings among farm workers and household workers can be found, however, in data regarding the participation of elderly individuals in the Supplemental Security Income (SSI) program at the end of their work lives. The SSI program is a public assistance program for the aged, blind, and disabled poor. An elderly person who does not have a sufficient amount of reported earnings to qualify for Social Security benefits or who receives a low level of Social Security benefits may be eligible for SSI.

Based on his 1991 study comparing elderly SSI recipients to all Social Security recipients age sixty-five and older,[10] Charles G. Scott observed:

> SSI recipients, especially males, were much more likely to have been involved in farming than those in the Social Security beneficiaries group. About 21 percent of male [SSI] recipients earned income in the agricultural sector, compared with only 3 percent of the overall group. . . .[11]

The study also found that about 21 percent of the women receiving SSI had worked in private households, compared with only 5 percent of all Social Security retirees age sixty-five or older. In addition, the study noted that there was evidence that wages earned by household workers often continued to be unreported after Social Security coverage was extended to these workers.

Research Needed on Unreported Earnings

Improving Social Security coverage of workers, particularly those who are least likely to have other sources of retirement income, can help to reduce poverty among the elderly. As previously noted, domestic and farm workers earn some of the lowest wages and thus are most in need of Social Security benefits but may not be covered by Social Security (or only minimally covered) because their earnings have not been reported. Research is needed to gain greater understanding of the nature and magnitude of the problem of unreported earnings.

As part of such a research effort, information is needed about the effect that the previously mentioned 1994 legislation on employer reporting requirements has had on the level and nature of nonreporting. The SSA has developed plans to conduct research on nonreporting but has lacked the funds to explore the issue. Resources should be allocated to the SSA to undertake research in two critical areas:

—the extent to which earnings are unreported and why

—the proportion of domestic workers who should be classified as self-employed and should pay their own payroll taxes.

This research needs to determine the number of people affected, the likely level of earnings not reported, the approximate number of employers involved, and the poverty rates of those with unreported earnings. It must also determine the reasons for nonreporting and examine the extent to which workers with unreported earnings due to their employers' failure to report are taking advantage of the provision to receive retroactive earnings credits.

If workers can provide evidence that they worked for a specific employer, the SSA will credit the worker for those earnings.[12] A signed statement from an employer can serve as evidence of past wages paid. Employers have rarely been penalized for nonreporting because the SSA and the Internal Revenue Service seldom attempt to retrieve unpaid payroll taxes from them.[13]

It can be complicated for workers to discern whether they are employees or self-employed. The Internal Revenue Service and the SSA apply a set of rules to make this determination.[14] For example, if the person for whom the domestic worker is doing a job provides the tools or equipment and sets the hours of work, the domestic worker may be an employee. Alternatively, if the domestic worker pays his or her own expenses, provides the equipment, and works for more than one employer, the worker may be self-employed.

If a worker is an employee, the employer is responsible for reporting the worker's wages and making the payroll tax contributions. By contrast, if a worker is self-employed, the *worker* is responsible for reporting his or her wages and making the payroll tax contributions. (In other words, the worker would contribute both the employer and the employee shares of the taxes, which equal 15.3 percent of the wages earned—12.4 percent for Social Security and 2.9 percent for Medicare Hospital Insurance; however, a portion of payroll tax contributions by self-employed individuals can be deducted for income tax purposes.)

This research also should examine ways to reduce nonreporting, to inform workers of their rights, and to inform employers (and the self-employed) of their responsibilities.

While there is a cost associated with conducting this research, it should nonetheless take precedence over other recent proposals that would incur substantial administrative costs. For instance, several bills have been introduced in Congress that would require the SSA to send certificates to current beneficiaries stating that their benefits would not be reduced in the future. The

Congressional Research Service has concluded that such certificates would be no more binding than current law. The SSA commissioner, Jo Anne Barnhart, has testified before Congress that sending these certificates may have the undesired effect of alarming workers who do not receive them, such as workers near retirement.[15] Moreover, the SSA estimates that the cost of mailing even a rather basic type of certificate would be $14–16 million.[16] A more elaborate certificate could double the cost.[17]

This money could be put to better use. A portion of the estimated cost of mailing certificates could be used to conduct research on unreported earnings. This research would inform policymakers about the extent of the problem and the means by which to address it so that individuals who have worked hard receive the Social Security coverage they deserve for themselves and their families.

Research and the Real World

The relevancy of this research cannot be overstated. Let me give you two personal examples. When my parents' health took a turn for the worse, I rushed to see about them. My definition of the sandwich generation is having to find a caregiver for my four-year-old daughter and also for my eighty-one-year-old father and seventy-six-year-old mother.

A major part of my visit to my parents was spent finding them caregivers. The ones who sounded great on the phone did not show up for the interview; the ones who presented well in the interview disappeared when I asked for references. But I persevered and found a woman with glowing recommendations, good experience, and a personality that even my reclusive father could tolerate. Just as I was rejoicing, she said, "I need to be paid off the books. I don't want you to deduct FICA or report my earnings."

I needed this caregiver, and I thought, "There must be a corollary to the little white lie that would make it all right for me to be a little bit hypocritical on this issue of unreported earnings." I found my answer in the SSA provision that allows employers to pay domestic workers for up to $1,300 without deducting FICA. I shifted this particular caregiver to emergency status, as a back-up and on weekends. I then had to hire more caregivers who were willing to work on the books.

My second story shows that our research really does have an impact on the lives of real people. I received a call from a woman who had heard me speak and talk about unreported earnings. She remembered that I said that even if workers' earnings had not been reported, they might still qualify for Social Security if they could document that they had worked.

The caller was working with an immigrant family with a twelve-year-old girl whose mother had died. The mother had been working off the books, but her employer agreed to write a letter indicating that the mother had worked. The problem was that the local Social Security office was not familiar with the rule that allowed for establishing work history retroactively in this way. Hence, I received a phone call asking me for documentation of the rule, which I provided. A second call from this woman confirmed that she had in fact been able to obtain survivor's benefits for this young girl.

Social Security has safety valves that help provide protection for workers even when employers have not followed the rules. It is important to assess reform plans for these same kinds of protections and, more generally, to assess the impact of reform proposals on people who might otherwise fall through the cracks.

Notes

1. Edith U. Fierst, "Household Employees without Social Security," unpublished, January 1999. *See also* Charlotte Muller, "The Distinctive Needs of Women and Minorities," in Robert N. Butler, M.D., Lawrence K. Grossman, and Mia R. Oberlink, eds., *Life in an Older America* (New York: Century Foundation, 1999), p. 108; Kilolo Kijakazi, "Social Security and Black Women after Fifty Years," National Urban League, Inc., Washington Operations, unpublished, 1985.

2. Social Security Administration, *Annual Statistical Supplement to the Social Security Bulletin, 2001*, Table 2.A1, p. 84.

3. Social Security Administration, *Annual Statistical Supplement*, p. 85.

4. See the Social Security Administration website (www.ssa.gov/OACT/COLA/CovThresh.html).

5. Social Security Administration, *Social Security Handbook, 2001*, 2001, p. 916. See also www.ssa.gov/OP_Home/handbook/ssa-hbk.htm.

6. To be fully insured for the Social Security program, a worker who reaches age sixty-two in 1991 or later must earn forty quarters of coverage. The number of quarters required for a worker who becomes disabled or dies before sixty-two is determined by the age of the worker at the time of disability or death, but a minimum of six quarters is required. In 2002 a quarter of coverage is earned for each $870 in annual covered earnings. A worker can earn a maximum of four quarters per year. The amount required for a quarter is adjusted annually for inflation based on changes in the Consumer Price Index. See Social Security Administration, *Annual Statistical Supplement 2002*, p. 12.

7. Ella J. Polinsky, "Women Household Workers Covered by Old-Age Survivors and Disability Insurance," *Social Security Bulletin*, July 1965, pp. 33–38.

8. Polinsky, "Women Household Workers," p. 34.

9. Social Security Administration, *Social Security Handbook*, p. 901.

10. Charles G. Scott, "Aged SSI Recipients: Income, Work History, and Social Security Benefits," *Social Security Bulletin*, August 1991.

11. Scott, "Aged SSI Recipients," p. 7.

12. Social Security Administration, *Social Security Handbook,* pp. 1726, 1421, and 1424(E).

13. Fierst, "Household Employees without Social Security," p. 2.

14. *Code of Federal Regulations*, Title 20, chap. III, 404.1007.

15. Jo Anne B. Barnhart, Social Security Administration, "Improvements for Women, Seniors, and Working Americans," testimony before the House Committee on Ways and Means, Subcommittee on Social Security, February 28, 2002.

16. Kilolo Kijakazi, *The Costs and Tradeoffs of Social Security Benefit Guarantee Certificates* (Washington, D.C.: Center on Budget and Policy Priorities, 2002).

17. Letter from Dan L. Crippen, director of the Congressional Budget Office, to Rep. Robert Matsui (D-Calif.), ranking member of the House Ways and Means Social Security Subcommittee, March 11, 2002.

Commentary on Part Three

Comment by Kim Hildred

As Republican staff director of the Social Security Subcommittee of the House Committee on Ways and Means, I was asked to provide a policy reality check on the material in this discussion of Social Security in a diverse America. That is, I was charged with discussing the usefulness of the research findings for policy analysts and reflect on whether this research fits with Congress's approach to Social Security in 2003 and might help move the debate toward consensus.

The first question policy analysts ask ourselves is: What is the research topic? If it is a topic not remotely on our radar either for the current session or for the near future, we may not have the time to give it extensive attention, given our limited resources.

The second question is: Is the research fair, balanced, and relatively impartial? Immediate clues include the use of politicized words. For example, the use of the word *privatization* raises questions as to the impartiality of the research.

Next, are the assumptions realistic? Can they be applied to the real world or does the research begin with assumptions that will produce expected results?

Is the methodology reasonable and academically sound? Can the results be replicated and stand the test of scrutiny?

Generally, research helps policymakers most when it analyzes current policy and identifies areas where policy could be improved to provide a better outcome for our society. Research should also provide analysis of the impact of politically viable solutions in comparison with one another. It should not be just an analysis of one solution without providing evidence of whether it is better or worse than other solutions.

Policy analysis and research should balance all considerations: cost of the proposal, balancing policy principles (for example, adequacy and equity), and the effect of a proposal on all populations, not just a few.

It is also helpful when research does not just oppose an idea. In other words, saying one idea is not a good one without proposing something better and backing it up may not be the most useful approach.

Ultimately in most policy discussions the real debate is not about absolute rights and wrongs, but about tradeoffs, as Pam Herd pointed out in chapter 10. Most of the time there is no perfect course of action, just the best possible course of action. Research best serves policymakers when it can help determine the best of several courses of action.

In chapter 9 Lee Cohen discusses the effects of disability on redistribution. The Social Security Subcommittee of Ways and Means is focused on the disability program. Research like this is helpful to use for educating members of Congress regarding those who benefit the most from particular proposals and, therefore, those who would be most impacted by change. This research works as a nice stepping-stone to the consideration of future changes in the program should they be necessary.

A number of excellent questions and examples of tradeoffs are raised concerning the extent that we can improve the retirement program without touching disability insurance (DI) as it exists today. While it is true that changes in Old Age and Survivors Insurance and DI affect each other, and that the financing of the two is intertwined, it is still possible for us to change one without affecting the other.

With respect to Pamela Herd's discussion in chapter 10 about reforming Social Security family benefits, this analysis certainly meets the general criteria for useful research that I outlined above. It identifies a policy problem and examines several solutions side by side. It also considers a balance between cost, equity, and adequacy. It is also extremely timely, as Congress considers changes to strengthen the Social Security program. As she mentions, child-care credits are being considered in a number of different proposals, and I certainly commend her for considering an option to offset costs. Such options are helpful to consider in these austere fiscal times.

However, within the politically viable category, if I suggested eliminating spousal benefits to the chairman of the House Social Security Subcommittee, Rep. E. Clay Shaw Jr. (R-Fla.), who often affectionately refers to his district as heaven's waiting room, I think I would have my head handed to me.

Pam Herd raises policy questions that are difficult to answer. The policy rationale values child care; others might value marriage. But the discussion is useful, especially as we look at impacts on different groups.

In chapter 11 Kilolo Kijakazi focuses on the impact of unreported Social Security earnings. This is a very interesting policy area and one that deserves much more research. Our subcommittee has and will continue to focus on related areas of employer wage reporting and the growing so-called suspense file where wages that cannot be credited to a worker's record are placed.

She also focuses on those wages that never enter the system. These are important issues that Congress is beginning to pay more attention to. It is important to understand the role of the Social Security Administration and the Internal Revenue Service (IRS) with respect to these issues, as it is the IRS that is responsible for unreported earnings, tax noncompliance, and tax rule changes.

Such research is also most helpful when it includes cost-benefit analysis. As we consider legislative proposals, different groups of people are affected in different ways. Research often helps us make certain decisions. For example, if we know a proposal might not positively affect everyone, we can attempt, through other provisions in the proposal, to make the difference needed.

Comment by Kathryn Olson

As the Democratic staff director of the Social Security Subcommittee of the House Committee on Ways and Means, I might be on opposite sides of the aisle from Kim Hildred, but I can hardly disagree with anything she said about our approach to research and how it is used in our process.

One thing I want to make clear is that it is very important to have outside policy researchers because congressional staff members do not have the time to do this kind of analysis. We rely on a variety of outside sources, including government agencies, academia, and others.

I have a few other comments about the ways we use research. In addition to its use in evaluating policy, it also is used as ammunition in our various policy wars with each other. Both sides use it this way—to support one policy or attack another.

In a more positive vein, research can raise issues that are very important to groups that lack a political voice, such as those workers who are the focus of Kilolo Kijakazi's chapter. So it is important that researchers are free to look at a variety of topics.

I will turn now to a policy perspective on some of the presentations. Pamela Herd's chapter on child-care credits was a clear presentation of three options. In particular, it got at the problem with simply dropping zero years, which is that this does not reflect very well people's actual work patterns. Few parents are able to leave the work force for a full calendar year.

With respect to the option of compensating parents by giving them a wage credit that is a fraction of the U.S. median wage, I observe that everybody receives this wage credit. It strikes me as a way of generally boosting benefits for low earners or low earners with kids, as opposed to a child-care credit that aims to compensate people who have lost wages due to child care or other family care responsibilities.

Another observation about child-care credits is that one of the traditional problems with such proposals is their administrative complexity. It requires going back and figuring out who had kids, what kind of proof is required, and that sort of thing.

Kim Hildred also stated the obvious about winners and losers. It was a very useful aspect of this analysis to show that a small group of people would experience no change, while there were large groups of people with big changes—either increases or decreases. That kind of reshuffling is very hard for Congress to deal with, even if Congress were inclined to eliminate the spouse benefit.

Finally, it is important to recognize that Social Security is not the cause of elderly poverty. It was not designed to be, by itself, a complete source of retirement income. There are multiple components of retirement income, and each plays a significant role. Social Security is the universal base that helps to even out the disparities seen in other sources of retirement income. It is also the one where it may be easiest to make a change that carries through to all workers. This is in contrast, for example, to the private pension system, in which not all workers participate, and which is voluntary. You can only change the incentives so much, in attempting to achieve a desired result in the private pension system.

Moving on to Kijakazi's chapter on the coverage of domestic workers and farm workers, in my experience there has not been much focus in the U.S. system on this type of noncompliance with the payroll tax. So it is good to raise this issue and raise the profile of it.

Some people believe that the problem is not significant because workers will receive Supplemental Security Income (SSI) benefits. However, SSI is not a good substitute for Social Security. It has an asset test, so it discourages savings. There are no early retirement benefits. There are no family benefits for surviving spouses and children, and there is no Medicare coverage, although many people with SSI do get Medicaid.

As I mentioned earlier, these workers are not well represented politically. So it is important for researchers to raise questions about whether their treatment under the Social Security system is adequate.

It is a vexing issue: employers do not comply, either out of ignorance or refusal, and workers themselves do not always know the value of contributing to the social insurance system.

In the agricultural sector there are some complexities associated with farm workers' not being paid in cash. I do not know how common that is, but that has come up periodically before our subcommittee. I recall something about beaver pelts as a form of pay and questions about how to tax them.

The big organizations that fund a lot of pension-related work internationally do not necessarily drill down to find answers to these sorts of problems, but that is potentially a promising thing to look at.

My last comments are on Lee Cohen's chapter on disability insurance (DI) and rates of return. This, too, fills an important hole in the research. Much of the rate of return analysis has looked only at Social Security retirement benefits, and to some extent at survivors. It is important to recognize, as this chapter implicitly does, that it is very hard to disentangle disability and retirement benefits. They are a unified continuum of protection. Workers go on disability and they survive to sixty-five. They convert to the retirement rolls. They use the same benefit formula. Disability benefits protect both the worker and the family.

There are also many categories of disability benefits. The worker can get benefits. A surviving disabled spouse who is elderly can get benefits. Children who have very severe impairments from their youth who survive to adulthood can get benefits, and not just out of the DI fund. Their benefits can also come from the old age trust fund, depending on the status of the parent on whose earning record they receive benefits.

Finally, does research help build a consensus or move the debate forward in Social Security reform? I see the debate about Social Security as fundamentally one of values and ideology as opposed to numbers. So policy research can inform us about potential policy change or issues to consider in designing a new system, but I am not sure that it convinces people to adopt different values or objectives in reform.

PART FOUR

State-Administered Programs and Diversity

This section draws attention to the state-administered social safety net. Millions of Americans are dependent upon the benefits provided by state-administered programs like Temporary Assistance for Needy Families, unemployment insurance, and Medicaid. Thus it is important to understand how these state programs address issues of diversity, equity, and adequacy, which are also pertinent to national programs.

Grantland Johnson, California's secretary of health and human services, moderated the session and set the stage by characterizing the budget realities faced by states as "the daunting distasteful set of options of cutting services, reducing the eligibility for our programs, raising taxes, or doing a combination of all three." He warned that the impact of such options disproportionately affects those populations that can least afford it, as they are particularly vulnerable due to the economic downturn.

In chapter 12 Cheryl Hill Lee of the National Urban League's Institute for Equality and Opportunity presents a review of disparities in access to state unemployment insurance programs. In chapter 13 Vicky Lovell of the Institute for Women's Policy Research describes the Temporary Disability Insurance programs that are available in five states and covered 36 percent of private sector workers in 1996. John Monahan of the Annie E. Casey Foundation describes in chapter 14 the diversity in types of state cash assistance programs and the diversity of caseloads. In chapter 15 Cindy Mann of Georgetown University's Institute for Health Policy Research Studies discusses Medicaid and other public-financed health insurance coverage for diverse populations under state-administered health care programs.

12

Impact of State Unemployment Insurance Programs on African Americans

Cheryl Hill Lee

The American unemployment system is primarily a state-based program. There is great variability in specific state policies, as states are able to adopt their own unemployment benefit levels, financial eligibility provisions, and qualification restrictions for their unemployment insurance (UI) systems. There are several factors that may influence an individual's eligibility for UI benefits, including hours worked and earnings prior to becoming unemployed. For instance, in most states part-time workers do not qualify for UI benefits, and many low-wage earners also do not qualify. Only nineteen states and the District of Columbia allow part-time workers to be eligible for UI benefits. While some states have implemented policies that allow more low-wage and part-time workers to qualify for UI benefits, many states continue to have policies that exclude all these workers, who tend to also be African American and Hispanic workers. This chapter examines whether African Americans are less likely to receive unemployment insurance benefits as compared to whites.

Discrimination in the labor market is a contributing factor to the low rate of unemployment insurance for African Americans. Darity and Mason state that there is substantial racial and gender disparity in the American economy.[1] Even though years of schooling, quality of education, years of work experience, and culture are contributing factors to earnings and employment status, they are not the only factors that explain wage differentials and employment patterns. Discrimination has persisted in the United States, and market pressures have not eliminated it, despite some theories that would suggest differently. Labor market discrimination increases the number of African Americans who may have earnings or work histories that would prevent them from being eligible for unemployment benefits.

If discrimination takes the form of creating a hostile work environment, African Americans may feel forced to quit their jobs, perhaps while pursuing discrimination claims. But by quitting they become ineligible for unemployment insurance. Workers who quit their jobs do not qualify for unemployment insurance because they must be involuntarily separated from employment in order to qualify for benefits.

Although more than 90 percent of employed workers held jobs that were covered by the unemployment insurance system, less than 30 percent of those who became unemployed received UI benefits in the early 1980s.[2] Current estimates place the share receiving benefits at 43.3 percent.[3] An even smaller proportion of low-wage unemployed workers received unemployment insurance. There has been a considerable reduction in both manufacturing jobs and union membership in the past decade, two labor practices that increased the likelihood that unemployed workers would apply for benefits. The prior positions of many low-wage unemployed were in retail trade and services industries—industries where workers are least likely to receive UI benefits.[4] Much of the low-wage and part-time work force is composed of African Americans, Hispanics, women, and the disabled. According to Current Population Survey (CPS) 2000 data, only 16.8 percent of the African American and Hispanic unemployed populations received UI benefits as compared to 23.5 percent of the white unemployed population. Men received unemployment insurance at a greater rate than women, but white men received UI benefits at a slightly higher rate than the national average.

The October 2002 unemployment rate was 5.7 percent for all workers, but whites had an unemployment rate of 5.1 percent. The 9.8 percent unemployment rate for blacks was almost double the rate for whites, while the unemployment rate for Latinos was 7.8 percent. Since African Americans and Latinos are more likely to be unemployed and to remain unemployed longer than whites, it is crucial for unemployment insurance to be equally available and accessible to them.

The wide variation in recipiency rates by state and region shows that state policy decisions regarding regular program legislation and administration have a greater impact on recipiency levels than do either current federal policy or economic and demographic factors.

Recipiency is affected by the tightness or looseness of state UI policy.[5] During the 1980s there was a significant decline in the number of unemployed workers who received benefits, due to changes in the federal-state unemployment compensation system. According to Baldwin and McHugh, less than 38 percent of U.S. unemployed workers received an unemployment benefit in 1990, compared to 75 percent coverage during the 1974–75 recession.[6] To bring state unemployment insurance trust funds in line with federal guidelines, state legislatures in many cases moved to reduce the costs of UI programs by adopting stricter eligibility requirements. Baldwin and McHugh reported that a survey of state law changes showed that thirty-five states adopted one or more increases in their minimum monetary earnings requirements between 1981 and 1987. Such stricter eligibility requirements are what cause most of the low-wage and part-time workers, a majority of whom are African American and Hispanic, to be ineligible for UI benefits.

This chapter is organized into three parts. First, an overview of research on unemployment insurance eligibility is provided. Second, the data used for the empirical analysis, the methodology, and the results from the model are described. Third, the discussion concludes with the implications of the research and some policy recommendations.

Literature Review

According to Lieberman, the labor market doubly disadvantages African Americans in terms of UI benefits because it excludes the most needy workers.[7] The higher unemployment rate for African Americans includes issues of being more likely to become unemployed and being less likely to leave unemployment. Consequently African Americans have longer periods of unemployment compared to whites, which means that African Americans who receive UI benefits are more likely to exhaust them. Occupational exclusion has been another disadvantage for African Americans. Historically, many black workers tended to be concentrated in industries not covered by unemployment insurance, such as agricultural and domestic work. The African American unemployment rate has historically been twice the white unemployment rate, and it continues to be the case.[8] During periods of economic recovery, the unemployment rate for blacks tends to decrease at a slower rate than that for whites, and that causes the unemployment ratio to increase. Therefore, the black-white unemployment ratio continues to persist at 2:1.

According to data from the CPS household labor force survey, unemployment increased in 2001 to 5.8 percent in December, due to the economic decline, especially during the second half of the year. The number of claims for UI benefits also rose. The number of claims from October to December 2001 was 1.3 to 1.5 million higher than during the same time period a year earlier.[9] Between 1998 and 2000 workers in the ten states with the highest UI benefits recipiency rates were three times more likely to collect UI benefits than workers in the ten states with the lowest recipiency rates. The high-recipiency states are mainly in the Northeast, the upper Midwest, and the West Coast. The low-recipiency states are in the Deep South, the Southwest, and the Rocky Mountain area.[10]

According to a recent report by the National Women's Law Center, women make up 70 percent of the part-time work force.[11] In 2000 there were more than 15 million women and only about 7 million men working part-time. Many women are unable to work full-time because they are caring for children, an elderly parent, or disabled spouse and they cannot afford child care or adult dependent care.

Part-time workers are not covered by UI in the majority of states. For example, under Texas law, all workers must be willing to work full-time in order to be eligible for UI benefits. Women, African Americans, and Latinos hold the majority of the part-time and low-wage jobs in Texas, and they also tend to be involuntarily unemployed for the longest periods. Emsellem, Allen, and Shaw reported that blacks on average are much less likely to receive UI benefits than whites, and Latinos fall behind whites as well in Texas.[12] As a result of the minimum earnings requirements imposed in Texas, approximately 30 percent of those who worked part-time in low-wage jobs did not qualify for UI benefits. Texas law also requires that an individual must have earnings in at least two calendar quarters during the base period in order to qualify for UI, but this requirement disqualifies most part-time workers. Part-time workers in Texas have only an 8.5 percent chance of receiving UI benefits, even if they worked an average of thirty weeks a year and thirty hours a week.[13]

It is also the case that low earnings and short work histories can lead African American workers to be eligible for unemployment benefits for fewer weeks than higher paid white workers. Therefore the recipiency rate for African Americans can also be shorter than for whites because higher shares of African Americans exhaust their benefits faster.

CPS Data

The data for this study are from the 2001 Current Population Survey March Supplement, taken by the U.S. Census Bureau to examine income and poverty in 2000. There were approximately 5,400 individuals in the sample who were unemployed during some part of 2000. Only 22.2 percent of the unemployed people within the sample reported receiving unemployment insurance benefits. Among those, 23.5 percent of whites received UI benefits compared to 16.8 percent of blacks and Hispanics. A larger percentage of men received unemployment insurance compared to women (22.9 percent versus 21.3 percent).

The differences in the receipt of unemployment insurance, controlling for both race and gender, are shown in figure 12-1. More white men and women

Figure 12-1. *Unemployment Insurance Benefits, by Race and Gender*

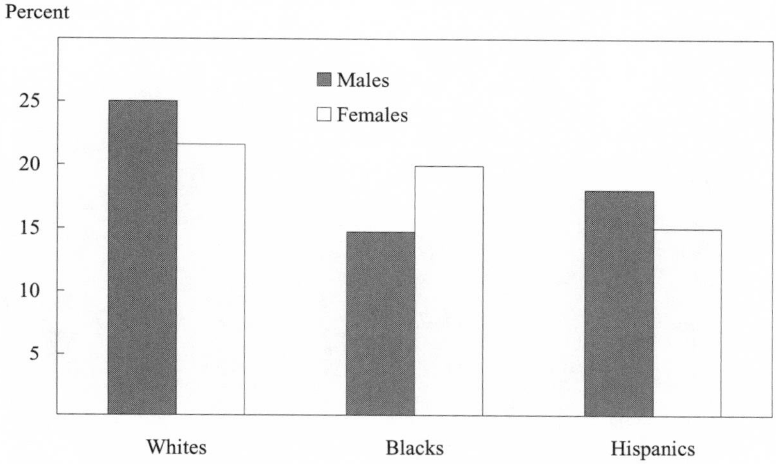

Percent

Source: U.S. Census Bureau, 2001 Current Population Survey, March Supplement.

received unemployment insurance than African American and Hispanic men and women. Black women received benefits slightly more often than Hispanic men, but Hispanic women received benefits more often than black men. Essentially, black men are the least likely group to receive unemployment insurance benefits.

Regionally, the highest UI benefits recipiency rates are in the Midwest (25.1 percent) and the Northeast (24.9 percent), followed by the West (23.6 percent) and then the South (17.5 percent). The disparities in the rates at which the unemployed receive UI benefits across the United States demonstrate the power of state-level policies. According to the CPS data, the largest proportion of the black population is concentrated in the South (30.1 percent). Only 16.3 percent of African Americans represented in the data reside in the Midwest, which is the region where the most UI benefits received were reported.

When one looks at a breakdown of recipiency rates based on the number of part-time weeks previously worked, only 10.1 percent of those who had worked part-time for nineteen to thirty-six weeks of the year received UI benefits. When the part-time work exceeded thirty-six weeks, the insurance recipiency rate was 14.8 percent, But 23.9 percent of individuals who reported working part-time for eighteen weeks or less received unemployment insurance benefits. Individuals who worked the least amount of part-time weeks most likely worked more full-time weeks, therefore making them more likely to receive unemployment insurance benefits.

Figure 12-2.   *Unemployment Insurance Benefits, by Union Status and Race*

Percent

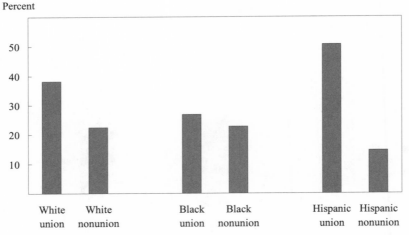

Source: U.S. Census Bureau, 2001 Current Population Survey, March Supplement.

When one looks at UI benefits by income level, the highest rate (50.7 percent) went to those who fell within the $50,000 to $75,000 income level. The rate for those who made between $25,000 and $50,000 was 46.5 percent, compared to 44.5 percent for those who made more than $75,000. The very low earners (less than $25,000) had a rate of only 15.8 percent.

Figure 12-2 shows how union membership increases the recipiency rates for all races, but especially for Hispanics. Union membership increases the likelihood of the Hispanic unemployed receiving unemployment insurance benefits to the highest of any group, while nonunion Hispanics are the least likely group to receive UI benefits. That statistic may also reflect language barriers, with unions helping Hispanics navigate through the bureaucracy of the unemployment insurance system.

When one compares the percentage of unemployed people who received unemployment insurance based on their marital status, singles have a rate of 32.6 percent and married/other have a 30.8 percent rate. Individuals who have never married are the least likely group to receive unemployment insurance (12.0 percent), and much of the African American population falls into that marital status category. However, people who have never married may also be less likely to apply for UI benefits, because they may not have anyone else to support financially.

The CPS sample also provided data on the recipiency rates for UI benefits based on the educational attainment of the unemployed people. Individuals

Table 12-1. *Probabilities of Receiving Unemployment Insurance Benefits,
Based on Coefficient Values*

Variable	Compared to white males		
	Black	Hispanic	Female
Black only	−0.0674		
Hispanic only		−0.0669	
Female only			−0.0248
Black, female, and Hispanic (basic model)	−0.0851	−0.0809	
Basic model and demographics	−0.0545	−0.0422	
Basic model and explanatory state policies	−0.0812	−0.0757	
Basic model and nonexplanatory state policies	−0.0893	−0.0935	
Basic model, explanatory, and nonexplanatory state policies	−0.0856	−0.0890	
Basic model and all state policies	−0.0858	−0.0880	
Basic model, all state policies, and state dummies	−0.0661	−0.0792	
Basic model, all state policies, state dummies, and demographics	−0.0291	−0.0301	

with less than a high school diploma were the least likely group to receive
unemployment insurance benefits, with a rate of 13.6 percent. All other groups
had rates more than 10 percentage points higher: 26.1 percent for high school
graduates, 24.0 percent for individuals with some college or an associate's
degree, 24.4 percent for those with bachelor's degrees, and 24.6 percent for
individuals with graduate and professional degrees.

Empirical Methodology and Results

The results of estimating the gap in the receipt of unemployment insurance
for African Americans, Latinos, and women are shown in table 12-1. Both
African Americans and Latinos have a gap of 6.7 percentage points compared
to white males, and there is a 2.5 percentage point gap between Latino women
and white males. The table then shows how different variables can help to
explain the gap.

For African Americans, when one controls for those African Americans
who are Hispanic and female, the gap in receiving unemployment insurance
actually rises to 8.5 percentage points. This is due to a higher share of African
American workers being female, along with the race and ethnicity disadvantages faced by black Latinos. For Latinos, the gap in receiving UI benefits
increases to 8.1 percentage points when one controls for Latinos who are black
and female.

Because blacks and Latinos are not evenly distributed across all states, a part
of their gap in receiving unemployment insurance is caused by being overrep-

resented in states that have more stringent barriers to getting unemployment insurance. Table 12-1 shows that controlling for this overrepresentation in states that have more limitations on getting unemployment insurance can reduce the gap from 8.5 to 8.1 percentage points for blacks. But, African Americans are also more likely to live in states that have policies that make unemployment insurance more accessible, so the gap grows to 8.9 percent when one controls for those policies. That is, given the differences in state policies and in where African Americans live, if African Americans were more equally spread across the states with whites, the actual gap in recipiency would look greater. The net effect of state policies and the current distribution of African Americans favors African Americans' receipt of unemployment insurance, so the gap is not caused by the net effect of the state eligibility requirements.

When one controls for overrepresentation in states that have more stringent barriers to getting unemployment insurance, the gap for Latinos is reduced from 8.1 to 7.6 percentage points. However, that gap increases from 7.6 to 9.4 percentage points when one goes from the policies that create more limitations on getting UI benefits to the policies that make UI benefits more accessible to Latinos.

This means that the administration of the states' laws affects the rate of receiving unemployment insurance. This is confirmed by adding controls for each state, not related to the specific unemployment insurance laws. The percentage gap for African Americans shrinks from 8.6 percentage points to 6.6 percentage points, which would mean that potentially 23 percent (the 2 percentage point difference between 8.6 and 6.6 relative to the 8.6 percentage point gap) of the difference is explained by differences between whites and African Americans in how the program is administered. The percentage gap for Latinos only shrinks from 9.0 to 8.1 percentage points when similar controls are added. This implies that there may be other reasons for why Latinos receive UI benefits much less frequently than whites.

The remaining gap of 6.6 percent for African Americans can be explained further by differences in the demographic makeup of the African American and white populations. Less educated, unemployed workers are far less likely to get unemployment insurance. This is because of their lower earnings in part, but it is also related to their difficulty in navigating the state unemployment insurance bureaucracy. Married and single workers are more likely to apply for unemployment insurance than never-married workers. Because African Americans have slightly less education than whites and are more likely to be never married, the demographic differences can help to reduce the gap to 3.0 percentage points. So, demographic differences can explain about 35 percent of the 8.6 percentage point gap in getting unemployment insurance.

Hispanics have a 7.9 percent gap remaining once the controls are added, so demographic information should help to explain that gap. However, unlike African Americans, the majority of Hispanics do not fall into the never-married category. More Hispanics have either been married or are currently married, according to their marital status distribution within the CPS data. A larger proportion of Hispanics have less than a high school diploma, compared to African Americans, which may explain much of that remaining gap. Therefore, based on lower educational attainment, Hispanics tend to earn even less than African Americans. Many Hispanics may not even apply for unemployment insurance because they may find the process intimidating due to a lack of education or lack of proficiency with the English language.

Another significant factor involving the lack of unemployment insurance for minorities is related to labor market discrimination. Blacks and Latinos with union membership can more readily handle labor market discrimination because the support from the union can help them navigate through the bureaucracy of the unemployment insurance system. Based on the empirical results, union members are more likely to receive unemployment insurance than nonunion members. However, African Americans without union membership are much more vulnerable to the negative effects of discrimination within the labor market. Unfortunately, there are fewer African Americans in union-supported jobs, such as manufacturing and construction, compared to decades ago. The fact that blacks are unemployed for longer periods than whites, and that blacks are denied employment in certain jobs more often than whites, shows that labor market discrimination plays a significant role in the lack of unemployment insurance for African Americans.

Discrimination within the administration of unemployment insurance and within the labor market, in general, is a feasible explanation for the existence of a gap in the recipiency rates for unemployment insurance between whites and minorities. After all the controls for state policies, demographics, and others were put into place to help to explain portions of the gap in the receipt of unemployment insurance, there still remained an unexplained portion. That remaining portion can be attributed to discrimination.

Policy Recommendations

States should be compelled to reevaluate their unemployment insurance eligibility requirements in order to remove racial and ethnic disparities in the receipt of unemployment benefits. Administrative problems, where unemployment officials can discriminate against African Americans when they apply for unemployment insurance benefits, need to be resolved and eliminated. To the extent that labor market discrimination has contributed to the lack of unemployment insurance benefits for minorities, safeguards should be put in place to ensure that African Americans qualify for benefits at a rate that would exist if there were no labor market discrimination.

Unemployment insurance also could become more equitable by requiring all states to institute extended benefits options for the claimants. Blacks tend to be unemployed for longer periods of time than whites and may only be eligible for benefits for a short period, so their unemployment insurance benefits are often exhausted. The unemployment insurance system should be designed to allow for an extension of benefits for individuals who are actively seeking employment but may have trouble finding work due to labor market discrimination and other barriers.

Conclusion

This chapter shows unemployed African Americans and Latinos are 6.7 percent less likely to get unemployment insurance than unemployed whites. There are several possible explanations for why whites receive unemployment insurance more readily than African Americans or Hispanics.

African Americans and Hispanics tend to be unemployed for longer periods than whites, and many states only provide unemployment insurance for a maximum of twenty-six weeks. Discrimination in the labor market often prevents African Americans and Hispanics from becoming reemployed before their unemployment insurance benefits are exhausted, if they are able to get past the bureaucracy of the system to qualify for benefits initially. Stringent state policies are only part of the reason why African Americans and Hispanics do not receive unemployment insurance as readily as whites.

A portion of the gap in receiving UI benefits can be explained by African Americans and Hispanics being overrepresented in states that have more restrictive barriers to getting unemployment insurance. Some state policies hinder minorities from receiving UI benefits, but other state policies actually help them.

There appear to be two major sources of variation within the states: (1) administrative problems, where unemployment insurance officials may be discriminating against African Americans; and (2) subtle barriers in navigating the bureaucracy—indicated by the difficulty that less educated unemployed individuals have in accessing the unemployment insurance system. Other barriers may exist that are related specifically to the workers. For example, individuals may choose not to apply for unemployment insurance based on their marital status. Individuals who have never married may not be compelled to apply for unemployment insurance since they may only have themselves to support.

Using data from the 2001 Current Population Survey, this chapter estimates the probability of an unemployed individual receiving unemployment insurance benefits. Individuals in this study were those who reported some spell of unemployment in 2000. Statistical controls were used to explain the gap in the probability of African Americans and Latinos in receiving unemployment benefits in 2000 compared to whites. Controls are used to understand the role of state policies that set eligibility criteria and for individual factors that may lower the application rates for unemployment insurance. The eligibility criteria included state-specific policies for quarterly earnings, hours, waiting periods, and alternative base periods. Individual factors that could influence the decision to apply for unemployment insurance are age, marital status, education, and union membership.

The inequities within the unemployment insurance system in the United States are not acceptable. Significant changes to the system need to occur in order for more African Americans, Hispanics, and women to qualify for benefits. Labor market discrimination contributes to the low recipiency rate for minorities, and many of the current state unemployment insurance policies add to the disparity. Major reforms need to take place within many of the states in order to create a more equitable UI benefits system.

Appendix A: Empirical Model in Detail

A logit model is estimated where the binary choice dependent variable is whether an individual receives unemployment benefits or not. The key demographic information within the model consists of race, age, gender, marital status, educational attainment, and union membership status of the unemployed individuals. Several state policy variables are included within the model to capture the effect of specific laws within the states regarding unemployment insurance (UI) eligibility. The logistic regression model that was estimated is of the following form:

$$UI_{benefits}\ [pr(Y=1)] = \beta_o + \beta_{1race} + \beta_{2Latino} + \beta_{3sex} + \beta_{4abp} + \beta_{5minwage} + \beta_{6parttime} +$$
$$\beta_{7maxbenf} + \beta_{8tur} + \beta_{9waitweek} + \beta_{10maxwage} + \beta_{11insured} + \beta_{12statedum} + \beta_{13minreq} + \beta_{14dminreq} +$$
$$\beta_{15highqtr} + \beta_{16dhighqtr} + \beta_{17age} + \beta_{18marital} + \beta_{19education} + \beta_{20union} + \beta_{21uerate} + \varepsilon_i.$$

Initially, we estimated the model with only race variables included to isolate the effect of race on the incidence of UI benefits. Additional variables were included to estimate the impact of the state policies on the unemployment insurance recipiency rates for minorities and women. Key demographic variables were also included to provide some additional explanation for why individuals may not even apply for UI benefits.

The following equation was used to calculate the probabilities in table 12-1, where $\Delta P / \Delta X = \Delta P$ since $\Delta X = 1$, which yields:

$$\Delta = \frac{P \cdot e^B}{(1 - P) + P \cdot e^B} - P,$$

where P is the probability of an individual receiving unemployment insurance, and ß is the coefficient on race in each of the respective regression models. The value for P was 0.1615 for calculation of the probabilities on the coefficients for blacks and Latinos. So the values within table 12-1 represent the probability of blacks, Latinos, and women receiving unemployment insurance compared to white men.

The actual coefficient values for the race and gender variables within the regression model are reported in table 12A-1. Depending on whether the demographic or state policy variables are included in the model, the values for the coefficients on race and gender vary. These results are indicative of how influential the specific state policies are in determining whether blacks, Latinos, or women receive unemployment insurance. The coefficients and standard errors for each of the independent variables within the regression model are reported in table 12A-2. Many of the demographic characteristic variables are statistically significant, but only one of the state policy variables is statistically significant.

Table 12A-1. *Coefficient Values for Race and Gender*

Variables	Coefficients on		
	Black	*Latino*	*Female*
Black only	−0.4328		
Latino only		−0.4300	
Female only			−0.1423
Black, female, and Latino (basic model)	−0.5305	−0.5073	−0.1567
Basic model and demographics	−0.3578	−0.2835	
Basic model and explanatory state policies	−0.5092	−0.4790	
Basic model and nonexplanatory state policies	−0.5527	−0.5751	
Basic model, explanatory, and nonexplanatory state policies	−0.5330	−0.5510	
Basic model and all state policies	−0.5340	−0.5457	
Basic model, all state policies, and state dummies	−0.4250	−0.4983	
Basic model, all state policies, state dummies, and demographics	−0.2013	−0.2073	

Table 12A-2.   *Coefficients and Standard Errors from Empirical Model*

Variable	Coefficient values	Standard errors
Race dummy	−0.433*	0.101
Latino dummy	−0.430*	0.085
Gender dummy	−0.142*	0.066
Age	0.027*	0.003
Union membership	0.583*	0.247
Single	−0.028	0.090
Never married	−0.813*	0.091
High school graduate	0.607*	0.099
Some college or associate's degree	0.515*	0.109
Bachelor's degree	0.462*	0.133
Graduate or professional degree	−0.133	0.207
State policy variables		
Base wage required for minimum benefit	−0.009	0.064
Alternative base period	0.122	0.094
Minimum wage worker qualifies for benefits	0.239	0.126
Part-time workers eligible	−0.213*	0.081
Maximum weekly benefit available	0.117	0.126
Extended benefits trigger is adopted	0.109	0.131
Waiting week provision	0.108	0.086
High quarter wages required for minimum benefit	0.069	0.078
Base period wages required for maximum benefit	−0.034	0.086
Wages must be in insured work	−0.127	0.095
State unemployment rate	0.095	0.053

*Statistically significant at the 95 percent confidence level.

Appendix B: CPS Data Explanation

This chapter uses the Current Population Survey (CPS) March Supplement, taken by the U.S. Census Bureau to estimate income and poverty in the previous year. A different set of data is more widely used in unemployment insurance (UI) benefit research, comparing numbers from the Current Population Survey Basic Survey, taken by the U.S. Census Bureau for the Bureau of Labor Statistics to estimate monthly unemployment and labor market conditions, in conjunction with data from the U.S. Department of Labor's Employment and Training Administration's (ETA) 203 Report, which is from state-level administrative data on unemployment insurance benefits. Those two sources of data do not necessarily cover the same individuals. In the majority of UI studies, data from the CPS survey are used to estimate the number of unemployed persons in a state. The ETA 203 data report the number of unemployment insurance beneficiaries in a state from state administrative data. The combination of the two provides an estimate of the share of unemployed workers receiving benefits. The ETA 203 data are the most widely used data for discussions concerning UI benefit recipiency rates. However, the ETA 203 data are not the best data to utilize when one compares unemployment insurance benefits received by race. The ETA 203 data are not reported as individual data, so it is not possible to control for differences between those who report receiving unemployment insurance and those who do not apply based on characteristics that make some people more, or less, likely to apply for unemployment insurance. For example, certain states within the ETA 203 Report, such as New Jersey and Washington, have no racial data reported. This would cause significant problems when one tries to calculate national averages for unemployment insurance recipiency by race. Therefore, the CPS March Supplement was used as the source of data so that the most accurate and consistent analysis based on racial differences could be conducted.

Notes

1. W. A. Darity Jr. and P. L. Mason, "Evidence on Discrimination in Employment: Codes of Color, Codes of Gender," *Journal of Economic Perspectives* 12, no. 2 (1998), pp. 63–90.

2. R. M. Blank and D. E. Card, "Recent Trends in Insured and Uninsured Unemployment: Is There an Explanation?" *Quarterly Journal of Economics* 106, no. 4 (1991), pp. 1157–89.

3. National Employment Law Project (NELP), "Expanding Unemployment Insurance for Low-Wage Workers: State Legislative Highlights (1996–2001)" (New York: NELP, 2001), pp. 1–9.

4. General Accounting Office, "Unemployment Insurance: Role as Safety Net for Low-Wage Workers Is Limited," GAO-01-181 (Washington, D.C.: 2000).

5. S. A. Wandner and T. Stengle, "Unemployment Insurance: Measuring Who Receives It," *Monthly Labor Review* (July 1997), pp. 15–24.

6. M. Baldwin and R. McHugh, "Unprepared for Recession: The Erosion of State Unemployment Insurance Coverage Fostered by Public Policy in the 1980s," Briefing Paper, Economic Policy Institute, Washington, D.C., 1992.

7. R. C. Lieberman, *Shifting the Color Line: Race and the American Welfare State* (Harvard University Press, 1998); W. E. Spriggs and R. M. Williams, "What Do We Need to Explain about African American Unemployment?" in Robert Cherry and William M. Rodgers III, eds., *Prosperity for All? The Economic Boom and African Americans* (Russell Sage, 2000), pp. 188–207.

8. Spriggs and Williams, "What Do We Need to Explain about African American Unemployment?"; M. V. L. Badgett, "Rising Black Unemployment: Changes in Job Stability or in Employability?" *Review of Black Political Economy* 22, no. 3 (1994), pp. 55–75.

9. W. Vroman, *Unemployment Insurance Primer: Understanding What's at Stake as Congress Reopens Stimulus Package Debate* (Washington, D.C.: Urban Institute, 2002).

10. Vroman, *Unemployment Insurance Primer*, pp. 1–11.

11. National Women's Law Center (NELP), "The Economic Stimulus Package Must Include Unemployment Insurance Improvements for Low-Wage Working Women," Special Report, NELP, Washington, D.C., 2001, pp. 1–6.

12. M. Emsellem, K. Allen, and L. Shaw, "The Texas Unemployment Insurance System: Barriers to Access for Low-Wage, Part-Time, and Women Workers," Special Report, National Employment Law Project, New York, 1999, pp. 1–12.

13. Emsellem and others, "The Texas Unemployment Insurance System," pp. 1–12.

13

Incomplete Development of State and Voluntary Temporary Disability Insurance

Vicky Lovell

Short-term or temporary disability insurance (TDI) is a critical component of a complete employment-based social insurance package. Unlike other social insurance programs, however, in the United States the provision of TDI has generally been made at employers' option, rather than as a matter of public policy. More than half the work force is not protected by TDI against short, unpaid work absences due to accidents and health issues that occur outside of employment.

When workers are covered by a continuum of social insurance programs, they are indemnified against the loss of earnings due to unemployment, work- and non–work-related injury and illness, and old age over their full lifespan. During involuntary unemployment, eligible workers receive benefits through the state/federal unemployment insurance program. For periods of injury and illness lasting six or twelve months, there are two state programs: Workers' Compensation for disabilities that are related to work and TDI for non–work-related accident and illness. Disabilities that are anticipated to be permanent or fatal and preclude any employment are protected under the federal Social Security Disability Insurance (SSDI) and means-tested Supplemental Security Income (SSI) programs. Finally, the Old Age and Survivors Insurance program of Social Security provides income for workers during retirement. Some of these programs also support workers' dependents and survivors. In addition, most of them may be augmented by policies purchased by workers or employers in private insurance markets.

What Is TDI?

TDI provides partial, temporary wage replacement to workers who are unable to perform their job duties because of a serious health condition or an injury that occurred outside work. It covers health conditions that are more serious than a common cold or minor surgery, since most plans have a one-week unpaid waiting period before benefits begin, but that have not been diagnosed as permanent. Benefits typically pay around two-thirds of the employee's usual wage, for up to twenty-six weeks.

TDI policies, including the programs mandated by some states (described below), are not accompanied by guarantees that employers will hold a job for recipients until their return to work. However, there is anecdotal evidence that employers often conduct their TDI programs as temporary leaves from which employees are expected to return.[1] In addition, workers on TDI may qualify for job-protected leave under the federal Family and Medical Leave Act of 1993 (FMLA), which would run concurrently with their TDI leave for an FMLA maximum of twelve weeks.

In the typical case, temporary disability insurance is not the first stage of a long-term disability insurance (DI) policy covering the same medical condition. For the most part, the two programs are geared toward substantially different circumstances, although in some cases workers receiving TDI fail to recover within the relatively short period covered by that insurance and transition to long-term disability. The likelihood of transitioning from TDI to DI or SSDI varies by health condition and age.[2] The two programs use very different definitions to assess eligibility: TDI provides benefits to workers who are unable to perform their customary occupation for a number of months, while SSDI is restricted to those with medical conditions that are expected to be terminal or to render them unable to engage in *any* employment for twelve months or longer.[3] In addition, SSDI and SSI recipients are more likely to suffer from more than one chronic condition and to feel pessimistic about their prospects for improved health than individuals receiving TDI.[4]

For women, TDI provides a kind of paid leave that employers have been reluctant to offer voluntarily: maternity leave. (Only 2 percent of private-sector workers are covered by paid family leave.[5]) Initially, most state TDI programs disallowed claims related to pregnancy and childbirth.[6] (The Rhode Island TDI program, the plan for railroad employees, and, to a more limited extent, California's TDI program were unusual in covering maternity disability as early as the 1950s.) In 1974 only 1 percent of private-sector workers with health insurance participated in plans that covered maternity in an equivalent manner as other disabilities.[7] Guidelines issued by the Equal Employment Opportunity Commission in 1972 clarifying that pregnancy-related disabilities were to be treated as other temporary disabilities under health insurance and disability policies were challenged later in the decade and settled by passage of the Pregnancy Discrimination Act in 1978, which clearly established refusal to cover pregnancy- and maternity-related disabilities under TDI plans as illegal discrimination.[8] Now, claims related to pregnancy and childbirth receive approximately one-fifth of total TDI payments.[9] In California, the guidelines for the state-mandated TDI plan call for benefits to begin four weeks before a baby's due date and continue six weeks postpartum for a pregnancy with no complications and longer as medically necessary.[10] In New Jersey, for an uncomplicated pregnancy and delivery, benefits are typically paid for four to six weeks before a baby is due and six to eight weeks after delivery.[11]

State-Mandated Temporary Disability Insurance Programs

Publicly mandated TDI has a different administrative structure than other social insurance programs and is less inclusive than any other. Unlike Social Security, TDI is not a federal program; nor is it a state program guided by federal oversight, the way unemployment insurance is. Like Workers' Compensation, TDI programs are initiated at individual states' discretion, with no federal involvement; but unlike Workers' Compensation, which is mandatory in every state except Texas, the state-mandated TDI concept was not widely adopted.[12] As outlined in table 13-1, five states have elected to either establish mandatory state TDI programs or require that employers provide TDI coverage: California, Hawaii, New Jersey, New York, and Rhode Island.[13] Except for Hawaii, these states all enacted TDI in the 1940s—within fifteen years of passage of the Social Security Act—to provide a more complete set of social insurance programs for workers in the rapidly industrializing United States. In these early years of social insurance, many jurisdictions were struggling to create programs to support individuals with employment histories who were unable to work. TDI was seen as a complement to unemployment insurance: both programs are targeted at workers who want to return to employment but, temporarily, cannot.

Experimentation with unemployment insurance (UI) by individual states in the early decades of the twentieth century eventually led to the current federal/state system in which states set most administrative and programmatic details of their UI programs under a federal umbrella that ensures fiscal soundness and sets some administrative guidelines. Federal involvement in UI includes a tax system that incentivized state programs, ensuring that each state would create a UI program. Although twenty-five states considered TDI legislation in the period from 1939 to 1951, neither state- nor federal-level interest developed to the extent that a federalized program or relatively similar universal state plans were adopted.[14] Thus publicly mandated TDI remains something of a social insurance anomaly, protecting workers in only a few states.

Since there is no overarching federal structure to the individual state TDI plans, each has its own administrative, financing, eligibility, and benefit provisions. The only constant among the five states is in the covered conditions: accidents and illness of a short-term nature that are not incurred on the job. (California recently expanded its TDI program to provide up to six weeks of paid family disability leave. When this program begins paying benefits in July 2004, workers will be able to take disability leave to care for ill family members or when they have a newborn, newly adopted, or newly placed foster child to care for.)

Three state TDI programs are financed through both employer and employee contributions, while two are wholly employee-funded. In California and New Jersey employers may purchase TDI coverage from a state program, elect to substitute an acceptable plan from the private insurance market, or self-insure instead; in Hawaii and New York the state does not run its own TDI plan (although New York has a special TDI program for unemployed workers). In Rhode Island all employers must subscribe to the state-run plan.

Eligibility criteria vary considerably among the state TDI plans. In California a worker is covered after earning only $300 during a specified set of weeks, while the Rhode Island threshold is $7,380 (or $2,460 for workers with a particular distribution of earnings over certain calendar quarters). Hawaii, New Jersey, and New York require 14, 20, and 4 weeks of employment, respectively; Hawaii also requires a minimum of 20 hours a week of work and $400 in earnings; New Jersey mandates a minimum of $103 in earnings during the required 20 weeks or total earnings of $1,030; and New York stipulates that the 4 weeks of work be consecutive.

The percent of each state's work force that is eligible for participation in the mandatory TDI plans varies according to eligibility criteria and worker exclusions written into the plans. Generally approximately 75 percent of workers are covered.

The statutory replacement ratio—that is, the benefit amount as a percent of a worker's average weekly earnings—is similar across the five state programs, ranging from 50 percent in New York to 67 percent in New Jersey. (With the exception of New Jersey, all the state TDI plans are slightly less generous than their Workers' Compensation programs, which typically have a replacement rate of 67 percent.) However, with maximum weekly benefit levels set as low as $170 (in New York), the actual replacement rate may be much less adequate. (Employers may choose to provide a plan with a higher benefit maximum. In New York, for example, employers with offices in both New York and California may offer New Yorkers a more generous package than is required by law as a way of maintaining employer-wide benefit equity.)

Some states tie their benefit caps to the state average weekly wage (as is done with Workers' Compensation programs), so the maxima adjust automati-

Table 13-1. *State Temporary Disability Insurance Programs*

Administrative structure and eligibility	California	Hawaii	New Jersey	New York	Rhode Island
Administering agency	Employment Development Department	Department of Labor and Industrial Relations	Employment security agency	Workers' Compensation Board	Department of Labor and Training
Financing	Employee	Employer (may share with employee, subject to maximum)	Employer and employee	Employer (may share with employee)	Employee
Carrier	State or acceptable private plan	Private (state plan for unemployed)	State or acceptable private plan	Private (state plan for unemployed)	State only
Percent of work force participating[a]	77.6	47.0	84.3	78.8	82.7
Eligibility requirements	$300 in earnings	14 weeks of work, min. 20 hours per week, $400 earnings	20 weeks of work and $103 earnings, or alternative	4 consecutive weeks of employment	Earnings of $7,380 or alternative
Covered conditions	Non-work-related accident and illness; 2004: family TDI	Non-work-related accident and illness	Non-work-related accident and illness	Non-work-related accident and illness	Non-work-related accident and illness

continues

Benefits					
Benefit amount as percent of weekly earnings	approx. 55–60	58	67	50	approx. 60
Maximum weekly benefit[b]	$602	$408	$450	$170	$543 plus dependency allowance
Average weekly benefit[b]	state: $230 private: $352	$365	state: $282 private: n/a	$185	$263
Average weeks per claim for 1998	state: 12.1 private: 10.5	3.2	n/a	7.1	9.6
Maximum benefit period	52 weeks (6 for family TDI)	26 weeks	26 weeks	26 weeks	30 weeks

Sources: U.S. Department of Labor, Comparison of State UI Laws (January 2001); available at http://workforcesecurity.doleta.gov); California Employment Development Department; Hawaii Department of Labor and Industrial Relations; New Jersey Department of Labor; New York Workers' Compensation Board; Rhode Island Department of Labor and Training; VPA, Inc. (www.vpaweb.com).

a. Author's calculations using U.S. Social Security Administration, Social Security Bulletin, Annual Statistical Supplement, 2001, table 9.C, and U.S. Bureau of Labor Statistics, "Geographic Profile of Employment and Unemployment," bulletin 2524, 1999, table 16.

b. Employed workers.

cally to wage increases; in others (California and New York), the top benefit amount is set by the legislature. Given differences among the TDI states in wages as well as in TDI benefit provisions, there is considerable disparity in average weekly benefit levels, which ranged in 1998 from a low of $185 in New York to a high of $365 in Hawaii.

Claim histories also vary greatly from state to state. With the exception of California, which allows up to 52 weeks of TDI, and Rhode Island, which sets a 30-week maximum, TDI plans usually provide benefits for up to 26 weeks. The average number of weeks of benefits paid per claim is 3.2 in Hawaii, 7.1 in New York, 9.6 in Rhode Island, and 10.5 for private plans and 12.1 for the state-operated insurance fund in California. (Comparable data are not available for New Jersey.)

Who Is Covered by TDI?

Thirty-seven percent of private-sector nonagricultural workers are protected by temporary disability insurance programs for which employers pay at least a portion of the premium (table 13-2).[15] An additional 12 percent participate in wholly employee-funded state-mandated programs in California and Rhode Island.[16] Sixteen percent of government employees have TDI coverage through state and local employment (TDI is not part of the benefit package for federal workers).[17] All in all, about 40 percent of the total public and private nonagricultural work force is covered by mandatory or voluntary TDI plans.

The pattern of participation in TDI plans across groups of workers is similar to that of other employment benefits. White- and blue-collar workers, those with full-time work schedules, union members, higher paid workers, and employees in larger firms are the most likely to be covered by TDI. Among industries, workers in construction, retail trade, and services are the least likely to have TDI.

There is little publicly available demographic data to indicate which workers are covered by TDI and which are excluded. An evaluation of New Jersey's program shows that 69 percent of eligible TDI claimants in that state are women; nearly 25 percent are women in the age group 25 to 34 (table 13-3).[18] Women aged 35 to 44 make up 18 percent of the eligible claimant pool; 13 percent are women between the ages of 45 and 54. (The preponderance of these claims is doubtless for pregnancy- and maternity-related disability.) Male claimants are most likely to be aged 35 to 44, although the age distribution of men receiving TDI is relatively consistent throughout the ages of 25 to 64.

Table 13-2. *Participation in Employer-Funded Temporary Disability Insurance Plans, by Worker and Establishment Characteristics (Private Industry, 2003)*
Percent

Characteristics	Workers in TDI plans
All	37
Occupation	
White-collar	40
Blue-collar	44
Service	20
Wage level	
$15 per hour or higher	52
Less than $15	27
Work hours	
Full-time	45
Part-time	12
Unionization	
Union	68
Nonunion	34
Industry[a]	
Construction	23
Manufacturing	59
Transportation and public utilities	49
Wholesale trade	43
Retail trade	20
FIRE	49
Services	31
Employer size	
1–99 workers	26
100 or more workers	50

Source: U.S. Bureau of Labor Statistics, *Employee Benefits in Private Industry, 1999* (USDL 01-473, 2001, table 2); U.S. Bureau of Labor Statistics, *Employee Benefits in Private Industry, 2003* (USDL 03–489, 2003, table 2).
a. Excludes mining; data are for 1999.
Note: Shading indicates group/establishment type with lower TDI coverage.

Most TDI claims involve three broad medical conditions: injuries and diseases of the bones and organs of movement; accidents, poisoning, and violence; and pregnancy and childbirth (table 13-4). Benefits are paid for an average of 96, 80, and 80 days, respectively, for these conditions. Claims relating to ailments of the digestive and respiratory systems are the least expensive and have the shortest durations; mental, psychoneurotic, and personality disorders have the longest average duration and the greatest average total benefit.

Table 13-3.   *Age and Sex of Eligible TDI Claimants, New Jersey, 2000*

Age	All	Women	Men
Under 25	7.8	6.0	1.8
25–34	28.6	23.2	5.4
35–44	26.5	18.3	8.2
45–54	20.1	12.6	7.5
55–64	13.5	7.5	6.0
65 and over	3.5	1.8	1.7
All	100.0	69.4	30.6

Source: New Jersey Department of Labor, Program Planning, Analysis and Evaluation, *Temporary Disability Insurance Workload in 2000: Summary Report* (2002), table 3.

The Impact of TDI on Diverse Populations

Regarding the question that was directed to this panel—"What do we know about the impact of TDI on diverse populations?"—the answer is that there are few data that allow us to look directly at demographic differences in access to coverage or denial of claims, to evaluate whether some medical conditions are routinely excluded from approval, or to assess the existence of racial and ethnic differences or sex differences in coverage or in benefit receipt. However, some conclusions can be drawn about differential access to TDI and qualitative differences in programs covering different workers that are directly related to the lack of universal TDI coverage.

—The most fundamental inequity in TDI coverage is that 22 percent of workers live in states with mandated TDI coverage, while millions do not. Thus, as a state-based social insurance program, TDI policy in the United States is built on a hugely inequitable foundation. For women, the happenstance of living in a non-TDI state may well mean not having paid leave for pregnancy- and childbirth-related disability.

—State TDI plans exclude fewer employees than private plans are likely to cover. Workers seeking private TDI coverage, whether employer- or employee-funded, may have difficulty obtaining policy coverage of preexisting conditions,[19] and private insurers may market TDI policies to the most profitable segments of the work force, leaving needier workers underinsured.[20] On the other hand, private policies typically offer higher wage replacement ratios.[21]

—Within states that have mandatory TDI coverage, some categories of workers are excluded: state employees in some states; domestic and family workers; the self-employed; and, in New York and Rhode Island, agricultural workers.[22]

Table 13-4. *Most Common Medical Bases of Completed TDI Claims, New Jersey, 2000*

Major morbidity group	Percent of cases	Average duration (days)	Average gross benefit (dollars)
Bones and organs of movement	18.7	96	4,300
Accidents, poisoning, and violence	16.7	80	3,484
Pregnancy and childbirth	14.9	80	3,353
Circulatory system	8.6	96	4,302
Neoplasms	8.2	100	4,463
Digestive system	6.6	47	2,103
Mental, psychoneurotic, and personality disorders	5.7	104	4,708
Respiratory system	5.2	39	1,777

Source: New Jersey Department of Labor, Program Planning, Analysis and Evaluation, *Temporary Disability Insurance Workload in 2000: Summary Report* (2002), table 5.

—Among the TDI states, benefit levels vary considerably, leaving New Yorkers, in particular, with woefully inadequate average benefit levels. Automatic adjustment of benefit maxima in Hawaii, New Jersey, and Rhode Island provides some protection against inflation in those states, and California recently passed substantial increases in its maximum benefits for 2004 and 2005.

—TDI states differ in their treatment of employer-paid sick leave during TDI claim periods. In Rhode Island workers can receive both TDI and paid sick leave; in New York any employer payment is deducted from the TDI benefit. California and New Jersey stipulate that the sum of TDI benefits and sick pay may not exceed a worker's regular earnings.

—Rhode Island's TDI program provides an extra benefit increment of $10, or 7 percent of the weekly benefit, for workers' dependent children, helping to increase benefit adequacy.[23]

—Beginning in July 2004 the most significant difference among the TDI states will be California's extension of TDI to provide family disability leave.

—The limited data available about TDI coverage show that the same workers who are most likely to have low wages and few employment benefits—low-wage workers; part-timers; those who are not union members; workers in the construction, retail, and service industries; and workers in smaller firms—have the lowest rates of TDI coverage. Three-fourths of all low-wage women workers are employed in retail and services, which suggests that their participation in TDI is disproportionately barred.[24] Uneven access to TDI exacerbates existing inequities in job quality and restricts many women's ability to take paid maternity leave.

Conclusion

Temporary disability insurance is a key component of social insurance, protecting workers against short-term earnings losses associated with non–work-related accidents and illness. In the absence of a national TDI policy, access to TDI benefits is distributed very unevenly, and available data suggest that workers at the greatest disadvantage in the work force generally have the lowest rates of TDI coverage.

Recent statutory changes in California, however, point the way toward improved TDI policies for workers in the five TDI states, through implementation of higher maximum benefit levels (which will increase the program's adequacy for higher-wage workers) and, perhaps more important, in expansion of the circumstances for which benefits may be paid to include care work provided to ill family members or newborn, newly adopted, and newly placed foster children.

Notes

1. Michele I. Naples, *Family Leave for Low-Income Working Women: Providing Paid Leave through Temporary Disability Insurance: The New Jersey Case* (Washington, D.C.: Institute for Women's Policy Research, October 2001), p. 3.

2. Christopher C. Wagner, Carolyn E. Danczyk-Hawley, Kathryn Mulholland, and Bruce G. Flynn, "Older Workers' Progression from Private Disability Benefits to Social Security Disability Benefits," *Social Security Bulletin* 63 (2000), p. 33.

3. Virginia P. Reno and Daniel N. Price, "Relationship between the Retirement, Disability, and Unemployment Insurance Programs: The U.S. Experience," *Social Security Bulletin* 48 (May 1985), p. 32.

4. John R. Kearney, "The Work Incapacity and Reintegration Study: Results of the Initial Survey Conducted in the United States," *Social Security Bulletin* 60 (1997), pp. 28–29.

5. U.S. Department of Labor, *Employee Benefits in Medium and Large Private Establishments, 1997* (1999); *Employee Benefits in Small Private Industry Establishments, 1996* (Washington, D.C., 1998).

6. U.S. Department of Labor, *Temporary Disability Insurance: Problems in Formulating a Program Administered by a State Employment Security Agency* (Washington, D.C., 1953), p. 26.

7. Daniel N. Price, "Cash Benefits for Short-Term Sickness, 1948–1981," *Social Security Bulletin* 47 (August 1984), p. 36.

8. M. Margaret Conway, David W. Ahern, and Gertrude A. Steuernagel, *Women and Public Policy: A Revolution in Progress* (Washington, D.C.: CQ Press, 1995), p. 161.

9. California Employment Development Department, "Disability Insurance Profile for SFY 96/97 and SFY 97/98," 1999.

10. California Employment Development Department, "State Disability Insurance (SDI): Frequently Asked Questions—Pregnancy" (www.edd.ca.gov/direp/difaq1tx.htm [accessed September 16, 2003]).

11. "Questions and Answers about Pregnancy Disability Benefits," New Jersey Department of Labor, Trenton, N.J., 1999.

12. Daniel Mont, John F. Burton Jr., Virginia Reno, and Cecili Thompson, *Workers' Compensation: Benefits, Coverage, and Costs, 2000 New Estimates* (Washington, D.C.: National Academy of Social Insurance, 2002), p. 2.

13. A separate program covers railroad employees. In addition, workers excluded from the state program are sometimes covered by elective programs or by secondary plans, such as California's Non-Industrial Disability program for state employees, which pays much lower benefits than the regular state plan.

14. U.S. Department of Labor, *Temporary Disability Insurance*, p. 3.

15. U.S. Department of Labor, *Employee Benefits*.

16. Author's calculation using U.S. Social Security Administration, *Social Security Bulletin: Annual Statistical Supplement, 2001,* table 9.C1, and U.S. Bureau of Labor Statistics, "Geographic Profile of Employment and Unemployment," bulletin 2524, 1999, table 16.

17. Author's calculation using U.S. Bureau of Labor Statistics, "Employee Benefits in State and Local Governments," bulletin 2531, 2000, table 29, and U.S. Bureau of Labor Statistics, "Geographic Profile of Employment and Unemployment," table 16.

18. New Jersey Department of Labor, *Temporary Disability Insurance Workload in 2000: Summary Report* (2002).

19. Keith Ouellette, "Wanted: DI Policies for Marginally Impaired Risks," *National Underwriter* 106 (February 25, 2002), p. 6.

20. Wagner and others, "Older Workers' Progression," p. 28.

21. Wagner and others, "Older Workers' Progression," p. 29.

22. Social Security Administration, "Temporary Disability Insurance," in *Social Security Programs in the United States* (Washington, D.C., 1997).

23. Rhode Island Department of Labor and Training, "Frequently Asked Questions about TDI" (www.dlt.state.ri.us/webdev/tdi/tdifaq.htm [accessed January 7, 2003]).

24. Marlene Kim, "Women Paid Low Wages: Who They Are and Where They Work," *Monthly Labor Review* 123 (September 2000), pp. 26–30.

14

Diversity among State
Cash Assistance Programs
and Populations

John T. Monahan

State cash assistance programs for low-income families with children vary substantially between states and, in some places, among jurisdictions within a particular state. This extraordinary variety can be seen in differing funding levels, eligibility criteria, program requirements, implementation strategies, and administrative structures. Indeed, from a national perspective, the defining characteristic of state cash assistance programs may be their striking diversity.

With regard to the characteristics of families receiving cash assistance, over the past ten years caseloads have changed in some ways but not in others. Overall, caseloads declined quite dramatically from 1996 to 2002 due to welfare reform and a booming economy. In terms of racial and ethnic characteristics, cash assistance caseloads became increasingly Hispanic—roughly reflecting national population trends.

Receipt of cash assistance by noncitizen legal immigrants declined precipitously due to changes in federal law enacted in 1996. When one looks at gender and family structure, cash assistance caseloads remain overwhelmingly female and largely composed of single-parent households. There is a paucity of systematic research about the disparate impacts, if any, of cash assistance policies by race or ethnicity or about effects on legal immigrants ineligible for benefits or services.

Purpose

This chapter provides a brief background on the nature and history of state cash assistance programs aimed at families with children and then examines ways in which those programs affect special populations identified for consideration by the National Academy of Social Insurance in developing its conference agenda in January 2003.

Background

The roots of current state cash welfare programs for families can be traced to the federal-state Aid to Families with Dependent Children (AFDC) program. Established during the New Deal, and originally designed to deliver assistance to widows and orphans, AFDC changed and grew in the ensuing decades. Even as it evolved, AFDC maintained its original framework within which the federal government matched state expenditures for cash welfare payments for low-income families. Federal matching rates were inversely related to state per capita income. AFDC also established an individual entitlement to cash payments for families meeting relevant federal and state eligibility criteria.

Within this core federal AFDC framework, states had considerable discretion on key issues, such as benefit levels. For example, table 14-1 demonstrates differences in AFDC benefits between states in 1996, including changes in real benefit values from 1970 to 1996.

When President Bill Clinton signed the Personal Responsibility and Work Opportunity Reconciliation Act (PRWORA) on August 22, 1996, AFDC was repealed. The Temporary Assistance to Needy Families (TANF) program took its place, providing each state with a fixed block grant that can be used for a broad range of purposes, including support for low-income families, marriage promotion, and teen pregnancy prevention. Each state's TANF allotment reflects its historic AFDC spending levels, and each state is required to demonstrate that it is maintaining 75–80 percent of its spending under AFDC. No individual is entitled to benefits or services under TANF.

After 1996, reflecting welfare reform implementation and a booming economy, cash assistance caseloads plummeted across the country. Some states experienced more dramatic declines than others.

As caseloads fell and states' TANF allocations remained fixed, state cash assistance programs found themselves with more resources available per recipient family than prior to federal welfare reform. However, due to the linkage between TANF block grant allocations and historic AFDC expenditure patterns, the amount of resources available to serve needy families varied among states.

As previously noted, states have enormous discretion in their use of TANF funds. However, there are several important federal requirements, including a five-year lifetime benefit (shorter at state discretion), complex restrictions on the ability of states to serve legal immigrants, and a requirement that states ensure that significant portions of their caseload are engaged in work activities (however, this had little practical impact during the 1990s because work participation rate calculations rewarded states for their caseload declines).

Table 14-1. *History of State Variation in AFDC Benefits, 1996*

State	Maximum for family of 3 (dollars)	Percent of federal poverty level	Real change, 1970–96
Median	415	40.8	. . .
High (California)	633	62.9	−37
Low (Mississippi)	120	11.5	−45

Source: LaDonna Pavetti, "Welfare Policy in Transition: Redefining the Social Contract for Poor Citizen Families with Children and Immigrants." In Sheldon H. Danziger and Robert H. Haveman, eds., Understanding Poverty (Harvard University Press, 2001), 234–35.

States used their newfound flexibility to deploy TANF funds for noncash assistance purposes, including child care and transportation. Less than 50 percent of TANF block grant funds are now spent on cash assistance.[1] Many states (for example, Colorado and North Carolina) delegated to counties and local governments authority to establish different rules for cash assistance. For example, states adopted work incentives (such as earned income disregards in forty-seven states), tough work requirements (such as immediate work activities in thirty-eight states), and tougher sanctions for noncompliance with program rules (such as full-benefit sanctions in twenty-one states).[2]

For families who left welfare, 60–70 percent of those who left went to work, although typically at relatively low wages, below $10 an hour.[3] Even if such families receive the Earned Income Tax Credit, food stamps, and Medicaid, their wages may not enable them to live at or much above the poverty level. While there has been virtually no evidence of widespread harm in the aftermath of welfare reform, areas of continuing concern include:

—impact of national and local economic downturns

—welfare reform's impact on nonworking, low-income mothers and their children who are not receiving cash assistance

—welfare reform's effects on adolescents

—the increasing share of child-only cases on state cash assistance rolls

—decreases in food stamp and Medicaid participation among otherwise eligible families due to TANF's delinkage of those programs from cash assistance.

Diversity among Cash Assistance Recipients

State cash assistance programs serve diverse caseloads. In the 1990s cash assistance caseloads became increasingly Hispanic, consistent with broader population trends. It also appears that the racial/ethnic composition of state caseloads continues to reflect trends in shares of low-income children belonging to particular racial or ethnic groups. For example, TANF caseload composition in 1990 mirrors the shares of children under 100 percent of the federal poverty level by race/ethnicity.

While the same analysis reflects a modest overrepresentation of African Americans on TANF in 2000 compared with shares of poor children by race/ethnicity, overall trends appear quite similar.

State Policy Choices

With regard to state policy choices, social scientists have conducted regression analyses of state cash assistance policies adopted subsequent to PRWORA. Illustrative is Gais and Weaver's finding that "policies restricting cash assistance—such as shorter time limits, more severe sanctions, and family caps—are more common among states that have a high percentage of African-Americans on the caseload. . . . High Hispanic caseload(s) are associated only with stiffer time limits."[4]

Families Leaving Cash Assistance

In looking at families leaving cash assistance, most studies have found that African Americans are underrepresented among those who leave. Further research is needed on reasons for leaving, including the possibility of racial disparities in the use of sanctions. However, following the first quarter after welfare exit, African Americans are more likely to be employed and have higher median earnings than other groups. Yet they are also more likely to return to welfare within one year of leaving the rolls. Patterns among Hispanics are unclear.[5]

Gender and Marital Status

Recent federal data reveal that 90 percent of TANF recipients are women. A breakdown of marital status for TANF adult recipients shows that 65.3 percent are single, 12.4 percent are married, and 22.3 percent are separated, divorced, or widowed. These data show that state cash assistance programs continue to serve, in large measure, female-headed households. This fact is consistent with trends under AFDC and underscores why cultural conservatives and others devote so much energy to marriage-promotion proposals under TANF.

Legal Immigrants

Federal welfare reform legislation severely restricted legal immigrants' eligibility for a wide range of public programs and benefits. These policy

Figure 14-1.   *Decline in Receipt by Noncitizens, of Four Welfare Benefits,*
1994–99

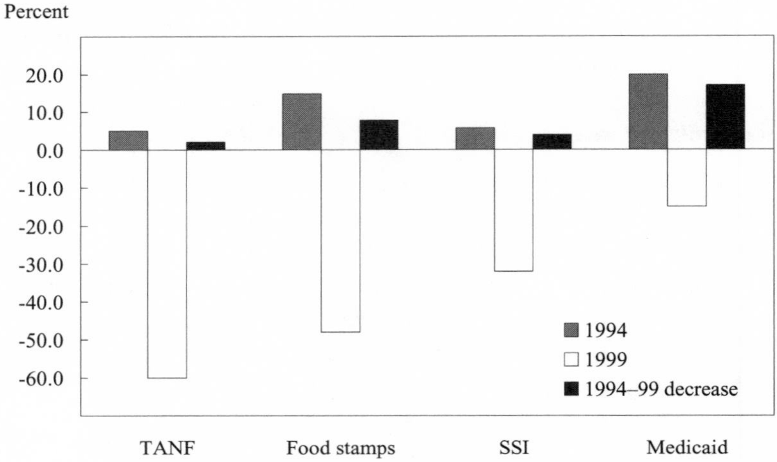

Percent

Source: The Urban Institute's analyses of the 1995 and 2000 Current Population Survey data.
Michael Fix and Ron Haskins. "Welfare Benefits for Non-citizens." In Isabel V. Sawhill, R.
Kent Weaver, Ron Haskins, and Andrea Kane, eds., *Welfare Reform and Beyond: The Future of
the Safety Net* (Brookings, 2002), 205.
Note: Numbers above the line are the percentage of legal permanent resident noncitizens
receiving each type of benefit in 1994 and 1999; numbers below the line are the respective
declines in benefit receipt.

changes achieved their intended effect of reducing receipt of public benefits by
legal immigrants. Figure 14-1 shows the percentage declines in benefit receipt
for four programs.

With respect to TANF, all states exercised their option under federal law to
provide TANF to all legal immigrants residing in the United States prior to
1996. Nineteen states also chose to use state funds to provide cash benefits to
legal immigrant families arriving after 1996. These state-only programs often
place naturalization and residency requirements on recipients.

As noted above, little is known about the well-being of legal immigrant
families that would have been eligible for cash assistance under AFDC but are
not able to receive it under TANF. Of special concern are citizen children
residing in families with noncitizens. While the eligibility of citizen children
for TANF and other public benefit programs was not affected by the 1996 law,
many immigration advocates fear that such families will not seek assistance
due to fear of immigration enforcement.

Conclusion

The National Academy of Social Insurance's conference theme of "diversity" accurately describes both the landscape of state cash assistance programs and the families served by those programs. With TANF scheduled for reauthorization in 2003, it will be important for policymakers to bear both aspects of diversity in mind.

Under TANF, states are exercising their broad flexibility to transform our social safety net for poor families with children, and this profound change is playing out in different ways across the country. At the same time, the racial and ethnic composition of American families is evolving rapidly and powerfully, and the low-income families may be expected to mirror those trends. Understanding how increasingly different state cash assistance programs serve the changing face of poor families will remain a question of continuing concern and inquiry.

Notes

1. Administration for Children and Families, Office of Planning, Research, and Evaluation, HHS, *2002 TANF Annual Report* (Government Printing Office, 2002), 2.

2. Thomas Gais and R. Kent Weaver, "State Policy Choices under Welfare Reform. In Isabel V. Sawhill, R. Kent Weaver, Ron Haskins, and Andrea Kane, eds., *Welfare Reform and Beyond: The Future of the Safety Net* (Brookings, 2002), 34.

3. Robert A. Moffitt, "From Welfare to Work: What the Evidence Shows." In Isabel V. Sawhill, R. Kent Weaver, Ron Haskins, and Andrea Kane, eds., *Welfare Reform and Beyond: The Future of the Safety Net* (Brookings, 2002), 79.

4. Gais and Weaver, 38.

5. Elizabeth Lower-Basch, "Leavers and Diversion Studies: Preliminary Analysis of Racial Differences in Caseload Trends and Leaver Outcomes," Office of the Assistant Secretary for Planning and Evaluation, HHS (Government Printing Office, 2000), 6–8.

15

The Impact of State Health Programs on Diverse Populations

Cindy Mann

This chapter looks at coverage of diverse populations under state-administered health care programs. Two stories are told: first, about the progress that has been made since the late 1990s in providing more people with opportunities for coverage, particularly publicly financed coverage, and second, a description of what has been happening since the economy began to sour, what some of the trends have been, and a little about what can be expected over the next period of time.

As Grantland Johnson's introductory comments indicated, the issue of state budget cuts looms very large whenever state-based programs and particularly the Medicaid program are discussed. Medicaid accounts, on average, for about 15 percent of state general fund expenditures. When states have budget problems, they will inevitably turn to their Medicaid programs for some of the solutions whether or not Medicaid is the primary source of those problems.

Background

Racial and ethnic minority groups are disproportionately represented among the nonelderly uninsured. In 2001 non-Hispanic whites accounted for 47 percent of the uninsured, while the remaining 53 percent was composed of Hispanics (30 percent), non-Hispanic blacks (16 percent), Asian and South Pacific Islanders (5 percent), and American Indians and Aleutian Eskimos (2 percent).[1] Minority groups are, moreover, disproportionately represented among the uninsured at all income levels. Figure 15-1 shows the high portion of racial and ethnic minorities, particularly Latinos both below and above 200 percent of poverty, although the extent of the lack of coverage is much greater for lower income individuals.

These are national data, but the uninsured rates among racial and ethnic minorities vary widely across states due in part to the diversity across the

Figure 15-1. *Uninsured Rates among Racial/Ethnic and Income Groups, 2001*

Poverty level

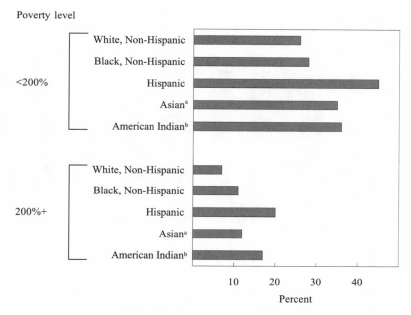

Source: Kaiser Commission and Urban Institute estimates based on March Current Population Survey, 2001.
Note: Less than 200 percent of poverty level = $28,256 for family of three in 2001.
a. Asian group includes Pacific Islanders.
b. American Indian group includes Aleutian Eskimos.

country in the breadth of state-administered health programs. Compared to the Temporary Assistance for Needy Families program (TANF), Medicaid has more federal guidelines and standards with respect to eligibility and benefits, but this still leaves a great deal of flexibility to the states. States largely determine how they will deliver services and what they will pay their providers. They also have broad discretion to determine eligibility levels, as long as they meet minimum federal standards, and states have considerable discretion to shape their benefit package for adults. As a result, Medicaid programs vary from state to state, and even greater disparities will likely be seen across states in coming years as some states make deeper budget cuts than others. The nonelderly uninsurance rates among Latinos between 2000 and 2001 show more than 35 percent of that population was uninsured in sixteen states, 25 to 34 percent in seventeen states and the District of Columbia, while less than 25 percent were uninsured in thirteen states. Among African Americans, the

Figure 15-2.   *Changes in Job-Based Health Insurance Coverage for Nonelderly by Race/Ethnicity, 1994–2001*

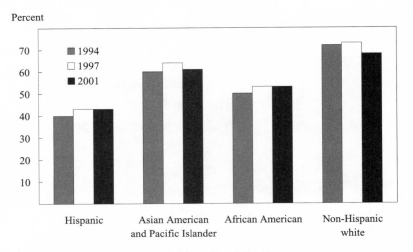

Source: March 1995, 1998, and 2002 Current Population Surveys.

nonelderly uninsurance rates for the same time period were 20 percent uninsured in fifteen states, 16 to 20 percent uninsured in another fourteen states and the District of Columia, and less than 16 percent uninsured in thirteen states.[2]

Sources of Coverage

Health insurance coverage rates among the nonelderly, low-income population depend largely on two factors: the availability of employment-sponsored insurance (ESI) and the availability of publicly funded coverage to fill in the often quite substantial gaps left by the employment-based system. Most people get their health insurance through their jobs. However, this is not true for low-income people, and it is particularly not true for many of those in racial and ethnic minority groups. The high level of uninsurance rates among African Americans and Latinos reflects their much lower rates of access to job-based health insurance coverage (figure 15-2). There was some improvement between 1994 and 1997, but this was followed by a decline or no change in ESI rates of coverage between 1997 and 2001. Based on trends in current private health care costs, these numbers will likely look even worse in coming years.

Lower rates of job-based coverage among African Americans, Latinos, and other racial and ethnic minorities result in part from the fact that these groups are more likely to have jobs that pay lower wages or that are temporary, seasonal, or otherwise less likely to offer health insurance. Wage levels are closely associated with an offer or take-up of employer-sponsored coverage. In 1998 only 50 percent of low-wage workers—those paid less than $7 an hour—had health insurance through their employer or their spouse's employer; 10 percent were offered coverage but did not take up the offer, largely because of cost, and 40 percent were not offered coverage (through their own employer or their spouse's employer) at any price. In contrast, 92 percent of high-wage workers—those paid more than $15 per hour—had health insurance through employers in 1998, 4 percent declined the offer, and 4 percent were not offered coverage.[3] Job-based health insurance coverage rates among low-income workers improved during the economic boom, but the gains seem to have disappeared quickly with the downturn in the economy.

Public Coverage of Parents and Other Adults

Has public coverage "stepped up to the plate" where employment-sponsored coverage has not been available? The answer to that question depends in part on the population group.

The Medicaid program is commonly thought of as a program that is available to all poor or low-income people, but that is not how it works. Eligibility for Medicaid is based on nonfinancial, as well as financial, eligibility rules. It is not enough to be poor or low-income; people need to fit within a certain eligibility category to qualify for Medicaid. Each category has its own minimum financial eligibility standards, and states have the ability to expand coverage for that category of people beyond the minimum standards, without limitation. Childless adults generally cannot be covered under Medicaid at any income level, unless they are pregnant, disabled, or elderly, as they simply do not fit into a federal Medicaid eligibility category. By comparison, children must be covered in every state at least up to the poverty line, and most states cover children through Medicaid at significantly higher income levels. All these eligibility standards for children are typically much higher than the eligibility levels that are in place for their parents.

Under the rules in place in April 2003, in fourteen states a parent with two children with earnings *below* 50 percent of the poverty line would be over-income for Medicaid, meaning that the parent would not qualify for Medicaid. (The children in the family would, however, be eligible.) A parent with wages at the poverty level would be eligible for Medicaid in only fifteen states and the District of Columbia.[4] Unfortunately, this picture is getting more, not less, bleak. Since 2001 three states have rolled back their parent eligibility levels substantially, due to budget pressures.

These low eligibility thresholds for parents have important and often unnoticed consequences. There was a large increase in labor market participation of poor parents between 1994 and 2000 due to changes in the economy and welfare policies. Figure 15-3 shows that labor force participation for poor, single mothers increased from 34 percent to 41 percent. At the same time, however, the uninsured rate for these mothers jumped by about two-thirds. In 1994 one of five poor, single mothers was uninsured compared to one of three in 2000.

Why did this happen? Poor women lost coverage because most had jobs that did not offer health insurance coverage or they were offered coverage at prices they could not afford. Yet, in many states, even women earning wages that kept their families below the poverty line could not qualify for ongoing coverage through the Medicaid program.

Until recently, this situation was beginning to turn around. In the late 1990s only a small number of states covered parents up to the poverty level, compared to twenty (including the District of Columbia) that covered this group in 2001. But, as discussed below, the progress has been stalled and, in some states, reversed since the economy began to sour.

Public Coverage for Children

Children's eligibility for coverage is more firmly rooted than that of parents in U.S. public coverage programs. The federal minimum eligibility standards for children are much higher than for parents, and, as previously noted, states have options to expand to even higher levels. Currently, one of every five children in this country is covered under Medicaid. The strong base of coverage offered by Medicaid was enhanced in 1997 when Congress enacted the State Children's Health Insurance Program (SCHIP). SCHIP encouraged states (through an enhanced federal matching rate) to boost their eligibility levels for children either in separate SCHIP programs or through Medicaid. As a result, most states now extend coverage to children up to at least 200 percent of the federal poverty line, and 84 percent of low-income uninsured children were eligible in 2000 for publicly funded coverage either through Medicaid or SCHIP. (Of these eligible children, 71 percent were eligible for "regular" Medicaid and 29 percent were eligible for SCHIP-funded coverage.) These 5.6 million children are not enrolled, however, and much remains to be done to improve participation rates in Medicaid and SCHIP. Nonetheless, the expansions in eligibility represent a significant change compared to 1996, when only six states covered children up to 200 percent of the poverty line. Who are the low-income children who are not eligible for coverage? Some live in states that

Figure 15-3.   *Trends in Employment and Health Coverage of Poor Parents,
1994–2000*

Percent

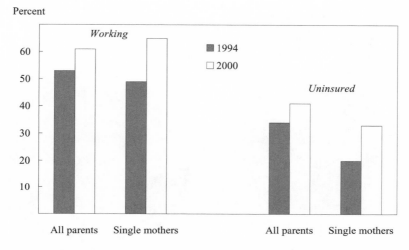

Source: Kaiser Commission and Urban Institute estimates based on the March Current
Population Survey, 1995–2001, unverified Current Population Survey estimates.

have not raised their eligibility standards to the 200-percent-of-poverty eligibility level, but many are immigrants who are caught in that same ban on
benefits for immigrant children that John Monahan describes in chapter 14
with respect to cash assistance.

Lack of Coverage for Newcomers

The federal law that prohibits states from using federal TANF dollars to help
newcomers—defined by the law as people entering the country after August
1996—applies to Medicaid and SCHIP as well. States cannot use federal
dollars in Medicaid or SCHIP to cover most immigrants (children and adults)
who have entered the country since 1996. This rule has broad implications. In
2001 noncitizens represented only about 20 percent of the nonelderly uninsured, but noncitizens were more than twice as likely to be uninsured as
citizens (figure 15-4).

The federal ban on using Medicaid and SCHIP funds to cover newcomers is
one of several factors that contribute to the sharp disparity in coverage rates
between citizens and noncitizens. Noncitizens who are eligible for coverage
may not be enrolled in Medicaid or SCHIP. Many do not know about programs
that are available to them or fear that enrollment may cause them or their

Figure 15-4.   *Sources of Coverage for Nonelderly Persons, by Citizen*
Status, 2001

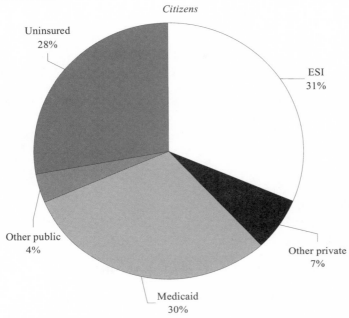

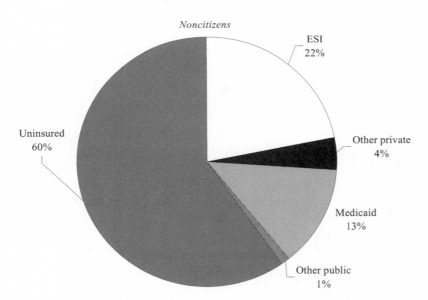

Source: Kaiser Commission and Urban Institute estimates based on the March Current
Population Survey, 2002.

families immigration-related problems. In addition, immigrants often must confront language barriers that interfere with their ability to access coverage for which they are eligible.

Lack of information about program benefits, misinformation about the impact of how receiving benefits might affect immigration status, and language barriers can be addressed if states have the resources and the political drive to overcome these obstacles. At least until recently, many states were making progress narrowing these gaps in coverage.

Budget Cuts Begin

This section looks at state actions in light of recent state budget pressures. Medicaid is jointly funded by the federal government and the states. Each state is reimbursed by the federal government for a portion of its Medicaid costs based on what is called the *federal medical assistance percentage*, commonly referred to as FMAP. The FMAP varies from 50 percent to about 78 percent. (The FMAP is higher—more favorable—for less wealthy states.) For example, in California or New York, for every dollar spent on Medicaid, the state will get 50 cents back from the federal government for a net state cost of 50 cents. Louisiana receives more than 70 cents for each dollar spent, for a net state cost of less than 30 cents for a dollar's worth of coverage. Although the federal government shoulders more than half (on average 57 percent) of the cost of the program, Medicaid is a large program and, therefore, costly for states. Not surprisingly, it has been a focus for budget actions in states across the nation.

There is considerable talk about runaway Medicaid costs, but the primary source of states' budget problems is steeply declining state revenues. Medicaid costs have been growing but, on a per person basis, more slowly than health care costs in the private sector. Figure 15-5 shows the annual percentage cost increases in Medicaid and private health care for 1996–2002. Given higher health care costs, particularly higher drug costs, and the medical needs of many of those served by Medicaid, Medicaid is actually doing a pretty good job of containing costs when compared to the private sector. Many state employee health benefit programs have seen per-person costs rise at a higher rate than Medicaid. Nonetheless, Medicaid costs have been rising, in part due to expansions and successful outreach efforts and in part due to the downturn in the economy. Because of Medicaid's size, any notable increase in costs will have significant budgetary implications. Medicaid accounts for a large share of state expenditures—it is a big program—and so when budget pressures are great and states are squeezed for dollars, they will inevitably turn their attention to Medicaid.

Figure 15-5. *Medicaid per-Person Costs versus Private Health Care*
Premium Costs, Annual Growth, 1996–2002

Percent

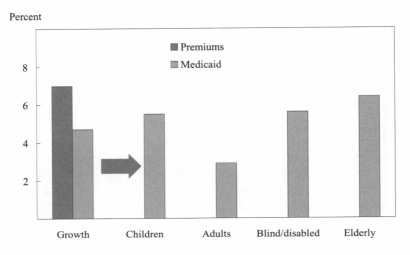

Source: Georgetown Health Policy Institute's analysis based on KPMG, 1996; Kaiser/HRET
Survey of Employer-Sponsored Health Benefits: 2000, 2002; Congressional Budget Office
Medicaid Baselines, 1997–2003.

Health Care Coverage at Risk during a Budget Crunch

Understanding how the Medicaid matching system works is important to
appreciating the depths of the cutbacks in coverage that can occur when states
are looking to save state funds. Table 15-1 contains a simple breakdown
showing the effects of state Medicaid spending reductions on federal Medicaid
payments to states. It shows what would happen in states, with differing match
rates, if they reduce their state spending on Medicaid by $125 million. At a 65
percent match rate, that $125 million in state savings will cost the state $232
million in federal dollars. The actual cut in coverage or services would
therefore be $357 million ($125 million plus $232 million). The loss of federal
funds will not help the state's economy, and the coverage or service reductions
must be at least twice as large as the state savings sought to be achieved. When
a state has a significant savings target, the implications for coverage can be
profound.

There are some troubling signs around the country that state proposals to
manage their budget shortfalls could have a serious impact on health care
coverage programs for low-income people. We are seeing:

—reductions in eligibility and benefits

Table 15-1. *The Fiscal Effects of State Spending Reductions*

	Federal dollars lost if a state reduces Medicaid spending by $125 million		Reduction in Medicaid services necessary to achieve state savings of $125 million	
Match rate (percent)	State funds saved (millions of dollars)	Federal dollars lost (millions of dollars)	State savings (millions of dollars)	Total reduction needed (millions of dollars)
50	125	125	125	250
65	125	232	125	357
75	125	375	125	500

—more limited access to care for those who have coverage

—resurrection of discredited barriers to enrollment and retention

—stalled progress on improving participation among those with limited English proficiency

—more disparities in eligibility and benefits across states

—more disparities in eligibility and benefits across population groups.

Over the past few years, state efforts to remove barriers to enrollment and retention in public programs have made a large difference in program participation rates. Figure 15-6 shows what happened to enrollment in Ohio after the state took a number of steps to improve participation rates in Medicaid. In 2000 Ohio fixed its delinking problem, where families leaving welfare were not always being properly continued on Medicaid; simplified its Medicaid application for families; dropped some of the more onerous verification requirements that families had to meet in order to apply for coverage; and adopted a relatively small eligibility expansion for parents and pregnant women. Largely as a result of increased participation rates among previously eligible families, enrollment shot up at the end of 1999 and continued to rise through 2001. For one golden moment, this was Ohio's pride—the state was hoping to improve participation rates, and, by eliminating some of the barriers to enrollment and retention, the state achieved considerable success. However, the growth in enrollment has become Ohio's nemesis. The state's revenues have plummeted and it is struggling mightily to pay for the coverage provided to these eligible families and pregnant women.

State budget pressures do not seem to be abating, prompting more and more states to make changes in their programs. Some of the changes are quite stark; some are more on the margins, although it is obviously not "on the margins" if you are the person who no longer has access to a needed service that you cannot

Figure 15-6.   *Ohio's "Regular" Medicaid Enrollment for Children,*
Families, and Pregnant Women, June 1997–June 2001

Monthly enrollment in thousands

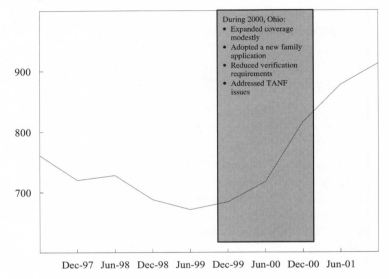

During 2000, Ohio:
• Expanded coverage modestly
• Adopted a new family application
• Reduced verification requirements
• Addressed TANF issues

Dec-97 Jun-98 Dec-98 Jun-99 Dec-99 Jun-00 Dec-00 Jun-01

Source: Data compiled by Health Management Associates from state Medicaid agencies for Kaiser Commission.

afford. States are also reducing or freezing payment rates to providers, actions that raise issues with respect to access to coverage. The Kaiser Commission on Medicaid and the Uninsured reported that twenty-two states cut Medicaid provider rates in fiscal year 2003 for at least one group of providers.[5] Medicaid is a poor payer in many states, and even lower payment rates will affect participation rates among providers and ultimately people's access to care.

What's Ahead?

Lest we lose sight over just how much is at stake, it is helpful to review the critical role that Medicaid, and to a lesser extent, SCHIP, plays for diverse groups of people who, for many reasons, find themselves without meaningful access to employer-based insurance. Consider two states—Florida and Massachusetts—with comparable ESI rates among the nonelderly: 36.6 percent for Massachusetts and 36.5 percent for Florida. Although their ESI rates are similar, the uninsured rates in these states are quite different—24.4 percent for

Massachusetts versus 38.5 percent for Florida—largely as a result of their policies and practices with respect to public coverage.[6] The combination of private and public coverage has led to a much higher insured rate in Massachusetts than in Florida.

The public program expansions in Massachusetts (and associated outreach and simplification efforts) have also helped to reduce the disparities in coverage rates among racial and ethnic groups. Medicaid and SCHIP provide health care coverage to 36 percent of nonelderly African Americans and 43 percent of nonelderly Latinos in Massachusetts, compared to only 19 percent of African Americans and 13 percent of Latinos in Florida. Largely as a result of these differences in public program coverage rates, the uninsured rates for nonelderly African Americans and Latinos are much higher in Florida than in Massachusetts—24 percent of African Americans are uninsured in Florida compared to 14 percent in Massachusetts, and 34 percent of Latinos are uninsured in Florida compared to 24 percent in Massachusetts.

Gaps in insurance rates between whites and racial and ethnic minorities persist, but the progress made in some states shows that these gaps are not intractable problems. They can be narrowed significantly when a state is thoughtful and aggressive about how to structure and manage its public coverage programs. The question is whether these gaps will widen and whether even more people will lose coverage in the coming years because a stable system for financing and assuring coverage for low-income people in times of economic downturns has yet to be put into place. In 2003 Massachusetts significantly cut back on its publicly funded coverage programs.

The variation in uninsured rates among nonelderly, low-income persons by state underscores the trade-off that we, as a nation, have made because we have chosen to rely on a "hybrid" system of coverage. Our system has both public and private elements and, on the public side, there is both federal and state funding and control over program rules. There are pros and cons to such a system, but there can be little doubt that this results in significant disparities in insurance rates across the nation and among groups of people. Any new era of health reform should not only consider how to manage costs and raise and maintain a sufficient level of resources to pay for coverage, but also consider whether the current divisions in state and federal responsibilities are well suited to the important task of assuring that all people in this country have access to quality, affordable health coverage.

Notes

1. Kaiser Commission and Urban Institute estimates based on the Current Population Survey March Supplement, U.S. Census Bureau, Washington, D.C., 2001.

2. Urban Institute and Kaiser Commission on Medicaid and the Uninsured analysis of March 2001 and 2002 Current Population Survey.

3. B. Garrett, unpublished data, Urban Institute, Washington, D.C., 2001.

4. Based on a national survey conducted by the Center on Budget and Policy Priorities for the Kaiser Commission on Medicaid and the Uninsured, published in 2003.

5. Vernon Smith, Rekha Ramesh, Kathy Gifford, Eileen Ellis, and Victoria Wachino, "States Respond to Fiscal Pressure: State Medicaid Spending Growth and Cost Containment in Fiscal Years 2003 and 2004: Results from a 50-State Survey," Kaiser Commission on Medicaid and the Uninsured, Washington, D.C., September 2003.

6. John Holahan, "Variations among States in Health Insurance Coverage and Medical Expenditures: How Much Is Too Much?" Discussion Paper No. 02–07, Urban Institute, Washington, D.C., June 1, 2002 (www.urban.org/url.cfm?ID=310520 [accessed September 25, 2003]).

PART FIVE

Medicare and Health Disparities

The implementation of Medicare has had a lasting effect on the health of elderly Americans and on the structure of health care in the United States. As the only near universal health care coverage program in the United States, Medicare has helped meet the health needs of American seniors since 1966. Providing coverage to all individuals, regardless of race, income, or geography, Medicare is considered a true social insurance program. Yet questions remain about whether Medicare provides the same quality of care for all participants. The chapters in this section examine and discuss the presence, scope, and impact of health disparities within the Medicare program.

There are two research-based chapters in this section. In chapter 16 Paul Eggers of the National Institute of Diabetes and Digestive and Kidney Diseases discusses what is known about Medicare disparities, and in chapter 17 Nicole Lurie of the RAND Corporation focuses on racial variation in the quality of care among Medicare+Choice enrollees. These are followed by commentaries by Linda Fishman, health policy director for the Senate Finance Committee; Brian D. Smedley, senior program officer for the Institute of Medicine; and James Randolph Farris, regional administrator of the Centers for Medicare and Medicaid Services.

16

Medicare Disparities: What Do We Know?

Paul Eggers

Since the initiation of Medicare in the mid-1960s, there have been gains in life expectancy at age sixty-five. However, the gains have not been equal. White males and females have had larger gains in life expectancy than their African American gender counterparts.

There have been a number of sentinel events that have improved our understanding of racial disparities within the Medicare population, including legislative changes, data improvements, and some research publications. Two of the more prominent legislative changes that have occurred were the implementation of the prospective payment system (PPS) in 1983 and physician payment reform (PPR) in 1992.

Because of the radical nature by which each changed the payment system to providers (hospitals for PPS and physicians for PPR), Congress mandated that the secretary of health and human services provide annual reports on their impact, including their impact on beneficiaries, particularly vulnerable groups.

It should be remembered that Medicare is essentially a very large insurance company, not a research or quality assurance organization (until recently). Consequently, for many years the information database on enrollment and utilization was limited to those data necessary for ensuring entitlement and paying bills. Research was, and remains, of secondary concern. In addition, the size of the databases was a limiting factor in what could be collected and effectively analyzed. Even in the 1960s there were more than 20 million beneficiaries, millions of hospitalizations, and hundreds of millions of physician contacts. Computer systems of that time period were not capable of handling such depth of information, particularly if it was not central to the mission of the agency.

Implementation of the PPS in the mid-1980s and the PPR in the early 1990s was premised on payment based on types of services and the condition of the patient. This resulted in a vast improvement in the overall quality of the payment data.

Race coding has also improved in recent years. With the exception of some end-stage renal disease (ESRD) beneficiaries, Medicare entitlement has been largely tied to social security entitlement. Because of this, Medicare has always based its enrollment database (EDB) on the Social Security Administration (SSA) enrollment database. From 1967 until the mid-1990s this database had minimal race codes—white, black, other, and unknown. In 1994 Medicare upgraded the EDB based on the SSA Numident file, which had some additional race codes—Native American, Hispanic, and Asian American. Although this improved race definitions somewhat, it still left many unknowns. The Health Care Financing Administration (HCFA) attempted to improve this in 1997 via a mass mailing to 2.3 million Medicare beneficiaries who were designated as unknown or other in the EDB and to all persons with a Hispanic surname. The 800,000 respondents improved the race codes to a marked degree. Medicare currently is working with the Indian Health Service to identify all aged Native Americans in the EDB.

In the 2000 Census there were 34.6 million persons in the United States ages sixty-five and over. The distribution by race and ethnicity categories was: non-Hispanic whites, 29.2 million; non-Hispanic blacks, 2.8 million; non-Hispanic Asians, 800,000; non-Hispanic Native Americans, 125,000; and Hispanics, 1.7 million. By race, 84.0 percent were white, 8.1 percent black, 2.3 percent Asian, 0.4 percent Native American, and 4.9 percent Hispanic.

The Medicare enrollment database had always adequately identified white and African American beneficiaries, and other race and ethnicity groups began to be identified in 1994. By 2000 about 50 percent of aged Asian Americans were identified by Medicare and more than 30 percent of Native American and Hispanic aged beneficiaries. Although this is far below universal identification, it still amounts to 400,000 Asian, 500,000 Hispanic, and 35,000 Native American aged persons.[1] No other database has such rich information on such large numbers of nonblack minority groups.

Although the literature is rich with articles on racial disparities, a few deserve special note. Martin Ruther and Allen Dobson were about the first to examine Medicare data specifically to look for changes in Medicare utilization by race over time.[2] Although the data available to them were fairly crude by today's standards, they presented a strong case that improvements in disparities had occurred during the first decade of Medicare.

Not surprisingly, the same trend observed in use rates is also seen in total Medicare expenditures.[3] Average Medicare payments in 1974 were about $500 for all gender and race groups. Beginning in the mid-1980s and accelerating during the 1990s, Medicare payments for black beneficiaries began to increase more than for white beneficiaries. By 1997 average payments for both male and female black beneficiaries were more than $7,000 per person, compared to about $5,500 for white beneficiaries. By 1978 total average Medicare payments for black beneficiaries had equaled average payments for white beneficiaries. By 1997 average payments for black female beneficiaries were 40 percent greater than for white females, while payments for black males were about 30 percent greater than for their white counterparts.

A. McBean and Marian Gornick took the analyses a step further by showing that, although overall hospitalization rates had improved for African American aged, when examined by cause of hospitalization and procedures, there were still evident access issue problems.[4] J. Ayanian and colleagues were among the first to look into cardiovascular disease procedure access and show major differentials in race disparities between African American and white beneficiaries.[5]

Gornick and colleagues tried to separate the effects of socioeconomic status (SES) from race in Medicare disparities. Based on work arising out of the physician payment reform reports to Congress, they were able to show that SES had little effect on explaining race disparities.[6] P. Eggers and L. Greenberg were among the first to use the expanded race codes (Asian, Hispanic, and Native American) in examining hospital use rates.[7] Finally, Gornick provides the best review of our current understanding of racial disparities in the Medicare population.[8]

Ruther and Dobson published one of the first looks at changes in racial disparities within the Medicare population in 1981.[9] Their study examined the use of services during the first decade of the program—from the first full year of Medicare in 1967 through 1976—and charted the change in the user rate (the number of beneficiaries per 1,000 who had any payment for service). In 1967 white beneficiaries used hospital insurance at a rate of 207 per 1,000 compared to 159 per 1,000 for nonwhite beneficiaries, a black-to-white ratio of 0.77. User rates increased for both groups during the next decade, to 233 for whites and 196 for nonwhites, increasing the black-to-white ratio to 0.84.

Similarly, for Supplemental Medical Insurance (SMI, part B), user rates increased over this time frame from 372 to 569 per 1,000 for whites and from 263 to 518 for nonwhites. The black-to-white use ratio increased from 0.71 to 0.91 during this time. Much of the increase for both groups reflected an increase in the percent of persons who met the part B deductible, which was $50 in 1966 and increased only to $60 in 1973. In 2003 the deductible stands at only $100, almost ensuring that any amount of physician care will result in Medicare coverage.

Figure 16-1.   *Total Hospitalizations of Aged White and Black Medicare Beneficiaries, 1970–2000*

Number of hospitalizations, per 1,000 persons

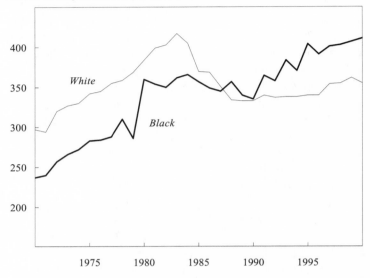

Source: National Center for Health Statistics, National Hospital Discharge Survey, public use files.

Ruther and Dobson conclude that Medicare was at least partly responsible for reducing racial disparities through (a) insurance coverage, (b) SMI buy-in provisions for state Medicaid programs, and (c) the legislative requirement that institutions provide care without discrimination.[10]

Two weaknesses of their analyses are that the measures are fairly crude—user rates per 1,000. This is not an actual measure of use of services, and the identification of nonwhite is merely all persons not designated as white.

A more accurate measure of hospitalization use rates are total hospitalizations per 1,000 persons. This trend is shown in figure 16-1 from data taken from the National Hospital Discharge Survey of the National Center for Health Statistics. In 1970 aged African American persons were hospitalized only 80 percent as much as white aged persons. By 1985 this measure of disparity had almost disappeared, and by 2000 African American seniors had hospitalization rates 16 percent greater than their white counterparts. This difference in use is more reflective of the relative difference in morbidity and mortality.

The effect of a legislative change was illustrated by Roger Evans and associates in their 1981 article in the *Journal of the American Medical*

Association.[11] Prior to Medicare coverage of ESRD in 1973, access to dialysis was extremely limited. The demographics clearly favored young, white males. However, within a few years after Medicare coverage, the demographics began to reflect what we believe to be the true underlying demographic variation in renal disease. Although numerous articles continue to show large disparities in access to transplantation, at least in terms of access to this basic life-saving therapy, Medicare coverage essentially removed the huge financial barrier.

Reports to Congress as a result of the PPS legislation led HCFA to develop a tracking system for elderly Medicare beneficiaries for hospitalization rates by age, sex, and race.[12] This system currently covers the calendar years 1986 through 2000 and has produced rates for twenty-eight diagnostic categories and twenty-six procedural categories. As demonstrated by McBean and Gornick, there were large differences in access by race, particularly for cardiac procedures.[13]

Trends from 1986 through 2000 in hospitalization of aged black and white beneficiaries for ischemic heart disease (IHD), cardiac catherization, percutaneous transluminal coronary angioplasty (PTCA), and coronary artery bypass graft surgery (CABG) show that there has been a modest increase (8 percent) in IHD hospitalization during these years. However, cardiac catheterization and CABG hospitalizations have more than doubled during these years, while PTCA rates have increased sixfold.[14]

By race, hospitalization for IHD has increased more for aged black beneficiaries (20 percent) than for aged white beneficiaries (7 percent), reflecting the same trend seen earlier in overall hospitalization rates. Still, by 2000 black beneficiaries were only 80 percent as likely to be hospitalized for IHD as were white beneficiaries.

Both white and black aged beneficiaries had large increases in the use of PTCA during the 1986 to 2000 time period (figure 16-2). However, while the white rate increased by more than 600 percent, the black rate increased by more than 1,100 percent. Consequently, the black-to-white ratio, which had been only 0.32 in 1986, had increased to 0.58 in 2000. Although a racial disparity still exists, the degree of disparity has decreased markedly.

The same relative trend can be seen for CABG rates. In 1986 aged black beneficiaries were only 28 percent as likely to get a CABG as were white beneficiaries. This ratio increased to 0.50 in 2000.[15]

As discussed earlier, Eggers and Greenberg analyzed cardiac hospitalization rates in 1998 for the expanded minority groupings. All nonwhite groups had fewer PTCA and CABG rates compared to whites. For PTCA the use ratios ranged from 0.48 among aged Asian beneficiaries to 0.82 among Hispanic aged beneficiaries. The use ratios for CABG followed a similar pattern.[16]

Figure 16-2.   *Increase in the Use of PTCA for Aged White and Black*
Medicare Beneficiaries, 1986–2000

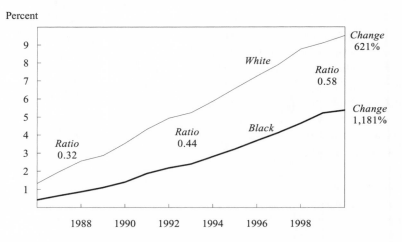

Source: Centers for Medicare and Medicaid Services, Hospital Discharge Monitoring
System.

However, none of the nonwhite groups had rates of hospitalization for IHD as
great as the white IHD rate. If IHD hospitalization is used as a proxy for overall
ischemic morbidity, the relative access rates are reduced. In particular, aged
Asian beneficiaries show access to cardiovascular procedures virtually identical
to that of white beneficiaries. Native American and black beneficiaries still have
access rates two-thirds to three-fourths as great as white beneficiaries.

Revascularization is typically premised on the results of a cardiac catheterization test. Many studies have found that, even adjusting for rates of catheterization, blacks are less likely to undergo revascularization than are whites. The
data from the Centers for Medicare and Medicaid Services (CMS) hospital
discharge monitoring system also show this to be true. Adjusting for rates of
catheterization, aged Asian Medicare beneficiaries have revascularization
rates equal to that of whites. Adjusted rates for black, Hispanic, and Native
American beneficiaries range from 10 to 40 percent lower than those of white
beneficiaries.

Physician Payment Reform Analyses

As a result of the implementation of physician payment reform in the early
1990s, the Office of Strategic Planning in HCFA developed a physician
monitoring system to track age-, sex-, and race-specific use rates over time

using 100 percent of physician billing. This included the development of the Berenson-Eggers Type of Service, a new service coding system that aggregates the 10,000 or so HCPC codes into 105 mutually exclusive and exhaustive categories.

Access to primary care is the starting point for overall health care access. In terms of total physician visits per year, there is little difference between white and black beneficiaries, with a black-to-white use ratio of about 0.96 to 0.97, consistently through the 1990s. However, the place of service differs greatly. Both white and black beneficiaries had increasing rates of physician office visits during the 1990s, but the differential between the races increased, from 12 percent in 1990 to 21 percent in 1999. Consistent with their higher rates of hospitalization, black beneficiaries receive more hospital-based physician care than do white beneficiaries.

Rates of emergency room use are about 40 percent higher for blacks than whites, but it should be noted that even for black beneficiaries, emergency room use only accounts for about 5 percent of total physician care.

Medicare Current Beneficiary Survey Analyses

Twenty percent of whites and 35 percent of blacks did not have supplemental insurance in 1976. Data from the Medicare Current Beneficiary Survey (MCBS) show that these rates of noncoverage have declined in the past quarter century, with 10 percent of whites, 22 percent of blacks, and 14 percent of Hispanics not having supplemental insurance in 2000. The source of supplemental coverage differed markedly by race and ethnicity. More than 60 percent of white beneficiaries had private supplemental insurance compared to approximately 30 percent of black and Hispanic beneficiaries.[17] Medicaid was the source of supplemental coverage for 31 percent of black and Hispanic beneficiaries but only 8 percent of white beneficiaries.

Access disparities also continue to exist with respect to the usual source of care. Almost 75 percent of white beneficiaries report a physician's office as their usual source of care, as compared to approximately 60 percent of black and Hispanic beneficiaries. Only 6 percent of white beneficiaries report using an outpatient department or the emergency room or having no usual source of care. The comparable figure for black and Hispanic beneficiaries is 15 percent. The percent of Medicare beneficiaries reporting no usual source of care declined during the 1990s for both whites and blacks, but whites had lower rates in all years.

Another measure of lack of access to care is the rate at which people do not see a doctor when they have a medical condition. The 8.8 percent rate for whites in 1990 declined to 4.6 percent in 1998; the corresponding rate for blacks declined from 12.3 percent in 1990 to 6.9 percent in 1998.

There are additional race and ethnic differences in health status. Elderly black and Hispanic Medicare beneficiaries are almost twice as likely to report their health as fair or poor as are white beneficiaries. Differences in activities of daily living are less pronounced, with about 50 percent of white and Hispanic beneficiaries and 40 percent of black beneficiaries reporting no limitations.

In terms of self-reported health conditions, black and Hispanic elderly have greater rates of hypertension and diabetes than white beneficiaries. On the other hand, osteoporosis and skin cancer are less prevalent among black elderly persons.

The MCBS is also being used to track trends in the use of preventive services in the Medicare population. From 1991 through 2000 overall use rates of flu shots have increased for all race and ethnic groups. In 1991 black and Hispanic beneficiaries were only 59 percent as likely as white beneficiaries to get a flu shot. By 2000 the black-to-white ratio had increased to 0.74.

As with flu shots, mammography rates have increased over the last decade. Aged black and Hispanic women receive mammography less frequently than aged white women, but the disparity has decreased over time. There is very little race and ethnicity difference in the use of Pap smears, with all groups having increasing rates between 1992 and 2000.

Beginning with the 2000 MCBS, aged male Medicare beneficiaries were asked about prostate exams. Preventive prostate exam use is about 10 percent lower among black beneficiaries and about 15 percent lower among Hispanic beneficiaries than among white beneficiaries.

Summary

Medicare has reduced many disparities in access to health care, but disparities still exist in cardiovascular care, primary care access, health status, supplementary insurance, and the use of preventive care. The immense data resources of CMS should continue to be used to monitor disparities and help guide intervention efforts.

Notes

1. S. L. Arday, D. R. Arday, S. Monroe, and J. Zhang, "HCFA's Racial and Ethnic Data: Current Accuracy and Recent Improvements," *Health Care Financing Review* 21, no. 4 (2000), pp. 107–16.

2. Martin Ruther and Allen Dobson, "Unequal Treatment and Unequal Benefits: A Re-Examination of the Use of Medicare Services by Race, 1967–1976," *Health Care Financing Review* (Winter 1981), pp. 55–83.

3. J. Lubitz, L. G. Greenberg, Y. Gorina, L. Wartzman, and D. Gibson, "Three Decades of Health Care Use by the Elderly, 1965–1998," *Health Affairs* (March/April 2001).

4. A. M. McBean and M. E. Gornick, "Differences by Race in the Rates of Procedures Performed in Hospitals for Medicare Beneficiaries," *Health Care Financing Review* 15, no. 4 (Summer 1994), pp. 77–90.

5. J. Z. Ayanian, I. S. Udvarhelyi, and C. A. Gatsonis, "Racial Differences in the Use of Revascularization Procedures after Coronary Angiography," *Journal of the American Medical Association* 269, no. 20 (1993), pp. 2642–46.

6. M. E. Gornick, P. W. Eggers, T. W. Reilly, R. M. Mentnech, L. K. Fitterman, L. E. Kucken, and B. C. Vladeck, "Medicare: Effects of Race and Income on Mortality and Use of Services among Medicare Beneficiaries," *New England Journal of Medicine* 335, no. 11 (September 12, 1996), pp. 791–99.

7. P. W. Eggers and L. G. Greenberg, "Racial and Ethnic Differences in Hospitalization Rates among Aged Medicare Beneficiaries, 1998," *Health Care Financing Review* 21, no. 4 (Summer 2000), pp. 91–105.

8. Marian E. Gornick, "Disparities in Medicare Services: Potential Causes, Plausible Explanations, and Recommendations," *Health Care Financing Review* 21, no. 4 (Summer 2000), pp. 23–43.

9. Ruther and Dobson, "Unequal Treatment and Unequal Benefits," pp. 55–83.

10. Ruther and Dobson, "Unequal Treatment and Unequal Benefits," pp. 55–83.

11. R. W. Evans, C. R. Blagg, and F. A. Bryan Jr., "Implications for Health Care Policy: A Social and Demographic Profile of Hemodialysis Patients in the United States," *Journal of the American Medical Association* 245 (1981), pp. 487–91.

12. Health Care Financing Administration, "1986 Annual Report to Congress: The Impact of the Medicare Hospital Prospective Payment System," pub. no. 03281, May 1989, chap. 4.

13. McBean and Gornick, "Differences by Race in the Rates of Procedures," pp. 77–90.

14. Unpublished data from the Centers for Medicare and Medicaid Services.

15. Unpublished data from the Centers for Medicare and Medicaid Services.

16. Eggers and Greenberg, "Racial and Ethnic Differences in Hospitalization Rates," pp. 91–105.

17. F. J. Eppig and G. S. Chulis, "Trends in Medicare Supplementary Insurance: 1992–96," *Health Care Financing Review* 19, 1 (Fall 1997), pp. 201–06.

17

Racial Variation in Quality of Care among Medicare+Choice Enrollees

Nicole Lurie

Racial and ethnic disparities in health and health services both have been well documented. Disparities exist in all clinical areas studied in nearly all health care settings researched so far. Causes for these disparities are multifactorial, and it is important that we continue thinking about solutions to eradicate them. The federal initiative to eliminate racial and ethnic disparities in health and health services was the impetus for the two studies discussed in this chapter.

Approaches to addressing disparities are easy to identify. They deal with access to health services, quality of health services, patient and provider communication, discrimination and bias, and cultural proficiency. Perhaps the most important disparities to be addressed are the nonmedical determinants of health.

It is helpful to define some of the disparities in care for Medicare beneficiaries in part as a quality of care issue. One reason is that Medicare and the American public are very focused on quality and equity. By defining disparities in Medicare this way, the emotionally charged aspects of the discussion are neutralized, which can lead to more productive and helpful communication about such disparities.

In order to understand disparities in Medicare as a quality of care issue, it is necessary to implement systems to measure and monitor use of health care and to report on the quality of care for different race and ethnic groups. Medicare is unique in collecting racial and ethnic data that can support these efforts, however imperfect.

In chapter 16 Paul Eggers described the tremendous strides that have been made over the last few decades in improving the data systems and the racial/ethnic data collection within Medicare.

In most of the private health care system, both fee-for-service and managed care, racial and ethnic data are sparse. Until recently most insurers and health plans thought it was illegal to collect such data or were afraid to do it for other reasons. Existing information is often incomplete and inaccurate, and problems remain.

Racial and ethnic data are important not only for quality of research but also for continued problem solving. It is shocking to see the results of both the Kaiser Family Foundation surveys; they remind us that much of the public and much of the physician community is seemingly unaware of the nature and magnitude of racial and ethnic disparities.

This chapter presents two studies utilizing different data sets that examine disparities in the quality of care for different racial and ethnic groups. The first study, conducted by Beth Virnig and colleagues, looked at the quality of care in the Medicare+Choice program. The second study was based on data from Consumer Assessments of Health Plans (CAHPS).

It is important to note that the data described here deal with the managed care side of Medicare, while the data presented in chapter 16 deal with fee-for-service Medicare.

Quality of Care in the Medicare+Choice Program

The first study looks at measures from the Health Plan Employer Data and Information Set (HEDIS) in Medicare+Choice plans. Eight different HEDIS measures were studied. These data are different from other data related to this type of research because, for the first time, they look at quality of care and disparities in quality for groups other than whites and African Americans. Data that would typically be lumped together in an "Other" category (such as from Asians, Hispanics, and Native Americans) were examined individually.

An important idea to remember is that the patterns of disparities that exist between African Americans and whites are not necessarily the same as the patterns of disparities that exist between and among other races and ethnic groups. Another point is that these categories are still too coarse and mask some important differences within different ethnic groups, particularly for Hispanics, Asians, and Pacific Islanders.

Table 17-1 shows the likelihood that people in various race and ethnic groups would receive these different measures of care. Included are rates of mammography, percentage of people involved in cholesterol management after an acute cardiovascular event and of those receiving a beta-blocker after an acute myocardial infarction (AMI), as well as rates for diabetic care, control of high blood pressure, and access to ambulatory/preventive care. Mammography rates for whites continue to lead those of African Americans and Hispanics. But, as stated in chapter 16, the rates for blacks are getting better and the rates for Hispanics also appear to be improving.

The numbers for American Indians or Alaska Natives are particularly appalling. (This is the first time such data have been available for this type of research.) In contrast, the rates for Asians or Pacific Islanders as a whole are the same as or better than the rates for whites. However, if these rates were decomposed into Asian or Pacific Islander subgroups, then the differences would be fairly startling. The recent data from the Commonwealth Fund Survey on quality of care for minority Americans looked at six different subgroups of Asians or Pacific Islanders and found big differences between Vietnamese Americans, Korean Americans, Japanese Americans, Chinese Americans, and others.

If management rates after AMI are examined, again the odds ratios for blacks are significantly lower than those for whites, indicating poorer quality care for African Americans. For Native Americans, even with better enumeration in the Medicare data, the numbers are too small to count in Medicare+Choice.

Although more complete enumeration of data and better identification of many racial and ethnic subgroups are available to researchers, when the subgroups are broken down even further into different disease categories, the numbers get uncomfortably small in terms of our ability to analyze some important components of quality (particularly in the area of managed care).

The unadjusted percentages for these same measures show the level at which quality is provided and not just the odds ratios. The point is that improvement in quality is needed across the board.

While it is important for this information to be framed in the context of the quality debate, it must also be framed in terms of interventions that will improve quality across the board. Particularly promising are changes in care systems that have been implemented to improve quality.

Table 17-1 looks at the HEDIS measures that describe quality of care for diabetes. This table also shows receipt of a hemoglobin A1C (or glycohemoglobin), which is a marker for the level of diabetes control. Also shown is the receipt of an eye exam, which standards of care suggest diabetics ought to have every year or two, and the receipt of cholesterol testing in the form of a low-density lipoprotein (LDL) cholesterol test.

Again, the data in table 17-1 show that the quality of diabetes care for African Americans is worse than it is for whites. Diabetes care for Asians is quite good, if every Asian ethnic group is lumped together, but again, these data likely mask important subgroup differences. Like the other measures, there is a lot of room for improvement across the board.

The performance in general for hemoglobin A1C and LDL cholesterol testing is noteworthy. Performance on these measures is better than it is for receipt of an eye exam. One could easily speculate that this is because blood

Table 17-1. *Likelihood That Persons of Various Racial and Ethnic Groups Would Receive Various Measures of Quality, Adjusted for Age and Sex, and Rate per 1,000 Medicare+Choice Enrollees, 2000*

Rate per 100 enrollees

Measure	White	Black	Asian	Hispanic	Native American	Other
Mammogram	75.61	72.24	76.47	69.67	56.55	76.17
Cholesterol management after acute cardiovascular event	67.71	57.24	71.58	60.00	—[a]	72.25
Beta-blocker after AMI[b]	88.75	83.40	90.15	88.46	—[a]	90.41
Diabetes care, HbA1C testing	80.19	74.65	84.10	79.08	77.45	83.23
Diabetes care, eye exam	67.37	61.63	79.07	67.34	78.16	75.09
Diabetes care, LDL-C screening	73.74	64.49	78.57	71.21	55.71	77.11
Control high blood pressure	35.76	31.97	41.51	39.45	49.98	37.63
Access to ambulatory/ preventive care	87.64	80.06	87.74	82.58	82.01	85.26

Source: Health Plan Employer Data and Information Set (HEDIS) 2000 individual-level data; and Medicare, 1999 Denominator data. From Beth Virnig and others. "Racial Variation in Quality Care among Medicare+Choice Enrollees," *Health Affairs* 21, no. 6: 224–30.

a. Numbers are too small to report.

b. AMI is acute myocardial infarction.

tests can be done in the doctor's office, whereas most patients need to be referred elsewhere for their eye exams. One easy solution might be to schedule both tests at the same time, reducing the chance of patients falling through the cracks by having to go somewhere else to have the eye exam, to negotiate another system, to deal with transportation and another copayment, and to face the other challenges that the health care system presents.

The last two measures are measures of quality related to the control of high blood pressure and use of ambulatory or preventive care. Again, African Americans do substantially worse, both in control of high blood pressure and in general access to ambulatory services, than whites. Asians do well, but the picture is somewhat mixed for both Hispanics and Native Americans.

As an aside, remember that relatively simple interventions can treat high blood pressure and stave off the development of coronary artery disease and renal failure. Simple treatments are often overlooked in our focus on high-tech health care.

Figure 17-1. *Ratings of Health Plan and Health Care*

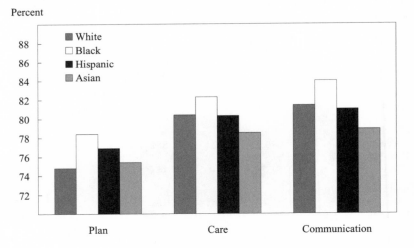

Consumer Assessments of Quality of Care

The second study is based on CAHPS data. My colleagues and I looked at a number CAHPS measures that addressed access to care and self-reported use of services. One of the beauties of CAHPS data is that the demographic and race and ethnicity data are self-reported, so researchers need not rely on claims data, with all their imperfections.

This analysis focused on people who were in the national CAHPS benchmarking data set, as well as those enrolled in Medicare+Choice plans. The former are people from a number of private health plans, as well as from the federal employee health benefits plan (FEHBP). This work began when some colleagues and I met with staff at FEHBP to discuss what role they play in addressing disparities. Their question to us was, "Do federal employees get disparate care?"

As in the previous study, this analysis also compares ratings for the different major categories of race and ethnicity. One additional thing that we were able to do was to examine whether the disparities were the same in all plans or whether there is plan-to-plan variation.

In figure 17-1, ratings of health plan and health care are presented on the left-hand axis. In general, blacks report slightly higher levels of satisfaction with their plan overall, with health care overall, and with communication with their provider. Asians have the worst ratings of care for all these measures. This

Figure 17-2. *Access to Care*

Percent

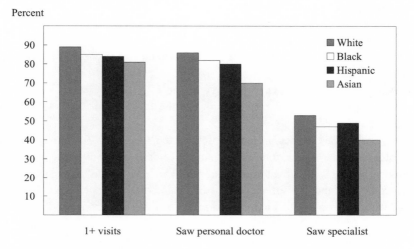

is consistent with a lot of data that suggest that Asian Americans report worse experiences with care and rate their care lower than other groups.

These data are in stark contrast to the data in figure 17-2 on access to care in which whites have better access, are likely to have more than one visit, are more likely to have a personal doctor, and are much more likely to see a specialist when needed than any of the other subgroups.

Despite the fact that blacks, in particular, report greater satisfaction and better experiences with care, they are less likely than whites to get care. Asians are the least likely to get care.

The next phase of research should focus on answering the question, "What are these differences about?" Is there something that plans that have no disparities are doing to achieve this result? Are plans with persistent disparities doing anything that could be inadvertently making disparities worse?

Thinking about solutions to disparities, and looking at this from a system of care and a quality perspective, it is important to remember that it does not have to be this way. Plans can address disparities, and there are some important examples around the country of plans doing just that.

Conclusions

It is pretty self-evident that significant disparities in quality exist in the Medicare+Choice program, as evidenced by self-reported experiences and HEDIS-derived measures. Managed care alone is insufficient to eliminate these disparities.

It is important to state, especially for CMS and Medicare, that ongoing federal leadership is critical in addressing disparities. But Medicare is not the only program in which federal leadership is needed and can be exercised.

If one were to combine all the federal health care programs—Medicare, Medicaid, the Veterans Administration, Department of Defense, FEHBP—the federal government is responsible for providing care to more than 50 percent of Americans of color. They are by far the biggest purchaser. Using the purchasing power to address disparities is the responsibility of the federal government.

I was delighted to see a recent article in the *New York Times* recounting Senator Bill Frist's statement that disparities remain an important issue in this country. What I was sad not to see, and what I wish he would have said, is that we need to link the performance of Medicare and disparities together, and that Medicare reform has to include taking serious steps to address disparities within the Medicare program.

Measuring and monitoring quality is critically important for improving quality. We need to continue to be aggressive about fixing the data problems that persist in the Medicare program. In the preceding chapter Paul Eggers described many positive things that have happened with data collection and data accuracy. The ability to identify different race and ethnic groups is getting much better in the Medicare program, but it still has a long way to go.

It is also important to remember that, at least right now, the Medicare program gets all its information from the Social Security Administration—so that agency continues to be a really important player in getting accurate data.

Quality improvement programs that CMS initiate and model for others throughout the country will be critically important. The agency ought to be able to use Medicare's purchasing power more wisely and to demand account-ability from plans and providers.

Finally, CMS can expand the array of measures for reporting on access and quality beyond those that currently exist in HEDIS. I believe that the public will respond to these efforts and that ultimately CMS will be able to support the kind of informed decisionmaking and consumer choice that most people so strongly advocate.

The federal government can provide data on the quality of care for people of color. This is obviously the goal of the Agency for Healthcare Research and Quality's National Quality Report and National Disparities Report.

CMS can demonstrate whether plans and providers are delivering high quality or equivalent care for all different race and ethnic groups. Ultimately if we can get consumers to use this information better, they will be able to make better decisions about their care.

Outside of the direct delivery of care system, better data can provide additional tools for U.S. citizens in general to work with political parties, plans, providers, health departments, Congress, and others, in addressing disparities and, if necessary, ultimately exercising their power as an electorate.

Commentary on Part Five

Comment by Linda Fishman

Paul Egger and Nicole Lurie have provided two informative discussions of the disparities among medical care beneficiaries in access to care and to quality.

In my position as health policy director for the Senate Finance Committee, I am aware that Majority Leader Bill Frist, himself a physician, has shown an interest in these issues and has presented research-oriented legislation on how incentives to reduce disparities of care might be incorporated in upcoming Medicare revisions. Most of my committee's time will be spent considering changes to Medicare that improve the program.

The Eggers and Lurie chapters clearly demonstrate that ethnicity and race are associated with differences in service use and health outcomes. A lot of progress has been made in this area, but more must be done to achieve equity. The focus cannot be on one ethnic group or one racial group but on the subgroups that Nicole Lurie has presented in her chapter.

It is important to note that the Medicare program in and of itself has increased access to care and improved quality and the well-being of all elderly and disabled persons. The peer review organizations, now called Quality Improvement Organizations (QIOs), and the regional offices of the Centers for Medicare and Medicaid Services (CMS) have played important roles in reducing these disparities. In his commentary, Randy Farris will present a few examples of what the regional offices of the CMS have done to benefit seniors in minimizing disparities.

A lot of money is spent on the Medicare program and, at least in Congress, we keep asking ourselves if we are spending it wisely and if the dollars are being targeted in the proper ways. The answer, as we examine these issues, is probably not. There probably is enough money in the system, but we need to target it better. A lot of people think that introducing and enacting a bill is a quick fix, but additional legislation is not always the answer.

From my personal perspective, and I served at CMS for a brief time as well, I believe the government needs to adopt more innovative approaches to addressing these problems, to target resources where they are needed, and to communicate better in terms of what benefits people get under the Medicare program and how they can use them most effectively. Out-of-the-box ways to communicate with these individuals need to be devised. It may be helpful, for example, to go to African American churches in order to assist congregants in using more fully the benefits they deserve.

We have to do a better job of getting seniors to use preventive services. Even though Medicare covers a number of them, it is clear that seniors do not often use them. Interventions like flu immunizations or pneumonia shots are covered by Medicare, but seniors and the disabled just have not used these services.

Medicare enrollees want the benefits, but they are not very well informed about how to go about using them. Medicare has been modestly successful in reducing disparities in some elements of preventive care like flu vaccinations. Randy Farris runs that program. CMS should get a lot of credit for that. Where the regional offices and the QIOs have been involved, there have been significant improvements.

Medicare+Choice plans presumably have better data than fee-for-service providers. They have conducted a lot of projects on reducing disparities, but Lurie's data show that there have been mixed results in those areas. It might be easier for Medicare+Choice plans to conduct these kinds of programs than the fee-for-service part of Medicare because they have coordinated care in a limited network of doctors and hospitals. We need to understand why there are continual disparities and how successful those projects have been.

My concern is that while programs and services are available to Medicare+Choice enrollees, only 15 percent of Medicare beneficiaries are enrolled in these kinds of plans. Our challenge is to capture the interest of those 85 percent of beneficiaries enrolled in the fee-for-service program and provide some incentives to direct them into effective programs.

At present, Congress has only very blunt tools. For example, some individuals in Congress would change the conditions of participation for providers through prescriptive legislation. That is a heavy hammer to use.

Changing the conditions of participation means Medicare providers would be barred from the program if they did not conduct certain kinds of projects or behave in certain ways, a strong tack to take indeed.

There are always monetary incentives. That is where Medicare could be changed in the Senate Finance Committee. CMS is still exploring ways to connect payments and quality, and I believe this connection is definitely the road to the future. There are some demonstrations ongoing that I do not think have come to full fruition, but they are certainly worth monitoring and evaluating.

I agree with Dr. Lurie that disparities in health care largely reflect differences in the quality of care. I was very interested in a January 15, 2003, article by Steve Jencks and colleagues in the *Journal of the American Medical Association* that looked at changes in quality measures from 1999 to 2001 by state. The authors noted that there had not been a lot of movement in the relative relationship of quality among the states.

My boss, Sen. Chuck Grassley, represents Iowa, and the people who live in Iowa are proud of the fact that Iowa ranks quite high in this particular study. Yet, if you look at Medicare spending in the state of Iowa—Medicare spending per enrollment, unadjusted for other factors—it is quite low.

Good health services research adjustments to the data make Iowa's position change. The bottom line, at least from a political perspective, is that Iowa's citizens feel they are being cheated under the Medicare program. Yet they appear to receive high-quality services.

This debate in Congress plays out in terms of how it affects provider payments. Provider payment equity is a big issue in terms of Medicare reform and Medicare payment concerns in the 108th Congress.

Nonetheless, changes in health delivery systems are needed to improve health outcomes. Disease management is a promising area, as it is limited and certainly needs some refinement.

While these programs can be effective in a Medicare+Choice environment, how to direct or channel people into disease management programs that might help them improve their health status is a rather tricky issue in the fee-for-service side of the program. My understanding is that CMS is trying to do some of that now in terms of specifically reducing health disparities among racial and ethnic groups. Targeting certain areas of the country where there is a high prevalence of chronic conditions, as well as a substantial population of minorities, CMS then approaches organizations to put themselves possibly at risk financially for the management of care of those individuals.

CMS would monitor their health outcomes over time to see, in fact, if they actually improved. This is an exciting idea in Medicare. The role of Congress is to provide a great deal of oversight and monitoring of how these projects would work.

What we really need to do, as opposed to legislative fixes, is address communication and outreach efforts. As I said, out-of-the-box thinking may result in creative solutions. CMS should target programs that are culturally sensitive and focused in the right places and let Medicare develop and flourish, in this area, all under the provision of congressional oversight directed toward monitoring quality over time.

Comment by Brian D. Smedley

Jill Quadagno's discussion (chapter 5) reminds us of government's capacity to do good. Clearly, Medicare has been an example of this kind of good. This program has gone a long way toward both equalizing access to health care for senior Americans and in reducing health care disparities, as Paul Eggers points out (chapter 16).

Variations in access and quality of care exist for both Medicare fee-for-service patients as well as Medicare+Choice patients. In chapter 17 Nicole Lurie demonstrates that the inequities consistently observed between African American and white populations, particularly in Medicare fee-for-service, do not necessarily apply for other racial and ethnic minority groups.

To be honest, in the Institute of Medicine (IOM) medical report on equal treatment we did not do a good job of making that distinction and pointing out the critical importance of additional data collection and research to understand the experience of quality of care for other racial and ethnic minority populations.

The IOM report called for more research to better identify these disparities related to access and quality of care for Asian American, Hispanic, American Indian, and Alaskan native populations. It also called for more detailed analysis of access and quality of care for some groups. This is another issue that Lurie pointed out. It is critically important because the issues of both access and quality may vary significantly for subgroups within what we presume to be fairly homogeneous racial and ethnic populations when, in fact, these groups are not homogeneous at all.

We know that there are significant differences in health status. Vietnamese American women, for example, experience the highest rates of cervical cancer among any racial ethnic group.

Among Americans, various groups experience significant access problems related both to language and insurance status. There may be some groups that do not experience the same level of barriers to care. Cuban Americans, for example, may experience fewer barriers to access and care than other Hispanic subgroups. It is critically important to get these subgroup data where possible.

This is easier said than done. Because of the small numbers in our data sets, we will experience difficulties in trying to determine the quality of care for these subgroup populations. Hopefully strata byte sampling in the Health Plan Employer Data and Information Set reporting process and other efforts should help in the future.

Lurie also pointed out that disparities obviously occur both in the Medicare fee-for-service and the Medicare+Choice plans, raising the important question of whether certain types of health systems may have differential effects on health care access and quality for minority Americans.

Borrowing from the Medicaid literature, as we pointed out in the IOM report, researchers have demonstrated that, following mandatory enrollment in Medicaid managed care plans, racial and ethnic minorities experienced diminished access to care relative to whites enrolled in the same types of health systems and relative to other racial and ethnic minority Medicaid patients who remained in fee-for-service systems.

In our IOM report the study committee expressed concern that some policies and practices of health systems, such as financial incentives to providers to limit services, may disproportionately and negatively affect minorities' access to certain types of services. Clearly we need to understand whether different attributes of health systems may pose disproportionate barriers to care for minority Americans.

Another important point that was raised is that we must move beyond documenting disparities to research to better understand potential sources of these disparities. It is well established that significant differences exist in the quality of care.

Several factors contribute to these disparities. As Dr. Eggers pointed out, many structural factors may contribute to disparities, including differences in where care is received. As he showed, African American Medicare patients are more likely to receive their care in emergency rooms or to have no usual source of care. Clearly there are differences in the rates of supplemental insurance for Medicare patients.

In putting together the unequal treatment report, our study committee tried to answer the question of whether and how these disparities occur. We tried to imagine how these disparities arise for patients even after they have accessed their doctor's office.

If an African American or Hispanic patient accesses the same private physician's office as a white patient, how do disparities emerge? There are many factors that may contribute to this problem.

Some racial and ethnic disparities are not unjustified or are not unexpected in that there are differences by race or ethnicity in patients' preferences for treatment and attitudes toward health systems. Some literature suggests, for example, that African American patients may be more likely than white patients to refuse certain kinds of interventions, particularly invasive interventions.

This may be related to lower levels of trust of health care providers or a lack of knowledge of intervention effectiveness. Other literature suggests that African Americans may present at later stages of disease progression than whites for some diseases, which obviously may limit treatment options. It should be noted, however, that studies that have assessed racial differences and acceptance of physician recommendations for treatment have generally found these differences in preferences for treatment to be small.

Even though mistrust of health systems may be present in some segments of the African American community, it is still incumbent upon health systems, health care providers, and policymakers to find ways to address mistrust and to undo the legacy of separate-and-unequal health care that clearly contributes to this mistrust.

Another set of factors related to health systems may also contribute to these disparities. Some issues that may apply for Medicare patients are differences in policies and practices of health systems and the failure of health systems to take into account the special needs of racial and ethnic minority populations. These include the possibility that, as I mentioned earlier, incentives to providers to limit services may disproportionately and negatively affect minority patients. Another possibility is that heavy patient case loads may have disproportionate and negative effects on minority patients when cultural or linguistic barriers also are present.

The lack of interpretation and translation services is a significant problem in some communities. This is a major issue in the Medicare program because reimbursement rates for these services are so low that providers in many cases are unable to recover costs.

Finally, some racial and ethnic disparities in care may emerge from the clinical encounter itself. The attitudes and behaviors of providers, as well as patients, may contribute to disparities. As part of our process in the IOM study, we uncovered a strong body of indirect evidence that shows that prejudice, bias, and stereotyping by providers may contribute to disparities in health care. Prejudice may stem from conscious bias, while stereotyping may be conscious or unconscious even among the well-intentioned.

Ambiguities, the interpretation of clinical data, and gaps in the evidence of the efficacy of clinical interventions may also contribute to these disparities. They also may promote the activation of prejudice and stereotypes in that uncertainty may allow stereotypes to enter into the clinical encounter.

These processes directly affect clinical decisionmaking and result in a consistent effect. Racial and ethnic minorities may receive care that is less well matched to their needs than for whites.

Given that this is a complex problem, comprehensive, multilevel strategies are needed to eliminate these disparities. We need to raise awareness among broad sectors of the public—not only health care providers but also patients, payers, health plan purchasers, and others—of health care gaps and disparities among racial and ethnic groups in the United states.

I found it stunning that the Kaiser survey pointed out that, I believe, approximately 75 percent of white physicians believed that these disparities are real beyond access-related factors. Conversely, about 75 percent of African American physicians believe that these disparities exist even when you account for access-related factors. Clearly we have to raise awareness among providers, as Lurie has pointed out.

Health systems should base decisions about resource allocation on published clinical guidelines, ensure that physician financial incentives do not disproportionately burden or restrict minority patients' access to care, and take other steps to improve access, including the provision of translation services where needed.

Economic incentives should be considered for practices that improve patient-provider communication and trust and reward appropriate screening, preventive, and evidence-based clinical care.

We also need to improve the health care work force to increase its ability to deliver high-quality care for racial and ethnic minorities. Community health workers need to be involved as liaisons between the community and the health systems that serve them. We need to support multidisciplinary treatment and preventive care teams and increase the proportion of underrepresented racial and ethnic minorities among health professionals.

In addition, both patients and providers can benefit from educational strategies. Patients can benefit from culturally appropriate education programs to improve their knowledge of how to best access services and participate in treatment decisions.

The greater burden of training lies with providers because they have the greater power in the clinical encounter. Cross-cultural curricula should be integrated early into the training of future health care providers and practical case-based, rigorously evaluated training should persist through practitioner continuing education programs.

Finally, I believe that data collection and monitoring will be the most important part of this comprehensive effort. As we have seen, there are a number of rich data sets available to track the quality of care for Medicare patients. We need to encourage collection, reporting, and monitoring of patient care by health plans and state and federal payers as a means to assess progress in eliminating disparities to help plans evaluate their intervention efforts and assess potential civil rights violations.

We need to look at differences in access and utilization as well as consumers' perceptions using the Consumer Assessments of Health Plans data and other data sets. CMS administrator Tom Scully once said that nothing changes behavior faster than data collection and monitoring. He was referring to nursing care and other Medicare providers.

I think the same principle applies here as well, for two reasons. First, if providers, health systems, and others know that the quality of their care is being monitored by the race or ethnicity of patients, that is going to be an intervention in itself. Second, the dissemination of data allows patients to vote with their feet, as has been shown with the reporting of data on nursing homes.

Comment by James Randolph Farris

This National Academy of Social Insurance conference has afforded me an opportunity not only to read the articles of various presenters, but also to review the work of Marian Gornick and various other documents that have come out over the last few years addressing the area of racial and ethnic disparities in the delivery of health care in the United States.

This subject has interested me in my various lives as an academic medical professional, as a private practitioner of internal medicine, as a public health physician in one of my former lives, and, most recently, as a policy person at the Centers for Medicare and Medicaid Services (CMS).

There is agreement that some, if not most, of the disparities that are seen in the U.S. health care system, are multifactorial in nature.

As they enter the health care system, patients bring with them those experiences they have had over the course of their lives that have flavored their interaction with the health care system.

Our health care system is, in some instances, difficult to negotiate for those members of our society who may not be as proficient with the language or who may not have the educational level of others. It can be a fairly daunting system to enter.

Finally, it is possible that there is some bias in the physician-patient encounter. There is also agreement that Medicare has helped through the years to eliminate disparities in the health care system.

I will share with you what CMS is doing and how CMS is changing to improve the quality of care for Medicare and Medicaid beneficiaries. I will also describe how CMS is using its data. CMS has a tremendous amount of data that are being used to help with the efforts to eliminate racial and ethnic health disparities. Additionally, I will specifically address measures that CMS is implementing in 2003 to eliminate racial and ethnic health disparities in the area of managed care for Medicare+Choice enrollees.

Since its inception almost thirty-eight years ago, Medicare has helped to reduce racial and ethnic health disparities by providing health insurance coverage for *all* Medicare beneficiaries. In 1960 very few people—probably in the range of 50 percent of people over age sixty-five—had any type of health care insurance, which meant that many of the citizens of this country had no health insurance. That playing field has been leveled by Medicare for all Medicare beneficiaries regardless of race and ethnicity.

Medicare has mandated that health care institutions provide care to everyone in a nondiscriminatory manner. The leadership and staff of the Centers for Medicare and Medicaid Services are committed to working to make a difference in the lives of Medicare beneficiaries, particularly those from vulnerable populations, which include African American, Hispanic, Alaska Native, American Indian, Asian/Pacific Islander, and low-income Medicare beneficiaries. Some would also want to include rural Medicare beneficiaries because we are learning about disparities that disproportionately affect population groups who live in rural settings.

Similarly, the CMS is committed to the Department of Health and Human Services's goal of eliminating racial and ethnic health disparities by the year 2010, as set forth in *Healthy People 2010*.

Since 1993 key indicators of health status in our nation have shown that the health of the nation has improved tremendously. The public health advances of the past century have added many years to our lives. The average American life expectancy in 2003 is about seventy-seven years, a marked improvement over the forty-seven-year life expectancy that existed in 1900.

The diagnostic armamentarium that is available to health care providers allows for early detection of disease, and new treatment modalities now render even devastating diseases amenable to cure. But despite this, vulnerable populations of Medicare beneficiaries continue to suffer from preventable death and disease at disproportionately high rates.

Research has shown that African American life expectancy lags behind the majority life expectancy in this country, but an even more important indicator is years of healthy life. African American years of healthy life are only fifty-six years as compared to sixty-four years for Caucasian Americans.

We have heard that Vietnamese American women suffer from cervical cancer at nearly five times the rate of Caucasian American women. Hispanic Americans have two to three times the rates of stomach cancer as Caucasian Americans. All vulnerable populations make less use of preventive health care services in our country. Thousands of lives could be saved every year by applying what we already know about the use of mammography to detect breast cancer early while it is still curable, by using influenza and pneumococcal vaccines to prevent morbidity and mortality from influenza and pneumonia and the diseases they aggravate, by delivering appropriate antibiotics early in the course of disease, and by managing diabetes with vigilance and addressing its complications earlier.

What is CMS doing to meet the challenge of eliminating disparities occasioned by race, ethnicity, and socioeconomic status among Medicare beneficiaries? Over the past several years, CMS has changed its focus from being a payer of health insurance claims to being a prudent purchaser of health care goods and services. CMS is making a conscious effort to be more visible and more focused on beneficiaries.

The name change from the Health Care Financing Administration (HCFA) to the Centers for Medicare and Medicaid Services is illustrative of this change in focus. Hardly anyone, including Medicare and Medicaid beneficiaries, knew what HCFA was. In fact, I recall the first meeting that I had with the secretary of health and human services, Tommy Thompson, and the CMS administrator, Thomas Scully. The secretary looked at all of us and said, "How can anyone love a HCFA? The first thing you need to do is change your name."

He gave Tom Scully the task of coming up with a new name, a name that would be much more representative of who we are and what we do. But he emphasized, and Tom Scully emphasized, that this was to be more than a cosmetic change. We needed to make ourselves more visible and to change our culture. To accomplish this we developed a number of new modalities to put us closer to the people, to the beneficiaries that we serve, and to the partners with which we work every day.

Every month CMS now conducts a series of open door meetings with various health care provider groups and constituent groups to hear their concerns firsthand and to collaboratively address their issues. Each of these open door groups is chaired by someone in a senior leadership position at CMS, including Administrator Scully and Ruben King-Shaw, the deputy administrator and chief operating officer, who chairs the Diversity Open Door Forum.

I have had the opportunity to travel around the country with both Tom Scully and Ruben King-Shaw and to attend meetings with health care providers, with beneficiaries, and with our various partners and the different associations with which we work. These are frank discussions about who we are and what we do, and about how we can better meet their needs.

In just the four years that I have been with CMS, we have hired about twenty new physicians. Not too long ago, there were only a few physicians at HCFA. Each of these physicians has real world experience, has practiced medicine, and has tried to balance having a life, having a family, making a living, and helping people.

In February 2002 we had our first meeting of central office and regional office physicians. Once upon a time there were very few physicians in regional offices. Now, each CMS regional office has a chief medical officer. I had the opportunity to bring together all the CMS physicians and brainstorm about what we can do and how we can address issues. Since those in the regional offices are more directly involved with issues of coverage, we need to make certain that the decisions that we make will be helpful to beneficiaries and providers.

As the health care market is changing, so is CMS. Efforts are being made in the area of health promotion. Each of the CMS regional offices has a regional flu coordinator, who works with individuals and coalitions to improve the immunization rates for influenza and pneumococcal disease in our country.

CMS is also trying to assure the delivery of appropriate care and improve the collection and use of standardized data. We are working with Secretary Thompson to update our outdated information technology systems. We collect a tremendous amount of data, but we do not do much with it. We are bringing in knowledgeable people from the private sector information technology industry to show us how we can utilize the data we currently possess to make a difference in quality, which will make a difference in the lives of the beneficiaries that we serve.

We are also trying to monitor the effectiveness of health interventions. This is where the quality improvement organizations (QIOs), formerly peer review organizations, play a vital role. Quality improvement organizations work with physician groups, hospitals, and in clinical settings to try to bring an educational, nonpunitive focus to the provision of health care. This educational focus allows a physician or a practice to see what others are doing. For example, many physicians are ordering hemoglobin A1Cs for their diabetic patients several times a year, while Dr. Smith has not offered one for his patients in the last two years. Perhaps Dr. Smith should look at how well he is keeping up with peers and read some articles to keep current.

The CMS has charged quality improvement organizations to work with practitioners, providers, and beneficiaries to improve the level of care that is being rendered in this country. We are looking at a number of different areas, including myocardial infarction, heart failure, pneumonia, diabetes, and breast cancer. But we also have one specific area of interest that we have tasked all of our QIOs to work with: the elimination of racial and ethnic health disparities between vulnerable populations and America's mainstream.

Under the *Seventh Scope of Work for Quality Improvement Organizations*, CMS expects every quality improvement organization to improve health outcomes for Medicare beneficiaries who are identified as belonging to vulnerable population groups. Further, the *Seventh Scope of Work* provides for a disadvantaged area support QIO to assist state QIOs by providing national leadership in the use of evidence-based materials to help eliminate disparities and influence delivery of quality health care. The CMS is also looking at claims data through the QIOs to make certain that we appropriately utilize those data.

Through the efforts of quality improvement organizations, we are also working with a number of other work groups within CMS. I am the cochair of the Historically Black Colleges and Universities (HBCU) Workgroup. The HBCU Workgroup also works along with QIOs to make certain that we design and develop culturally appropriate interventions to be used in the African American community in areas such as influenza and pneumococcal immunizations. Another workgroup at CMS looks at Asian/Pacific Islanders and works with QIOs to develop materials for that group; a Hispanic workgroup does the same thing.

We are also trying to put together initiatives that will allow us to address real problems among racial and ethnic groups. One of these is the Racial and Ethnic Adult Disparities and Immunization Initiative (READII). This initiative is a joint venture involving all U.S. Department of Health and Human Services agencies, including the Centers for Disease Control and Prevention and CMS. READII is a project that is designed to increase influenza and pneumococcal immunization rates among African American and Hispanic American populations over the age of sixty-five. This project has already been launched and is working well in five demonstration areas around the United States.

We recently began an initiative in which we are working with the Indian Health Service and tribal organizations through a network of satellite broadcasts to make certain that appropriate Medicare preventive health information is provided to Indian Health Service facilities so that they can continue to render good care to the Native American population. Leslie Norwalk, who is counselor to the CMS administrator and currently serving as acting deputy administrator, describes in chapter 18 other CMS efforts, particularly in the area of research involving various racial and ethnic groups.

CMS recently began a demonstration project on eliminating racial and ethnic health disparities and cancer. Congress has put about $25 million into this initiative because there is a realization that some racial and ethnic groups suffer more disease and death from cancer than other groups.

In the area of managed care, we are initiating a number of projects that will allow us to improve what managed care organizations are doing in terms of eliminating racial and ethnic health disparities. Part of this will involve projects focusing on linguistic problems. We are looking at those people who have limited English proficiency and making certain that Medicare+Choice organizations provide translators as well as materials to these persons in the language they understand. Projects have been enacted to design and develop culturally and linguistically appropriate services and hire culturally and linguistically appropriate staff and practitioners to be able to address the specific health needs of the populations that they serve.

I have tried to describe how we are utilizing our data, how we are working with our partners, and how we are trying to assure the delivery of appropriate care. We are promoting better health care and working to eliminate disparities.

Let me close with one thought. The greatest opportunities for improvement and the greatest threats to the future health status of this nation reside in population groups that have historically been disadvantaged economically, educationally, and politically.

PART SIX

Turning Diversity Research into Action

Policy-related research often yields rich data that can help legislators make better program decisions and inform the general public about the direct implications of programs and policies. Information generated by research can spur mass mobilization and social change. Despite the potential power of action inspired by quality research, there has been a general disconnect between quality research, policy debates, and public discourse. The chapters in this section discuss how to use research findings to empower decisionmakers, bureaucrats, and citizens to act in a manner that improves the circumstances of diverse populations.

The moderator of the conference panel was James Carr of the Fannie Mae Foundation, who noted that "the keys to social and economic mobility have not changed in more than 100 years. . . . They include meaningful and dependable employment; quality education; decent, safe, low-cost housing; low-cost financial services, including wealth-building opportunities; and a reliable social safety network." He framed the session's question as: "Is it that we do not have enough research and good policy ideas, or is it that we do not engage the research in a policy context in a manner in which the public fully understands and appreciates the value of [our] moving forward on the racial divide?"

This question was addressed from the organizational contexts of two government leaders and one foundation president: Leslie Norwalk, acting deputy administrator of the Center for Medicare and Medicaid Services; James B. Lockhart III, deputy commissioner of the Social Security Administration; and Ruby Takanishi, president of the Foundation for Child Development.

18

Meeting the Challenge of Diversity at the Centers for Medicare and Medicaid Services

Leslie Norwalk

As President George W. Bush has observed: medical care costs too much, and many Americans have no health coverage at all. The Department of Health and Human Services (HHS) and the Centers for Medicare and Medicaid Services (CMS) are committed to ensuring that everyone—no matter where they live, who they are, or whatever their financial status—gets the high-quality care they deserve.

Although CMS spends one of every three dollars in the health care system nationally, we do more than just pay health care bills. While CMS pays for services to 70 million beneficiaries through the programs we administer—Medicare, State Children's Health Insurance Program (SCHIP), and Medicaid—we want to be certain that all eligible Americans receive the care they need.

We estimate that 12 million of the nearly 40 million Medicare beneficiaries may not be able to access the health care services they need as a result of cultural and language barriers. We do not view this as a minority health issue; the people are not minor, nor are our efforts.

As my colleague Randy Farris commented in his article in part V, all of us at CMS are committed to the national goal of eliminating long-standing disparities by the year 2010 and continuing the progress this nation has already made in improving the overall health care of the American people. In doing so we are working to eliminate disparities caused by differing access to health care. There are three priorities for access as stated in the Healthy People 2010 project supported by HHS: health insurance, an ongoing source of primary care, and reducing barriers. These barriers include the lack of insurance coverage, nearby facilities, and professionals, as well as the presence of cultural or language differences.

CMS continues to make significant progress in many areas that affect Asian American and Pacific Islanders, African Americans, Hispanics, Native Americans, and Alaskan Natives. We are hoping to provide greater access to preventative health services through outreach in education, research, and data collection.

It is quite clear that the outreach and education component is critical in terms of reducing disparities across all different types of social insurance. We are spending a lot of time and money on this education campaign. CMS aims to print our publications in as many languages as possible.

At CMS, we believe that if we improve knowledge about our programs, communities will let us know how we can better help them. It is really a partnership.

We are reaching out to these communities in a variety of ways. Tom Scully, the CMS administrator, has set up a number of open-door forums where the general public, providers, and the community at large can call into a 1-800 number and ask questions. The diversity open-door forum, which I chair, will address anything relating to health disparities.

These open-door forums allow for guidance and input from individuals who might not normally be paying a lobbyist to come to see us. We think this is a way to open up the organization to the outside.

CMS has also established several partnerships with organizations and educational institutions from the five major ethnic and racial groups to assist us in communicating and educating all beneficiaries. For example, an ongoing outreach campaign has been developed for the Asian American and Pacific Islander communities to improve the quality of life by increasing their participation in federal programs. Similarly, a Chinese section has been established on our *medicare.gov* website.

It is critical that we strengthen our ability to meet the needs of the African American population, which is certainly vulnerable. CMS is looking at new ways to reach out to them, such as an outreach effort to African Americans in the rural areas of Mississippi and South Carolina, which presents a particular challenge for us. To support this initiative, CMS is partnering with historically black colleges and universities and other state agencies to disseminate publications across all our lines of business, which is to say Medicare, Medicaid, and SCHIP, and the publications include state-specific information.

CMS partnered with the School of Professional Studies and the Department of Nursing at Bowie State University to develop and conduct a pilot project to address diabetes in the African American community. Through this project we were able to evaluate the effectiveness of our diabetes management intervention strategies and provide information more generally about diabetes in the African American community.

As a result of our commitment to address health disparity issues in the Hispanic American community, CMS and Hispanic-serving institutions are developing a pilot community participatory intervention project for type II diabetes. This intervention project will measure the participants' attitudes, knowledge, and behaviors associated with diabetes prevention, treatment, and control.

With nearly one million Hispanic Medicare beneficiaries in the United States—and that number is, in fact, rapidly growing—CMS is planning a conference on elder Hispanic health. This conference will provide a unique opportunity to collaborate with federal agencies, Medicare+Choice organizations, hospitals, clinics, social service providers, and all those serving Hispanic communities in particular. This collaboration will help CMS better understand how to relate to the needs of elder Hispanics and plan for the future to eliminate health disparities in this population.

As noted earlier, we recognize the need to provide Medicare health information to our beneficiaries in languages other than English. As our non–English-speaking beneficiary populations continue to grow, it is important that we provide our *Medicare Handbook* and *Guide to Health Insurance* in languages in addition to Spanish, which we already provide.

As for our Native American and Alaskan Native population outreach, we have been working with the Indian Health Service (IHS) for a number of years to make sure that Medicare and Medicaid payments to IHS facilities reflect the full cost of providing those services. This methodology, together with better efforts to enroll Indian people and expand the scope of covered services, has increased health insurance reimbursement by 146 percent since fiscal year 1995.

CMS has established a partnership with the Salish-Kootenai Tribal College to improve enrollment among Alaskan Natives. They are developing a long-term care tool box containing a series of guides on how to implement various types of long-term care in the American Indian community, such as home health agencies, hospice care, and home- and community-based services. With this, communities will be encouraged to reach out to their tribes and individuals to identify the long-term care needs of the communities and then build whatever is required to address those needs.

CMS has many other activities that benefit the Asian American, African American, Hispanic American, and Native American communities, such as cancer prevention and treatment demonstration programs, and encourages a number of quality improvement projects. Medicare+Choice organizations must put together national quality assessment and performance improvement projects. At a multicultural workshop sponsored by CMS, knowledgeable health providers, educators, researchers, and representatives of advocacy and professional organizations of the five major racial and ethnic groups at the national, state, and community levels suggested ways for CMS to implement strategies that will eliminate disparities, enhance diversity, and foster cultural and linguistic competency at CMS.

Identifying racial disparities in access to health care service is a key focus at CMS. During the past few years several research projects have been initiated to improve our understanding of health disparities among racial and ethnic groups in order to address the goals of the president's Healthy People Initiative.

Several experts are helping us plan our future research agenda by providing guidance on how to eliminate health disparities among the groups mentioned earlier. The contractors are developing recommendations and strategies for shaping our future research agenda. We will use this information to develop program activities to help reduce health disparities.

Research projects currently under way include a consortium of academic institutions we fund that train health services researchers to use Medicare and Medicaid claims data. The original three institutions were the University of Minnesota, Boston University, and Dartmouth College, but a number of years ago CMS asked Morehouse School of Medicine to become the fourth academic partner so that they could educate our researchers on how to use Medicaid claims data to support the study of minority health issues. In addition, they conduct special outreach efforts to encourage minority health researchers to use our Medicare databases.

CMS funds two current studies that use the Medicaid database. A multistate study is analyzing the association between pregnancy-related care and outcomes and the ethnic and racial characteristics of women who had a Medicaid-covered delivery during 1995. The project will evaluate the use of health services from prenatal care through delivery and into the first three months postpartum. We expect the study to identify and explain the patterns of disparities in prenatal and postpartum care and the outcomes provided to women covered by Medicaid.

A second Medicaid research project will analyze the utilization of health care services related to cancer prevention for women on Medicaid. We understand the magnitude and patterns of utilization for preventative services for cancer among female beneficiaries. This is critical because in the United States cancer is the second leading cause of death, and the number one cause of death for women in the thirty-four to forty-four age group. The Healthy People 2010 breast cancer goal is to reduce the breast cancer death rate from 27.0 breast cancer deaths per 100,000 in 1999 to 22.3 deaths per 100,000 females by the year 2010.

Presently few data exist on the utilization rates of preventative services for women on Medicaid. Using the Medicaid administrative claims files this project will provide a better picture of the utilization patterns for preventive services, how they relate to cancer treatment, and health outcomes for female Medicaid beneficiaries. We will also identify areas for additional collaboration with the states to improve awareness and other outreach activities related to cancer prevention and screening.

Another research study we are beginning will determine the proportion of eligible American Indian and Alaskan Native populations that are currently enrolled in Medicaid, SCHIP, and Medicare. The study will analyze data to determine the extent of possible underenrollment in our programs across fifteen states on a county-level basis. The project will identify barriers to enrollment and effective strategies for outreach and assistance to help people enroll.

We are also looking at gender and racial disparities among Medicare beneficiaries with chronic diseases. We aim to expand our knowledge base in women's health and chronic diseases by using our Medicare administrative claim files. Cardiovascular diseases—primarily heart diseases and stroke—are among the major chronic conditions affecting people over sixty-five and are among the leading causes of death irrespective of gender or racial origin. Cardiovascular disease is responsible for more deaths in women over sixty-five than any other cause, including cancer. Findings from this project will help CMS target policies, programmatic changes, education outreach, research, and demonstration projects that may help improve health outcomes for female Medicare beneficiaries.

Chronic diseases contribute to the morbidity and mortality of older Americans. Diabetes is the seventh leading cause of death in this country, so CMS is working on a study that will use our Medicare Current Beneficiary Survey to develop a database, create analytical files, and provide programming and analytic support for studies on beneficiaries with diabetes. The study focuses on racial, gender, and ethnic differences for respondents to the survey who have reported having diabetes. The project will provide a mechanism for ongoing analyses from the survey and Medicare administrative files that are linked for the survey participants. Through this means, studies on Medicare beneficiaries with diabetes can be conducted using several years of data from the survey.

CMS and the Department of Health and Human Services are allied in trying to eliminate racial and ethnic disparities in health care. As we strive to make inroads in developing cultural competency in the way we administer our programs, it is imperative that we continue to obtain detailed information on racial and ethnic composition of our beneficiaries.

To reduce health disparities, we need to move away from a "silo" mentality between programs, incorporate what we have learned from our research into our day-to-day thinking, and regularly consider minority health issues as we implement Medicare, Medicaid, and SCHIP. We seek to improve access to health insurance, improve quality of care, and reduce unnecessary barriers to care so that all Americans can access the health care services they need and deserve.

19

The Challenge of Diversity at the Social Security Administration

James B. Lockhart III

Christopher Columbus's voyage to the New World is an apt example of success through diversity. Here was an Italian sailor on a Spanish ship with a crew from every corner of Europe and an African navigator, and he sailed to a land where Native Americans and, perhaps, Asians were waiting. It makes the point that the United States has always been a richly diverse nation and continues to be. The Census Bureau reports that the current number, if not the percentage, of first- and second-generation Americans with roots outside the United States is the highest in history.

This truth about this diverse culture and experience is important to the Social Security Administration (SSA), which administers programs that touch the lives of almost all Americans. SSA employees interact daily with the public. More than 80 percent of the agency's 65,000 employees work in either the field and hearing offices or the teleservice centers. We must be aware of the diversity of our beneficiaries so we can serve them better.

This chapter describes the racial, ethnic, and economic diversity of SSA beneficiaries and how SSA's service delivery reflects this diversity. It also explains how SSA's research and reform efforts are attuned to the diversity of these beneficiaries.

SSA Beneficiaries

Social Security's beneficiaries are as diverse as is the aged population. Sometimes Americans think that Social Security is just a retirement program. However, 30 percent of Social Security beneficiaries receive survivors' and disability payments. The Supplemental Security Income (SSI) program represents a safety net for America's aged or disabled poor. SSA pays monthly Social Security or SSI benefits to more than 50 million people, including more than 10 million people with disabilities.[1]

There is great diversity within subgroups of beneficiaries. Social Security retirees have different levels of income, which varies depending on their marital status and their race and ethnicity (figure 19-1). Their median income ranges from more than $31,000 for married beneficiaries down to about $12,000 for nonmarried women. Aged white beneficiaries have a median income of almost $20,000 compared to only a little more than half of that for Hispanic beneficiaries.[2]

Among aged beneficiaries, the shares of income from various sources vary sharply by income. It is not surprising that the beneficiaries in the lowest quintile rely most heavily on Social Security, which accounts for 82 percent of their total income. In contrast, Social Security represents only 19 percent of the income for beneficiaries in the highest quintile. This group receives as much aggregate income from pensions (19 percent) as from Social Security, and more of their income from assets (24 percent) and earnings (35 percent).[3]

Another indicator of the diverse population that SSA serves is the fact that English is not always the beneficiaries' primary language. About 9 percent of claimants—2.1 million—preferred to be interviewed in a language other than English. More than 74 percent of the language demand was for Spanish.[4] The greatest percentage of SSA's clients preferring to do business in a language other than English is among those applying for SSI aged benefits: nearly 35 percent preferred a language other than English.[5]

SSA's Service Delivery

The Social Security Administration's service delivery efforts have to reflect the diverse needs of the beneficiary population. As a result, SSA has one of the most diverse, well-qualified work forces in government.

SSA continues to recruit and train staff who can work effectively with the non–English-speaking public. Since FY 1993 approximately 35 percent of new hires for SSA field offices and teleservice centers have been bilingual. More than 1,000 bilingual workers were hired in 2001. The agency now has 6,600 bilingual employees who speak 87 different languages.[6] About 10 percent of field office employees and 23 percent of teleservice center employees are bilingual. We give callers immediate access to an interpreter if needed.[7]

In addition, we have expanded non-English publications and services available at our Internet site (socialsecurity.gov). Through our "Multi-Language Gateway," the public can access public information materials, such as a sample Social Security Statement and program fact sheets translated into fifteen languages. We also have formats that are accessible to people with disabilities.

Figure 19-1. *Median Income of the Aged Population, by Demographic Characteristics*

Thousands of dollars

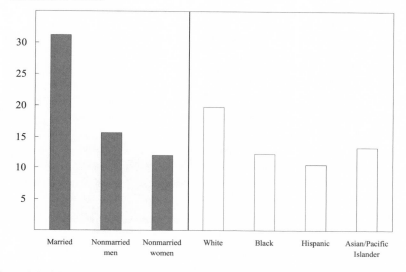

Source: Social Security Administration, *Income of the Aged Chartbook, 2000*, p. 16, and additional data from U.S. Census Bureau, Current Population Survey.

It is instructive to compare our work force diversity to the rest of the federal government and to the civilian labor force. African Americans represent a larger percentage of our work force than in either the federal government as a whole or in the civilian labor force (figure 19-2).

The percentage of Hispanic employees is also higher at Social Security than in the federal government. Asians are a smaller percentage of SSA's work force than the other two groups, but we are successfully working hard to recruit more. Native Americans are a greater percentage of the SSA work force than in the civilian labor force. People with disabilities are well represented, making up 8.2 percent, compared to 7.1 percent in the total federal work force.[8]

SSA's Research and Reform Efforts

Our research efforts also reflect the diversity of our beneficiaries. We assess the effects of our programs on current and future beneficiary groups. For example, we analyze the effects of policy changes on racial and ethnic groups, men and women, immigrants and nonimmigrants, as well as other economic and demographic groups.

Figure 19-2. *Diversity in the SSA Work Force*

Percent of work force

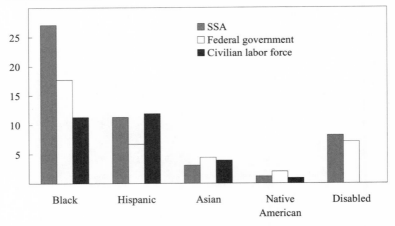

Source: U.S. Social Security Administration, as of January 2003 (unpublished).
Note: White employees: SSA (57.2%); federal government (69.1%); civilian labor force
(72.0%).

We do this because we recognize that the lifetime experiences of different
groups affect their retirement income. By lifetime experiences we mean
earnings and savings behavior, marital histories and family composition, and
mortality. In particular, Social Security benefits depend directly on those
lifetime experiences of individuals, which can vary widely across groups.

For instance, earnings and savings behavior varies. At every level of income
and education, the percentage of black and Hispanic households holding
potentially higher returning assets such as equities is considerably smaller than
in white households. This pattern could adversely affect the retirement incomes of minority workers and families in the future.

Mortality and morbidity are significant factors in assessing the equity of the
Social Security programs. Black males are somewhat more likely to die at
younger ages than males of other races. As a consequence, black males are less
likely to receive Social Security retirement benefits. However, they are more
likely to receive Social Security disability insurance.

We have developed several models for analyzing the distributional implications of various changes to the Social Security program. Modeling Income in
the Near Term, or MINT, is a microsimulation model that focuses on the baby-
boom cohort as retirees in 2022.

Owing to the rich detail in the model, we can examine how policy options
would affect Social Security benefits, as well as total income of individuals,

Figure 19-3.   *Social Security Funding Shortfall, 2002–76*[a]

Trillions of present value dollars

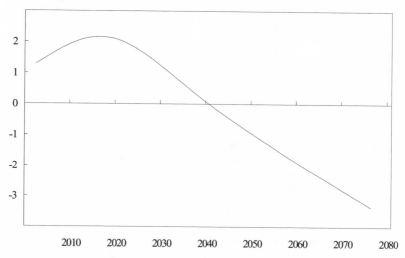

Source: Board of Trustees of the Federal Old-Age, Survivors, and Disability Insurance Trust Funds, *2003 Annual Report*, p. 11.
a. Cumulative net cash flow with interest at present tax rates and scheduled benefit levels.

under various proposals. We look at effects on benefits and total income by race, age, marital status, education, beneficiary type, and income quintile. In chapter 9 Lee Cohen provides good examples of how the MINT model handles differences in incomes, family formation, disability, and mortality by race.

Having research capabilities to determine how different populations would be affected by policy changes is particularly important given the need to reform the Social Security system. The current pay-as-you-go system is unsustainable in the long run. The ability to keep Social Security solvent for the next seventy-five years would require payroll tax increases of more than 50 percent or benefit cuts of at least 30 percent. Any reform should achieve sustainable solvency and allow beneficiaries more choice to reflect diverse circumstances.

The graph in figure 19-3 demonstrates the funding gap of the current system over the next seventy-five years and the need for reform. Assuming presently scheduled benefits and tax rates—in present value terms—the program's shortfall is $3.5 trillion, which is roughly equivalent to the total U.S. government debt held by the public today. That figure includes the $1.4 trillion trust fund, which means that over the seventy-five-year period the needs of the program exceed taxes by $4.9 trillion and, of course, it only gets worse thereafter.[9]

If we adopt personal retirement accounts, as President George W. Bush and his bipartisan commission have suggested, we need to keep in mind the reform issues related to diversity, including the following:

—*Life expectancy:* Individuals who expect to live two years after retirement will feel differently about annuitization of personal accounts than will those who expect to live twenty years.

—*Inheritable wealth:* How should account balances be distributed? Those who emphasize the importance of inheritable wealth will oppose annuitization, while those who focus on income adequacy for the long-lived will favor mandatory annuitization.

—*Benefits for widows:* Widows make up a disproportionate share of the elderly poor. Widows currently can receive up to 100 percent of their husband's benefit, depending on the age when they start receiving benefits, but that could change in various ways under reform proposals.

—*Low-income subsidies:* Should low-income beneficiaries be subsidized beyond SSI? Accumulating personal account balances will be difficult for people with spotty work histories and long periods out of the labor market.

—*Disability benefits:* Should disabled beneficiaries have access to their accounts prior to full retirement age? A rule that no one can access his or her personal account until full retirement age would disproportionately affect persons with disabilities.

—*Financial literacy:* Recognizing that more responsibility would be shifted to the individual, how do we teach financial literacy? There is an old joke in financial circles that for too many people economic understanding begins and ends with their ATM PIN number. Unfortunately, there is also truth in this. We need to change that. We need to work extra hard to provide valuable information so that everyone faces similar opportunities to see their retirement contributions grow.

Conclusion

We are proud of the role that our programs play in the lives of tens of millions of Americans from diverse walks of life. We work hard on communication and outreach efforts to let people know about Social Security and SSI benefit entitlement and we are committed to continuing these efforts. We are also committed to continue building our research capabilities. I am pleased to announce that recently the General Accounting Office removed SSA's research and policy development from the list of SSA's major management challenges. We recognize that change is needed in the Social Security program, and the importance of knowing how different beneficiary groups might be affected by those reforms.

Notes

1. Social Security Administration, *Monthly Statistical Snapshot,* May 2003 (www.socialsecurity.gov/policy/docs/quickfacts/stat_snapshot/index.html [accessed September 8, 2003]).

2. Social Security Administration, *Income of the Aged Chartbook, 2000,* p. 16.

3. Social Security Administration, *Income of the Aged Chartbook, 2000,* p. 22.

4. Social Security Administration, *Plan for Providing Access to Benefits and Services for Persons with Limited English Proficiency* (www.ssa.gov/multilanguage/LEPPlan2.htm [accessed September 8, 2003]).

5. Social Security Administration, *FY 2001 Limited English Proficient (LEP) Management Information* (unpublished).

6. Social Security Administration, *2002 Status Report on Service to SSA's Limited English Proficient (LEP) Public* (unpublished).

7. Social Security Administration, *Number of Bilingual Public Contact Employees* (unpublished).

8. Social Security Administration, Office of Civil Rights and Equal Opportunity, *Composition of SSA Workforce Compared to the Civilian Labor Force and the Federal Government.* (unpublished). See also U.S. Office of Personnel Management, *Federal Civilian Workforce Statistics, The Fact Book,* 2002 ed.

9. Board of Trustees of the Federal Old-Age and Survivors Insurance and Disability Insurance Trust Funds, *2003 Annual Report,* p. 62.

20

The Challenge of
Diversity for Foundations

Ruby Takanishi

This chapter touches on three areas. First, how research findings can be used to address economic disparities and cultural diversity through social insurance policies. Second, how American social policy can be informed by research on the needs and contributions of immigrant families. Third, how the first two areas can be addressed from the perspective of the foundation sector.

As a disclaimer, being president of the Foundation for Child Development, I could not possibly represent the foundation sector, since more than 55,000 foundations of different kinds exist in the United States today. They vary greatly in their assets and values, the issues they address, and the range of their grantmaking from the national to the local levels. The remarks here should be taken in the context of philanthropic diversity.

Connecting Research and Policy

Research findings can be used to address economic disparities and cultural diversity through social insurance. Foundations of different kinds, including the Foundation for Child Development, use strategies to make that connection between research and action.

One area in which foundations work is communication strategies, and the Henry J. Kaiser Family Foundation is one of the premiere examples. An important intermediary between research and action are communications strategies that organizations use to frame and promote their message in ways that are acceptable or appealing to key policymakers. Polling is part of this connection. Policy development is another and has been well represented through the research and policy analyses that have been presented throughout this volume. Using some of that research for policy analysis and policy development is also important. The Foundation for Child Development supports research, policy analysis, communication strategies, and advocacy groups related to child and family policy.

Attending to Immigrant Children and Families

Social policy can benefit from connecting research on the needs and contributions of immigrant families to policy options. Nationally in the year 2000 one in five children under the age of eighteen was a child of an immigrant or living in an immigrant family, which is defined as having at least one parent born outside the United States. Approximately 14 million children in the United States would be considered to be living in immigrant families in 2000, and that number has increased.[1]

From 1990 to 2000 the number of children in these immigrant families increased seven times faster than children in native-born families. In New York City more than 60 percent of the children below the age of eighteen live in immigrant families.[2] In Los Angeles County, the comparable number is about 70 percent. The Public Policy Institute of California recently conducted a study in which researchers found that in the entire state of California, one of two children from birth to age five is a child of an immigrant.[3]

As Nancy Gordon (chapter 6) and others have noted, these numbers are likely to grow barring any changes in immigration policy. Therefore, the work force in the near future will be essential for funding the social and health insurance programs of a large, aging baby boomer population that is culturally and ethnically different from this work force.

It is in our collective self-interest that America has social policies to ensure that this group of children and youth, who are going to become our prime work force and support us in our old age, be healthy and well educated. Policies are needed that welcome and integrate them into American society, since many of them will also become voters.

Five of every six children in immigrant families have origins in Latin America or Asia: 58 percent come from Latin America and 23 percent from Asia.[4] By about the year 2040, 50 percent of all children in the United States will be members of Hispanic, Black, Asian, or American Indian families or backgrounds. At that same time, 75 percent of the elderly will be non-Hispanic white, compared to only 50 percent of the children.

Of the children today, one of five children has fathers and mothers with no more than eight years of schooling.[5] If we believe that parents' education has a lot to do with educational prospects of their children and the income and employment mobility of parents, this obviously is a very serious situation.

Children in immigrant families are more likely than children with U.S.-born parents to live in poverty. This declines by generation, but in the first generation 26 percent of immigrant children live in poverty.[6] Poverty is especially high among children in immigrant families from Mexico, Central America, the Caribbean, and Southeast Asia. In 1989 official poverty rates ranged from about 26 percent for children from Haiti, 31 percent from Vietnam, 46 percent from Cambodia, and 51 percent from Laos.

Two-thirds of children in immigrant families speak a language other than English in the home.[7] This is a snapshot of who these children are, and these facts have been known for some time. In California especially, some of these analyses were available about fifteen years ago. The future is now much closer.

It is imperative that ongoing and future national surveys and studies take into account the changing faces of America's children and families. What is still troublesome is that in some important national surveys or those claiming to be nationally representative surveys of American children—such as the Early Childhood Longitudinal Study (ECLS-K), starting from kindergarten, or a more recent one starting from birth, Early Childhood Longitudinal Study (ECLS-B)—children who do not speak English or parents who do not speak English tend to be excluded so that the categories of Latino and Asian families that are reported in ECLS-K, for example, are not a representative sample of those particular labeled groups.[8] The extent to which African immigrants are included in the African American category is unknown. Those who immigrate from non-Anglophone countries are likely to be excluded.

Research on immigrant children and youth, given their growth and numbers, is relatively sparse. This situation must be changed. Thus the Foundation for Child Development has launched a Young Scholars Program that focuses on the changing faces of America's children to stimulate research on immigrant children and families during their first ten years of life. Much more is needed.

Social Policy Options

Immigrant families constitute one-third to one-half of American families who are low-income, low-wage workers who do not earn adequate incomes that enable them to raise their children well. The 2003 welfare reauthorization should include immigrants who were excluded in 1996 into the social insurance programs that can assist them to achieve a decent standard of living for themselves and their children. The Urban Institute studied immigrant families and workers with respect to health insurance coverage. In Los Angeles 40 percent of noncitizen children and 22 percent of citizen children in immigrant families were uninsured compared to 6 percent of children in California's citizen families. In New York City 28 percent of noncitizen children and 8 percent of citizen children in immigrant families were uninsured versus 6 percent of children in citizen families. Approximately 75 percent of children living in immigrant families are citizens of the United States, that is, they were born in the United States and are citizens.[9]

These findings suggest that health insurance rates for children depend on their citizenship status. But they also suggest another important finding, that New York State has been much more successful in enrolling large numbers of children in immigrant families than California has. This point has to do with state disparities in their policies that affect children's access to health care and other key resources. Child health insurance policies at the state level create disparities in outcomes, in this case, in health insurance coverage.

The restoration of food stamps to legal immigrant children in May 2002 was a promising step and should be sustained. Many immigrants work in the low-wage sector where family leave policy, sick leave, and vacations are practically nonexistent. This is an important situation to be addressed. Three foundations—including ours, the Foundation for Child Development; the David and Lucile Packard Foundation; and the Ford Foundation—supported a study at the National Academy of Sciences that is scheduled for release in 2003 that focuses on work-family policies, particularly in the low-wage sector.[10]

Access to health care is critical for the well-being and for the learning of children. It is clear that mothers who are about to give birth have very different access, coverage, and outcomes with respect to health care depending on the state in which they are living.

Education and training are aspects of social insurance that need more attention. Access to good quality education, both for children and for adults, is an important part of a social insurance system that depends on the productivity of its prime work force.

It is clear that attendance in good early education programs results in better outcomes for children, not only in the near term but also in the long term for their life prospects. With this, immigrant children are more ready for school and have a better grasp of English. However, if you look at the existing studies, like those on ECLS-K and Head Start, you will see that immigrant children, particularly Latino children, are less likely to participate given their numbers. Research has to determine why this is the case. Nonetheless, it is a fact, and one could speculate that this has consequences for children and their readiness for school entry.

There also needs to be renewed attention to undocumented immigrants. A clear distinction that has not been made is that the strategies among advocacy groups tend to focus on restoring benefits to legal immigrants versus undocumented ones. While such a strategy may be more politically viable, the numbers of undocumented immigrants are significant.

Economic security, the minimum wage, and living wages are needed for all families. While these policy options are most likely to benefit immigrant families, they will also be beneficial to all families in the low-wage sector.

The United States does not pay sufficient attention to social integration policies. Israel, Denmark, France, Sweden, and other countries that have significant numbers of immigrants have clear policies that focus on integrating immigrants into their societies. Immigrant integration policies include, for example, language classes that benefit immigrants in their job seeking and employment mobility and also have good consequences for their children and communication with schools. This could lessen the enormous pressures for language services. There is no way that you are going to find translation services for more than one hundred languages in the New York City public school system, for example. What is really significant is that if you look at polls, like the most recent one from the Public Agenda Foundation, immigrants say that learning English is one of their most important needs because they realize that immigrants who speak English have better earning prospects.[11]

Many of the countries mentioned above invest public resources and funds when immigrants come to their countries to learn the language. While I am a firm believer in multilingualism, it is also important to think about how immigrants are integrated into American society, and learning English is a very important part of this.

Conclusion

The changing demography of the United States requires a fundamental rethinking of social insurance in American society. We must step back and be informed by data. We should concentrate on incremental changes. However, we must recognize that American policies regarding social insurance that were developed in 1934 are not necessarily suited to 2003 and beyond.

The 1996 welfare legislation specifically excluded legal and undocumented immigrants, and that must be reconsidered. The United States can learn about the impact of our immigration policies by comparing them with other countries mentioned earlier. I find it deeply troubling that current U.S. policies allow state disparities in resources allocated to children and families. As a result, some states are better places for children and families to live. Those states that invest in children and youth tend to have better outcomes for their children.

Public policies can make an enormous difference in the lives of children and families. I hope the National Academy of Social Insurance and all agencies dedicated to improving the lives of our diverse population can better align the changing demography in the United States with our social insurance policies.

Notes

1. Foundation for Child Development, *Our Basic Dream: Keeping Faith with America's Working Families and Their Children* (New York: Author, 2000).

2. Research Forum on Children, Families, and the New Federalism, Mailman School of Public Health, Columbia University, "Lack of Appropriate Research Leads to Gaps in Knowledge about Children in Immigrant Families," *The Forum,* 5, no. 1 (February 2002), p. 3.

3. Deborah Reed and Sonya Tafoya, *Demographic, Social, and Economic Trends for Young Children in California* (San Francisco: Public Policy Institute of California, 2001).

4. Michael E. Fix and Jeffrey S. Passell, "U.S. Immigration: Trends and Implications for Schools," Urban Institute, Washington, D.C., January 28, 2003, p. 17 (www.urban.org/url.cfm?ID=410654).

5. Fix and Passell, "U.S. Immigration: Trends and Implications," p. 5.

6, Fix and Passell, "U.S. Immigration: Trends and Implications," p. 18.

7. Fix and Passell, "U.S. Immigration: Trends and Implications," p. 21.

8. *Entering Kindergarten: Findings from the Condition of Education 2000* (Washington, D.C.: Department of Education, Office of Education Record and Improvement, 2001).

9. "Immigrant Well-Being in New York and Los Angeles," Urban Institute, Immigration Studies Program, Washington, D.C., August 2002, p. 2

10. Eugene Smolensky and Jennifer Gootman, eds., *Working Families and Growing Kids: Caring for Children and Adolescents* (Washington, D.C.: National Academies Press, 2003).

11. Steve Farkas, Ann Duffett, and Jean Johnson, *Now That I'm Here* (New York: Public Agenda, 2003).

Epilogue

21

What Can We Anticipate from America's Diverse Public?

Ray Suarez

In these closing remarks I offer some perspectives from outside the field, from outside the practitioner's world and the academic world. I am glad that organizations such as the National Academy of Social Insurance (NASI) are trying to strip away the sentimental hooey and political passion that often gets encrusted onto a fundamental societal question: How do we take care of each other today, next week, and thirty years from today?

The NASI conference was held just blocks from the national legislature and a stone's throw from the president's home. It was held at a time when we are renegotiating what it means to be an American. According to the latest statistics, there are currently almost 30 million foreign-born people living, working, and growing up in America. Some social scientists and nongovernment organizations estimate that number is much higher.

It is the largest number of foreign-born in absolute and percentage terms that this country has seen in more than seventy years. At the time of the 1930 census, the United States was in the midst of digesting the largest influx of immigrants ever taken on by a nation state. These were people from every corner of the world, but mostly from Europe; they spoke a dozen languages, professed a wide array of religions, and had grown up under a wide range of political and social systems.

What we did not, could not know in 1930 was that a long and stubborn Depression, nothing less than capitalism's nervous breakdown, would be followed by the most horrifying and destructive war in the history of humankind. This would be followed by quotas and a reviving Europe, keeping another big influx of immigrants from happening for generations.

By 1960 the number of foreign-born had dwindled. Ellis Island was sitting abandoned and decaying in New York Harbor, and the children of immigrants now dominated our popular culture and politics, our sports and literature.

That long interval between immigrant flows made assimilated Americans out of Frank Capra and Mike Nichols, Knute Rockne and Hyman Rickover.

By the mid-1960s it was apparent that the quotas, percentages, and targets of existing immigration law were outdated, outmoded relics of those earlier immigrant generations. By 1965 few French wanted to come to the United States. Few Welshmen, Scots, or Germans wanted to come. But Mexicans, Filipinos, Koreans, and Chinese surely did want to come.

Once the artificial constraints and European biases of the quotas were removed by Congress, the story of American immigration was changed utterly and totally once again.

In 1850 the top ten birth countries of the foreign-born Americans of the day were, in descending order, Ireland, Germany, Great Britain, Canada, France, Switzerland, Mexico, Norway, the Netherlands, and Italy, number ten. By 1990 the top ten were, in descending order, Mexico, China, the Philippines, Canada, Cuba, Germany, Great Britain, Italy, Korea, and Vietnam.

Of the 28.5 million foreign-born Americans counted in the 2000 census, fully half were from Latin America; of those, more than half—almost 8 million—came from a single country, Mexico.

As someone who is a close observer of American culture, someone who writes a lot about American history, I am amused by the idea that this country's unity, its cohesiveness as a functioning state, is under threat from the people who speak to each other and to God in languages other than English.

If we could walk through the real life, teeming ethnic ghettos of big cities 100 years ago, in 1903, we would hear the voices of Japanese, Chinese, Yiddish, Italian, Polish, and Ukrainian immigrants on the crowded streets of San Francisco, Chicago, Baltimore, Pittsburgh, and Cleveland. The newsstands would be bursting with newspapers in all these languages and more; in fact, there would be multiple newspapers in many of these languages because there was one newspaper for Democrats, one for Socialists, one for union members, and so on.

The grandchildren of the children who ran the streets in those old ethnic ghettos are some of the same people worrying openly about what these new immigrants will mean to our country. From everything I have seen, my best advice is not to worry.

If you watch Spanish-language television or listen to Creole radio in Miami or Brooklyn, you will hear ads for night schools, for taped language courses for the car, and for CD-ROM language courses for the whole family. No one is developing these products, paying for the ads, and buying the courses for kicks or entertainment.

Virtually no Latino family doubts that the acquisition of English for themselves and their families is absolutely vital for climbing off the bottom rungs of the socioeconomic ladder to get someplace better, more comfortable, and more secure.

Reams of public opinion research and stacks of social science data have already shown this. Recently only 7 percent of foreign-born Latinos told public opinion researchers from the Kaiser Family Foundation that it is possible to get ahead in America speaking only Spanish.

Having said that, watching as a place like Queens, New York, morphs in one generation from "Archie Bunker Land" to an outer borough of the United Nations General Assembly, we have to wonder about the wider impact of this.

More people are coming from more different places than ever before, but do not underestimate America and do not underestimate the people who are coming. The immigrant is transforming America in 2003, but the immigrant is transformed by America as well.

Those who worry about diversity and assimilation should remember that in Brooklyn, my home town, which was settled by the Dutch, we did not measure land in morgans instead of acres. Nigerian immigrants in Chicago are not haggling over cattle or kola nuts as part of upcoming wedding plans. They are not using the Napoleonic code instead of English common law in East Flatbush or in Haitian neighborhoods in South Florida. They have been transformed.

Having said that, we still have a substantial challenge ahead. Big chunks of the social networks that help the immigrants of a century ago did not make it all the way to 2003, at least not in their original form. The hometown societies—the *landsmanshaften*, the private language schools, the armies of well-born and well-educated women looking for meaning outside of home and marriage who headed into the Lower East Side or Humboldt Park in Chicago, bringing the keys to assimilation and a map to the opportunity structure in this country—are a little harder to find today. But they are there. They are just not there in quite the same way.

The need has not changed. The median level of education for a new Mexican arrival to the United States is eighth grade. More than 60 percent of Central American–born residents of the United States do not have a high school diploma. The foreign-born make up 20 percent of the approximately 41 million Americans that do not have medical insurance, and another large portion of the medically underserved are the children of the uninsured.

Does all of this affect us? Sure it does. It affects all of us, as citizens, as educators, as scholars, as policymakers, and finally—and we sometimes forget about this—as human beings who care about the future of the country.

As a reporter, I am neutral on the matter of immigration. Its level, where it comes from, how it gets here—I'm not for or against, but I know what it is doing. Maybe we could take a utilitarian view of the debate over immigration rather than an emotional, nationalistic, or sentimental view. If people are here, is it better that they are trained or untrained?

Is it better that they have the possibility of making a stronger contribution to your local economy or that they remain shadow people, economically marginal and exploitable?

If they are here, which kind of life provides a better set of life chances for the children they inevitably have and are going to have in the coming years?

If those children are growing up here, making their lives here, I suppose we could have an abstract argument about whether they belong, whether we can handle this rate of influx indefinitely, and whether the essential character of the country is going to be altered.

Honest people who are not hostile or racist or nativist can disagree on these questions, but these people are here. It is too late for "what if?"

Now, since they are here, what is the best way to proceed?

The dropout rate for Latinos born outside the United States is 44 percent, according to a study from the House Committee on Education in the Workforce. How can we calculate the lost gross domestic product, the shortened years of life expectancy, the reduced life chances of their children, the lower taxable value of their property and the impact that that has on municipal governance, the smaller savings for retirement, the higher dependence on welfare, the businesses that are not started, and on and on and on? It is probably an incalculable figure.

Latinos will constitute 23 percent of the school population for grades nine to twelve in twenty years. That is the feedstock for a big chunk of the future work force. Today only 33 percent of Latinos are enrolled in college prep academic programs compared to 50 percent of whites and 43 percent of blacks.

This is a fascinating time to be writing urban history, social science, and ethnography; to be watching the interaction between immigration and the economy and immigration and the work force, especially when you try to assess the impact of that new Latino presence in America.

For one thing, this immigration defies easy categorization. The immigrants come from twenty-four countries, after all. The push and pull factors vary, and they varied certainly over the last twenty years as we ended the cold war and began something else.

Many of the countries that experienced turmoil and consequent economic calamity at home because of the cold war ended up sending large numbers of people here. There were people who came to escape political repression, and there were people who came on a search for opportunity.

Central Americans are the largest feeder group in the Washington, D.C., area and lately, because it is not that easy to emigrate from Cuba, they are the largest feeder population in Miami as well. They have had a roller coaster ride as different administrations and shifting political stands have given Hondurans, Salvadorans, and Nicaraguans a constantly changing set of legal hurdles, reception to asylum claims, based on the American opinion of home country governments.

These new populations are bringing striking changes to places like Fayetteville, Arkansas; Lumberton, North Carolina; the Yakima Valley in Washington; and Kalamazoo in western Michigan—places that you did not think of as good places to find a Mexican restaurant. Yet they have settled in these cities and are assimilating.

The immigrants and the sons and daughters of previous immigrant flows are disproportionately still making their lives in large metropolitan areas, even though the character of some of those smaller places is definitely being changed. But the six largest metropolitan areas in the country account for 60 percent of the Latino population and a huge, disproportionate percentage of all the foreign-born in the United States. They are coming to cities, even coming to past-their-prime cities, which is an important thing to think about. They come from rural and urban settings back in their home countries, which means they bring different sets of problems upon arrival.

This is a human flow that began in effect when Americans came to Spanish-speaking North America. And that immigration continues, unlike Germans, Italians, Norwegians, Scots, Irish, and any of the big immigrant groups of the late nineteenth and early twentieth century.

The Latino presence in the United States is constantly assimilating and renewing all at the same time. That is why it is so hard to figure out just what it means when the Census Bureau says that Latinos are now the largest minority group in the United States. I am not sure what that means because this is a vast array of people who do not even think that they have anything to do with each other if you ask them.

States like Texas, California, and New York are home at the same time to large, suburbanizing, increasingly English-dominant, and white-collar Latino populations, as well as low-skilled, non–English-speaking populations. How do you make social common cause? How do you make political common cause between a rural Dominican newly settled in the South Bronx and a Puerto Rican supervisor in a municipal hospital who lives in White Plains in Westchester County whose parents came fifty years ago?

Is there a natural solidarity between a family that pronounces their name "Martin-ez," lives in South Chicago, and whose forebears came to the United States at the beginning of World War I fleeing the Mexican Civil War and the

Martinez family that just moved to Pilson, the port of entry neighborhood in that same city, coming to the United States to escape small town poverty in Durango? Will the same issues affect and appeal to those very different Americans?

Amidst the staggering diversity of this population there are some commonalities that burden and challenge Latino life whether it is lived in the shadow of the Brooklyn Bridge or in the shadow of the Cascade Mountain range in central Washington State. There is a kind of triumphalism that you hear in the tone of Fannie Mae and various administrations and lending organization that remind us that black and Latino home ownership rates have reached historic highs.

But we also know that the assessed valuations of the homes they own are much, much lower than those of other Americans, which makes creating intergenerational transfer of wealth very difficult. This also has tremendous consequences for school systems in a country where a majority of school districts still generate their revenue from taxes on what? Real estate.

Latinos are more segregated residentially than blacks, which results in a higher rate of social isolation for Latino school kids. The minority population of a local public school as a rule overstates the presence of that same group in the neighborhood, as a rule of thumb by about two to one. So, in a 25 percent Latino neighborhood, the public schools—certainly the kindergarten through grade six schools—are likely to be 50 percent Latino.

Latinos go to school in some of the oldest buildings still left standing as schools in America. Lack of political clout and weakness in the tax base make it difficult to force the construction of new buildings, even as elementary school enrollments shoot past the previously unimaginable peaks attained at the height of the baby boom.

I went to the New York City public schools at a time when they could not put enough chairs in the rooms for us to sit in. Now the censuses at those same schools are higher than they were in 1962 when I was in kindergarten, which they thought was the high tide—the goat moving through the anaconda. You were never going to see that again, but here it is.

Latinos have higher work force participation rates than other Americans. Household incomes are lower than the American average, even though the average Latino household includes more employed people than the average American household.

Those working adults are more likely to work in agriculture, light assembly, and low-skilled industrial labor than other Americans. They are more likely to not have obtained a credential of any kind, either a diploma or a GED.

Although they work more, they are less likely than blacks and whites to work at jobs that include employer-offered health care plans, in part because of the industries in which they are overrepresented, in part because of their historically low labor union membership.

This shows up in urban areas as a heavy dependence on publicly supported clinics for basic health care. In rural areas it results in chronically underserved groups. This allows some illnesses that are cheap to treat at the outset to go untreated or undertreated for a long time. It creates diabetes and hypertension rates that not only lower life expectancies, but also lower the quality of life during what life span is attained, keeping workers out of the work force for more years of their lives.

At all income levels, Latinos are less likely than white families to have a credit card or a bank account. The heavy presence of new Latino populations in dense, older, metropolitan areas has had mixed results for Latino workers. It has meant in places like San Francisco and the adjacent San Jose-Silicon Valley area fast expansion in service employment, creating a lot of entry-level jobs, but also at the same time creating a tight labor market that helped increase hourly rates of pay.

But within that positive picture, social isolation remained high when you viewed it through the lens of residential and school patterns. High exposure to one set of industries may end up meaning higher unemployment than in the general population when there is a cyclical downturn, and San Jose is a perfect example. It is a metro area that was going great guns during the 1990s, but the outlook is less clear today.

One thing that the Latino chattering classes, such as they are—and I am kind of a member of them—talk about is whether the black model of the 1950s and 1960s for organization for political progress, for gains, is a valid and recommended model for Latino communities today. Because of the peculiar pattern in the history of Latino immigration, where there is no bell curve or an isolated spike in the flows, there is no model that is really valid for Latino immigration.

Latinos have never punched their weight politically in Texas, California, and New York, but that day may be coming. So stay tuned.

Are the big cities where Latinos are concentrated today maxed-out, economic entities for those on the bottom rung of the ladder? Unlike the situation that faced the Irish, Italians, and Eastern Europeans, the perilous state of today's city and state governments may make it impossible to use municipal employment, for instance, as a rung on the ladder to the middle class.

Is the same speed of upward mobility still possible in an era of offshore production and a labor marketplace that is no longer countywide, statewide, or even regionwide, but now has no borders? People who are sewing jeans in Chinatown right now in Lower Manhattan are not competing against people who sew jeans elsewhere on the eastern seaboard, but people who do it in Saipan, Hong Kong, and South Korea.

Can the models of intergenerational advancement that worked for Irish, Italian, and Russian Jewish families a century ago guarantee the mass movement of Latinos into the middle class in return for similar effort, in return for similar investment in personal and family capital in the form of education, in the form of savings, and in the form of deferred consumption in order to make family purchases that help them project upwards into the next generation?

One of the most interesting aspects of assimilation over the coming twenty years or so will be how race and the American way of thinking about race may or may not impose itself on individual Latino fortunes. In the way these 35 million or so people have been discussed in politics, in the popular press, they are a third race: blacks, whites, and Latinos.

But you know they are not. Kaiser researchers talked to thousands of Latinos from different national groups and asked them to self-identify ethnically and racially. Fifty-five percent of Cubans called themselves white as their first choice, not Cuban, Hispanic, or anything like that. They said, "I am white."

Only 12 percent of Dominicans and 19 percent of Puerto Ricans on the mainland identified themselves as white. But when filling out their long form in the 2000 census, 85 percent of Puerto Ricans on the island identified themselves as white.

What happens when they get on an American Airlines plane and fly to Newark Airport? They meet a society and a culture and a structure that tells them they are this new thing that they did not think they were before. This bears further examination.

Surprisingly large numbers of Caribbeans and Central Americans told researchers that other Latinos discriminated against them and their family members based on skin color. Will new opportunities be open only to a slice of urbanized, lighter skinned Latinos and denied to darker skinned families picking cherries in Western Michigan, butchering hogs for low wages in Iowa, or scraping together a desperate living with multiple adults working at sweatshop wages in fly-by-night clothing factories in Los Angeles?

Will an already wide gulf get wider between those who eat in nice restaurants, work in white-collar jobs, and buy swell houses and those who are not able to climb into the American middle class?

What is the nature of the solidarity that exists between the Latino professional eating in a hotel dining room with a non-Latino colleague or client and the busboy who silently takes away dirty dishes, fills water glasses, and evaporates into a back room?

When I interviewed Dr. Harry Pachon, executive director of the Thomas Rivera Center in California, he said Latino assimilation will move quickly if there continues to be rapid economic growth as there was in the 1990s. If there is not, Latino separation from the wider society and gulfs inside that population will continue to widen.

The fate of millions of people is riding on just that question. Their current situation at the bottom rungs of all kinds of institutional and workplace ladders will be less transitional and more permanent. They will remain less likely to master English, less likely to graduate from high school, less likely to vote, and less likely to own a personal computer.

When researchers look at their models, at population distributions by age and other measures, there are some pieces of good actuarial news and some not so good.

What does the immigrant profile look like when it is graphed by age? It is a very young group. This bodes well for statisticians worried about the fate of Social Security.

The newcomers are people coming into the work force at two extremes. They are more likely to have very few years of schooling and also more likely to have advanced degrees than native-born Americans. They are less likely to be covered by insurance and less likely to be vested in private pension plans. A breathtaking number of these families have no net household wealth.

These newcomers will beef up payments into Social Security and Medicare during the years when they are still a relatively young age group, and they will place demands on all kinds of systems in the later years.

Millions of old ages that would not have been spent in America, millions of childhoods that never would have happened at all, and millions of individual claims to society's overall wealth are going to be made by these immigrants.

For a time, the benefit profile is going to be a little different. There will be higher dependence than other Americans on government-backed, old-age pension programs, but this will be for a shorter time due to lower life expectancy.

Among legal or in-status workers' families, there will be more government-backed survivors, benefits, and disability payments because of the concentration of these workers in dangerous and life-shortening jobs. At the same time, more workers will begin or continue their working lives here and they have never experienced a dime of county, state, or federal tax-supported benefits until they got off the plane.

A Somali cab driver, a Jamaican tax preparer on Flatbush Avenue in an H&R Block storefront, a Bangladeshi seamstress, and an Indian electronics store owner all arrived here as adults and began paying into the tax and social insurance system.

We do not reliably include in our accounting or policy debates the notion that, while these people are going to cost us something down the road, they have cost us nothing up front. Their education has been paid for by families that take their sustenance from other national economies. They are educated by the strapped and overburdened state systems of developing countries and then achieve their value added here at very little cost to us.

Here are some important statistics about the largest component of that foreign-born population living in the United States. Of the 14 million foreign-born Latinos, 47 percent, almost half, are Spanish-language dominant. But when you look at the three youngest birth cohorts—younger than ten, eleven to seventeen, and eighteen to twenty-five—only the ten and under group is comfortable with English.

The Spanish-dominant rates are 66 percent for the eleven to seventeen group and 84 percent for the eighteen to twenty-fives. While one-quarter of all Latinos describe themselves as English dominant, the percentage is tiny among the foreign-born. Among the third generation (their grandchildren, theoretically), 78 percent are English dominant.

When asked about Latino children who are now growing up in the United States, 80 percent of the foreign-born respondents said the children would get a better education than they had. Seventy-six percent said Latino children would grow up to have better jobs or make more money. Sixty-eight percent said those children would be as close to their families as they are themselves, but only 56 percent said these children would have the same moral values that they did.

And so, America is confirmed as a land of opportunity, with the opportunity to be corrupted.

Embedded in all these statistics is something so optimistic, so cheering, that it should be reassuring to all other Americans. It is an essentially sunny view of the possibilities of coming here, held even by people for whom the United States has meant low-wage work, long, long hours, and little chance for personal advancement—tremendous opportunity for family advancement, but little opportunity for personal advancement. That generally optimistic view of what getting into the United States is really all about is an essential part of the make-up of the immigrant from anywhere.

Linda Chavez, who was briefly President George Bush's nominee for secretary of labor, has long written that Latino assimilation will eventually resemble that of the Irish, Italians, Poles, southern Germans, and any large immigrant group that was Catholic, arrived from farms, and then started the struggle to fit in. I have to part company with Linda Chavez there.

Other historians and theorists suggest that the proximity of the countries of origin and the long duration of arrival, unlike those earlier immigrations that graph with that spike in the middle, will create a model of assimilation unlike anything we have ever seen before. Today the Koreans who chat on their cell phones in their stores are not just on with somebody at home around the block. They are talking to somebody in Korea.

Look at the signs in convenience stores for those phone cards. When you came from Palermo or Stavanger, Norway, or Vilnius in 1903, there were no phone cards that said, "Call Lithuania for 12 cents a minute."

Barbadians not only send home millions in remittance income, but they also go home frequently and take their children with them. So the child grows up with not just sepia-toned stories of old people about what that place was like, but with a living, breathing association with what that place really is. The mother tongue may be maintained longer in families and in commerce and in prayer. Social forms, like extended family links, may persist longer, especially when those times form the legal basis for chain immigration. You might not be so crazy about your cousin, but your cousin keeps in touch if you are going to be the way he gets into America.

Latinos were significantly less likely than other Americans to agree with the statement: You can be more successful in American work places if you are willing to work long hours at the expense of your personal life. Were they rejecting hard-driving "Yuppiedom" in that bit of social science research? Today many are working those long hours and not getting ahead. So perhaps it is from hard-won experience rather than a vision of mainstream American culture that they are less likely to agree that there is something worthwhile in being at the job and not being home.

Latinos are far more likely than other Americans to believe that relatives are more important than friends and that it is good for children to live at home until they get married. Right now they do not institutionalize their elderly at the same rate as the wider population. But as they are here longer, as they make more money, we will get a chance to see whether that difference is the product of this generation simply not having the money to put Mommy and Poppy in the home or whether there really is something different that persists and forms a pattern of choices that illustrates something basic about who they are beyond things like what food they eat on holidays, which is what a lot of American ethnicity has boiled down to.

These potential differences and whether they persist is important, but really ephemeral, I would suggest. It is an exciting time to be alive. I know that a lot of people just make their bread and butter moaning about how terrible it is all going to be, but I find it pretty exciting.

In response to questions, Mr. Suarez made the following points.

I was born in a Brooklyn neighborhood that was becoming an ethnic ghetto, Crown Heights. When I was about to start school, my parents decided it was a good time to leave that neighborhood to get me into a better elementary school. We moved to a neighborhood called Bensonhurst, also in Brooklyn, which was not particularly welcoming to Puerto Ricans in 1961. So I managed to provide all of the local color in my elementary schools. It was not always great; it was not always terrible. At that time Bensonhurst was a very big neighborhood, bigger than most American cities, and was pretty much entirely Jewish and Italian. It was populated by the grandchildren of arriving Eastern European Jews who were on their second home in the new world and the children of Italian immigrants who were often in their first stop in the new world.

Bensonhurst is not anything like that anymore. There are people walking on the streets speaking Urdu and Russian and Spanish. The interesting thing about Bensonhurst is that, unlike other neighborhoods, this change did not come in a violent, wrenching way that destroyed capital and neighborhoods and left arriving populations with the shells and the dregs, requiring a resegregation that we saw in urban neighborhoods all across the old cities of America. In Bensonhurst, change happened so slowly that nobody remembered to get scared. It was interesting to watch how that contrasts with a place like Crown Heights, where it was happening at 10 or 15 percent a year.

So you turn around, and you do not even recognize the neighborhood you grew up in anymore. This change in Bensonhurst works. Now, it is not like Epcot Village, and people are not singing "Kumbaya" and holding hands. It is sort of rough and elbows out and sometimes uncomfortable, but it works. The main commercial road through the neighborhood, 86th Street, is still an intact, thriving commercial area, but now 20 percent of the signs are in Cyrillic letters. It is a really weird thing to watch happening.

That certainly colors my perception of all of this. Working as a reporter in Chicago and getting very lucky and winning a fellowship to the University of Chicago, where I was a student of William Julius Wilson, was a good opportunity for me. I wrote what I think was a very creditable thesis on the patterns of gentrification in urban neighborhoods, adding another overlay of ways to look at the effects of immigration.

Then I did a lot of coverage of the Immigration Reform and Control Act of 1986 and watched people trying to make paper pasts for themselves, when all of their energies used to go into erasing all the paper pasts for themselves, I watched how difficult and challenging, but ultimately tremendously rewarding, that whole process became for a lot of families.

By living around Chicago, Los Angeles, New York, and Washington, D.C., you only have to keep your eyes open and you can learn a lot. And luckily, as reporters, you are the ultimate outsider or you should be.

The last twenty years have just been an amazing time in this country. We have had to recalibrate a lot of our assumptions about what it means to be here and what it means to be from here.

This is happening now with new populations, and people are going to places because pioneers went out ahead and got the stakes in the ground. There is not any particular reason why the Twin Cities, Minneapolis-St. Paul, is the largest reception region for Somalis. There is nothing about the landscape of the Twin Cities that reminds them of Burbura, Mogadishu, or anyplace else.

So it is interesting to watch this and see how people put one foot ahead of the other, figure out what is expected of them, figure out how to work the system, figure out what open school night is, and all that information. If people watched it a little more closely, they would understand just how American this experience is.

Somalis going to open school night have already done a tremendous amount of buy-in into the system. Yet we cherish this notion that modern immigrants are not buying in in the same way as European forebears did.

Pat Buchanan famously said that he would find it a lot easier to assimilate 50,000 Englishmen than 50,000 Zulus, and having traveled in and written extensively about Southern Africa and having worked as a reporter in London, I beg to differ with Pat.

I think the language would be easier for the Englishmen, but people who grew up in a system that was providing all their health care and when their house got shabby the local council would repaint their house might have more culture shock when they got to Dayton, Ohio, than Zulus, who grow up in a system where they know not to expect much of anything from the central government and to rely on clan links, familial links, and ethnic links to create bonds of interdependence that have worked a great deal for them.

The journalism profession has not made a conscious decision, but perhaps an unconscious one, to not handle the issue of immigration. There are a few broadsheet papers that are doing serious longitudinal reporting on immigrant populations, on issues of diversity. The *New York Times* series, "How Race Is Lived in America," is an example. Apart from a couple of efforts like that, usually in just the biggest handful of metropolitan areas, there is no serious inquiry about what this all means.

Immigration is covered in the way that ethnic festivals are covered, with a sort of "gee, whiz" tone. "What's Dewali? Well, we went down to find out"— that kind of thing.

That Epcot Center ethnicity unfortunately has infected a lot of reporting. It is not because reporters are stupid or incurious or anything like that. They are just given so little time to do anything. You have to produce, you have to produce on demand, and you have to produce this afternoon. So there is no time to really conduct in-depth reporting.

There are stabs at it, taken especially by papers in metropolitan areas where there has been a sudden arrival of an unexpected, large group that now becomes a challenge to the social service networks in that area, like Hmungs in Minneapolis and the Pacific Northwest.

In the Minneapolis-St. Paul papers and the Seattle papers there has been some serious journalism on what happens with that. But there has not been very good coverage, and there has not been very much.

The only thing that will change the coverage is audience demand. Audiences do not have a reliable way of making their appetites known to the ever larger companies that are delivering information to them, because these large companies are trying to achieve economies of scale by writing one-size-fits-all news.

The idea that news is going to be heavily tailored to the interests and needs of discrete communities is also a tough sell. Right now the tide in the business is moving against serious ongoing inquiry about what this all means. So, really, it is all experiential on the part of day-to-day, rank-and-file Americans.

In response to the question of whether the immigrant population is less involved in the political system, it is true that they are less involved in the political system. But if you dig a little deeper, this is not surprising at all when you look at the age structure of this population, because we know that young people are less likely to vote than older people, and the bias of this population is heavily weighted toward young people.

We know that rich people are more likely to vote than poorer people, and the bias of this population is heavily weighted toward lower rather than median income. We know that educated people are more likely than less educated people to vote, and the bias is heavily weighted toward fewer years of educational attainment.

So I think a longer time in country will take care of a lot of this just naturally. I do not think immigrants are permanently less involved, and I do not think it reflects a lack of interest. In New York they elected to great fanfare the first Dominican member of the New York City Council, and that was a big thing for Dominicans to do because there is a fairly low rate of naturalization.

So you have to really work hard to express your political will when a large group only has a small number of voters. But when Councilman Guillermo Linares was elected, that was a big achievement.

Caribbean blacks in Brooklyn are filling the Democratic clubhouses and slating people for Democratic National Committee and state committee positions, as well as state representative and state assembly jobs.

There was a very big election involving a candidate born in India who was running for political office in Iowa. During a campaign debate one of her opponents said that this candidate could not understand the concerns of everyday Iowans. The interesting thing was how badly that backfired on the opponent who said that. Once upon a time people probably would have nodded their heads and said, "Yeah, she probably does not understand the concerns of everyday Iowans." But that just is not on the list of acceptable anymore. The person who said that lost, and so it was that the first Asian-born member of the House in Iowa was elected. It is a big deal. In Iowa—not a place you think of as a large immigrant port of entry—they are wrestling with this.

The political effects of immigrants is a great dissertation topic if you want to spend a lot of time in Los Angeles. The political in-fighting that is going to go on over the next ten years between disproportionately represented, long-entrenched, long-wired black politicians in Los Angeles and the nearby municipalities that cluster around the southern end of Los Angeles, trying to hold on in electoral districts that are becoming more and more Mexican by the minute, will really rock that world.

The whole idea about those you struggle against and those you have to beat in order to grab a share of power has always been an "us" versus white people thing in that part of the world. Now Mexicans and black politicians are in these death matches over state assembly and state senate seats in southern Los Angeles County. That is forcing a lot of people who always thought of "the man" as their shared enemy to reconsider who their natural allies are in the urban, progressive political movements. Now it turns out that it is not even our "man." It is a Mexican woman who thinks that she should run for your state representative seat.

That is a very interesting situation. A similar dance is going on in south Florida between Cubans and newer arrived Central American populations. Cubans are aging. They are moving out of the core city of Miami and into wider Broward County and even farther up the coast. Their grip on politics is going to change.

Puerto Ricans are suburbanizing in New York at a rate that means they are not going to be the largest Latino population in New York by the 2010 census. But this was the only place that they were the people who could throw their weight around politically. With that population dispersing into the other counties in the huge megalopolis, losing their concentration in the Bronx and without that same concentration in Manhattan and Brooklyn, they are not going to be able to collect a lot of the goodies that go with the urban spoils system that is available once you finally amass enough numbers to grab your piece of the pie.

In response to the party affiliation of Latinos, if I knew the real answer to that question I could sell it for millions of dollars to the Republican and Democratic national committees, but I can give at least some informed speculation. I think the Republican Party oversold their entree into large Latino populations in places like Texas and California. It is only the hangover from the cold war that keeps the Republican Party in the game in Florida because this is disproportionately a working-class population. It is just not a natural Republican Party population yet.

Parts of the Latino population will become just like any group of Americans over time, with acquisition of the traits that are easily measured and observed that make people more likely to vote Republican. But right now Latinos, in general, are less likely to embody those traits generally.

The Republicans have tried appealing to strong social conservatism and alliance to the Catholic Church as a way of making political common cause. I think it is fair to say that California's Proposition 186 did more in the other direction than 1,000 rallies around Catholic Churches could have done in the other direction. You may go to mass, but you are still might be interested in getting food stamps. If you have suspicions that one party is going to take care of you in that regard and another party is not, it is likely that you are going to stay with that party.

I do not see the Latino supermajority in urban areas for the Democrats changing very much very soon. Of course it is going to change. It already has begun to change, but a lot of it is smoke and mirrors and the distorted use of statistics. Republicans celebrated the fact that the current president got 30 percent of the Latino vote—to Al Gore's 70 percent—and that was played like a win because Bill Clinton got 72 percent four years earlier. So, their margin rose from 1996 to 2000, but he did not even carry Latinos in Texas.

I think it is very easy to oversell. The Democrats have probably made some stylistic and marketing errors in this regard as well by seeing their future so heavily in the hands of "soccer moms" and suburban commuters that some Latino politicians felt that they had been sold out in the last couple of election cycles and did not feel very inclined to turn out their people.

We did not see big turnouts. In 2000 Latino turnouts were higher than those of the population in general, which admittedly is not that much of a feat anymore, but this did not happen in 2002. It was not just that midterm elections tend to bring out voters at lower levels. This overstated even that drop-off from the presidential year.

I think it is not some sort of religious, theological, or emotional link that keeps the Latino vote squarely in the Democratic camp for now. It is the bread-and-butter stuff; if you ask these voters, they will tell you that they think the Democratic Party is going to take better care of them in that regard for now.

Again, this is all very transitional. Ask me again in ten years. It will be a different answer, but for now I do not see anything disturbing that Latino supermajority for the Democrats.

Contributors

Xavier Becerra is a Democratic member of the U.S. House of Representatives from California, with an assignment on the Committee on Ways and Means.

Kathleen Buto is vice president for health policy, government affairs, at Johnson & Johnson.

Adam Carasso is with the Urban Institute.

Donna Chiffriller, vice president, human resources-benefits, is responsible for the strategy, design, and management of Verizon's benefits for workers and retirees.

Lee Cohen is an economist at the Social Security Administration's Office of Research, Evaluation, and Statistics.

Cecilia Conrad is associate professor of economics at Pomona College in Claremont, California.

Paul Eggers is program director for kidney and urology epidemiology at the National Institute of Diabetes and Digestive and Kidney Diseases.

James Randolph Farris is regional administrator of the Dallas office of the Centers for Medicare and Medicaid Services.

Linda Fishman is health policy director for the Senate Finance Committee under the chairmanship for Sen. Chuck Grassley (R-Iowa).

Nancy M. Gordon is associate director for demographic programs at the U.S. Census Bureau.

J. Lee Hargraves, senior health researcher at the Center for Studying Health System Change.

Pamela Herd is currently a Robert Wood Johnson Foundation scholar in health and health policy at the University of Michigan.

Kim Hildred is the Republican staff director of the Social Security Subcommittee of the House Committee on Ways and Means.

Audrietta Izlar is a health care management benefits specialist for Verizon Communications.

Kilolo Kijakazi is with the Ford Foundation.

Cheryl Hill Lee is research analyst for the National Urban League's Institute for Opportunity and Equality.

Robert C. Lieberman is associate professor of political science and public affairs at Columbia University.

James B. Lockhart III is the deputy commissioner of the Social Security Administration, a Senate-confirmed position.

Vicky Lovell is study director at the Institute for Women's Policy Research.

Nicole Lurie is senior natural scientist and Paul O' Neill Alcoa professor of policy analysis at the RAND Corporation.

Cindy Mann is research professor at Georgetown University, Institute for Health Care Research and Policy.

Jerry Mashaw is Sterling professor of law and professor at the Institute of Social and Policy Studies, Yale University.

John T. Monahan serves as senior fellow with the Annie E. Casey Foundation.

Samuel L. Myers Jr. is Roy Wilkins professor of human relations and social justice at the Hubert H. Humphrey Institute of Public Affairs, University of Minnesota.

Leslie Norwalk is acting deputy administrator for the Centers for Medicare and Medicaid Services.

Kathryn Olson is the Democratic staff director of the Social Security Subcommittee of the House Committee on Ways and Means.

Martha Priddy Patterson is director of employee benefits policy analysis for Deloitte & Touche's Human Capital Advisory Services.

Jill Quadagno is professor of sociology at Florida State University, where she holds the Mildred and Claude Pepper eminent scholar chair in social gerontology.

Maya Rockeymoore is vice president of research and programs at the Congressional Black Caucus Foundation.

Brian D. Smedley is senior program officer in the Division of Health Sciences Policy of the Institute of Medicine.

William E. Spriggs is director of research and public policy at the National Urban League, as well as director of its Institute for Opportunity and Equality.

Eugene Steuerle is with the Urban Institute.

Ray Suarez is senior correspondent on *The News Hour with Jim Lehrer*.

Ruby Takanishi is president of the Foundation for Child Development, a national privately endowed philanthropy based in New York City.

Conference Program

National Academy of Social Insurance
Fifteenth Annual Conference

Strengthening Community:
Social Insurance in a Diverse America
January 30–31, 2003
National Press Club
Washington, D.C.

Thursday, January 30, 2003

8:15 a.m.	Registration and Coffee
9:00 a.m.	Opening Speaker: The Honorable Xavier Becerra, U.S. House of Representatives
10:00 a.m.	Session I: What Are the Implications of Growing Diversity?

Moderator: Lisa Mensah, The Aspen Institute

Presenters:
Cecilia Conrad, Pomona College
Nancy M. Gordon, U.S. Census Bureau
J. Lee Hargraves, Center for the Study of Health
  Systems Change

Discussants:
Donna Chiffriller, Verizon Communications
Jerry Mashaw, Yale Law School

12:00 p.m.   Luncheon Dialogue: The Impact of U.S. Social
                               Insurance on Disparities over Time
                               Moderator: Christopher Edley Jr., Harvard Law
                                    School

                               Speakers:
                               Robert C. Lieberman, Columbia University, author
                                    of *Shifting the Color Line: Race and the
                                    American Welfare State*
                               Jill Quadagno, Florida State University, author of
                                    *Promoting Civil Rights through the Welfare
                                    State: How Medicare Integrated Southern
                                    Hospitals*

1:30 p.m.   Session II: Social Security in a Diverse America
                               Moderator: Margaret Simms, Joint Center for
                                    Political and Economic Studies

                               Presenters:
                               Lee Cohen, Social Security Administration
                               Pamela Herd, University of Michigan
                               Kilolo Kijakazi, Center on Budget and Policy
                                    Priorities
                               Maya Rockeymoore, The National Urban League
                                    Institute for Opportunity and Equality

                               Discussants:
                               Kim Hildred, Republican staff director,
                                    Subcommittee on Social Security, Committee on
                                    Ways and Means, U.S. House of Representatives
                               Kathryn Olson, Democratic staff director,
                                    Subcommittee on Social Security, Committee on
                                    Ways and Means, U.S. House of Representatives

3:45 p.m.   Session III: State-Administered Programs and
                               Diversity: What do we know about the impact of
                               state programs on diverse populations?
                               Moderator/Commentator: The Honorable Grantland
                                    Johnson, secretary, California Department of
                                    Health and Human Services

                               Presenters:
                               Cheryl Hill Lee, The National Urban League
                                    Institute for Opportunity and Equality
                               Vicky Lovell, Institute for Women's Policy Research

	John Monahan, Annie E. Casey Foundation Cindy Mann, Georgetown University
5:30 p.m.	Reception
6:30 p.m.	Dinner Master of Ceremonies: Lawrence H. Thompson, NASI president

John Heinz Dissertation Award ceremony
Jeffrey R. Lewis, executive director of the Heinz
    Family Foundation, and Robert Hudson, chair of
    the Heinz Dissertation Awards Committee

Dinner Speaker
Ray Suarez, senior correspondent, *The News Hour
    with Jim Lehrer,* "What Can We Anticipate from
    America's Diverse Public?"

Friday, January 31, 2003

8:00 a.m.	Members' Breakfast
9:00 a.m.	Roundtable Sessions Chronic Care and Medicare in the Twenty-First Century David Blumenthal, Study Panel chair

Health Insurance and Disabled Workers
Janet Shikles, Advisory Committee chair

Family Benefits under Social Security
Joan Entmacher, National Women's Law Center

Media-Friendly Research Findings
John Williamson, Boston College

Ideas for Improving Social Security Projections and
    the Annual Trustees' Reports
Robert Clark, Social Security Advisory Board
    Technical Panel on Assumptions and Methods

10:15 a.m.	Opening Speaker
10:45 a.m.	Session IV: Medicare and Disparities: What Do We Know? Moderator: Marsha Lillie-Blanton, Henry J. Kaiser Family Foundation

Presenters:
Paul Eggers, National Institutes of Health
Nicole Lurie, The RAND Corporation

Discussants:
Linda Fishman, U.S. Senate Finance Committee
Brian D. Smedley, Institute of Medicine
James Randolph Farris, Centers for Medicare &
     Medicaid Services

1:00 p.m.   Luncheon Speaker: Samuel L. Myers Jr., Roy
                Wilkins professor of human relations and social
                justice, Hubert Humphrey Institute of Public Affairs,
                University of Minnesota

2:00 p.m.   Session V: The Challenge of Diversity: Turning
                Research into Action
                Moderator: James H. Carr, Senior Vice President for
                     Innovation, Research and Community
                     Technology, Fannie Mae Foundation

Panel:
Leslie Norwalk, policy director and counselor to the
     administrator, Centers for Medicare & Medicaid
     Services
James B. Lockhart III, deputy commissioner, Social
     Security Administration
Ruby Takanishi, president, Foundation for Child
     Development

3:15 p.m.   Closing Remarks and Wrap-Up by Co-Chairs

Index

Access to health care, 72–76, 211–15. *See also specific health care programs (Medicaid, Medicare, etc.) and specific ethnic or racial groups*

AFDC (Aid to Families with Dependent Children), 171. *See now* Temporary Assistance to Needy Families (TANF)

Affirmative action policies, 1, 3, 4

Africa and AIDS assistance, 38

African Americans: and cardiac procedures, 195–96; CMS programs for, 224; and diabetes, 71, 202; and disability insurance, 232; economic vulnerability of, 79–92; educational demographics, 29–30, 34; employment trends among, 86–89; family structure of, 83–86; and government-provided health care, 206; and health care disparities, 20, 197–98, 201–03, 212–13; income sources of, 89–90; income trends among, 81–83; life expectancy of, 69–70, 216, 232; and mammography rates, 21, 198, 201; middle class, 55; population demographics, 29; prostate exams, 198; and quality of health care in Medicare+Choice program, 201–03; regular health care provider among insured vs. uninsured, 73–76; salary demographics, 30; and Social Security reform, 48; in SSA work force, 231; and unemployment

insurance programs, 16–17, 143–57; uninsured demographics of, 30, 177–78; and unreported Social Security earnings, 127–39; and wage differentials, 30, 35; and welfare exit, 173. *See also* African American women

African American women: and breast cancer, 94; marital status compared with white women, 115–16; as single parent, 79, 116; and Social Security benefits, 12–13, 115–17, 123

Age: diversity growth, 34, 64–65; retirement age, 38–39

Agency for Healthcare Research and Quality's National Quality Report and National Disparities Report, 206

Agricultural workers. *See* Farmworkers

AIDS assistance, 38

Aid to Families with Dependent Children (AFDC), 171. *See now* Temporary Assistance to Needy Families (TANF)

Alaskan Natives: and CMS program, 225; underenrollment in government health care programs, study of, 227

Allen, K., 146

American demographics: educational, 29–30; minority, 29–30; population, 29; salary, 29–30; uninsured demographics, 30

Asian Americans: and cardiac procedures, 195–96; and cervical

271